THE REAL ESTATE IRA

THE REAL ESTATE IRA

JOHN J. SCAVUZZO

Dodd, Mead & Company
New York

To my wife, Marion, my daughter Donna,
and her husband, Dr. Gary Fantini

First Edition

1 2 3 4 5 6 7 8 9 10

ISBN 0-396-08913-5

Library of Congress Cataloging-in-Publication Data

Scavuzzo, John J.
  The real estate IRA.

  Includes index.
  1. Individual retirement accounts—Taxation—
Law and legislation—United States—Popular works.
2. Real estate investment—Taxation—Law and
legislation—United States—Popular works. 3. Tax
shelters—Law and legislation—United States—
Popular works. I. Title.
KF6395.R35S32   1986   343.7305'23   86-31916
ISBN 0-396-08913-5   347.303523

A sincere debt of gratitude is extended to a number of people. To Robin Bartlett, friend and editor, whose faith in the project was steadfast. To Rod Linder, for first opening the door to real estate, and to Dick Coleman, who guided me through the insurance and financial world. To my able assistants—Richard DeSalvo, for his technical support, Dan O'Connell, for his creative support, and Terry O'Brien, for her patience and perseverance. To my associates, Gil Mauerstein, Rich Krabbeler, Ed Carlough, Dr. Kenneth Hall, Britt Frank, and Ed Wood, for their encouragement. And last but not least, for the excellent writing and editing skills of Susan Tucker and John Sturman.

Contents

Three
Savings and Investments, 27

Four
The Debt-Free Replacement House, 41

Five
The IRA: What It Is and What It Isn't, 49

Ten
How Much Real Estate Can You Purchase With an IRA? 114

Eleven
The Ultimate Payoff: Converting Your Homesites into a Debt-Free Home, 135

Twelve
The Embattled Renter, 150

Thirteen
Your Map to the Treasure, 156

Appendix A:
Money and Tax Principles, 160

Appendix B:
How the IRA Works? 184

Appendix C:
Retirement Need Analysis, 195

Questions and Answers, 205

Index, 215

Introduction

Before the seemingly great promise of the real estate IRA is examined, we will focus on the impact the tax reforms of 1986 have had on the IRA, and what those reforms may portend for the future.

During the summer of 1986, Congress did the unthinkable—it attacked the IRA. The specific target was the tax-deductibility of contributions. After months of media coverage, the average citizen was confused because the messages conveyed the impression that:

- The tax deductibility of the IRA was being repealed.
- The value of the IRA was to be diminished.

Could this be true? These important questions warrant our concern. The issue is vital—the answers may surprise you. Let's turn the clock back just a little.

In 1986, Congress enacted the most sweeping tax changes since the income tax was introduced in 1914. As first envisioned, the objectives of the new legislation included lowering the tax rates, reducing the number of tax brackets, shifting the tax burden to corporations, and eliminating most or all tax shelters. The tax shelters, in particular, were a high profile target for the legislation; the new law cancelled provisions in the tax code that had permitted promoters to use tax dollars to shore up risky and economically marginal business offerings. These tax shelters produced paper and/or bookkeeping losses for investors and real losses for the Treasury Department. The majority of the shelters have fallen to the executioner's basket—a deserved fate.

But many enterprises escaped similar harsh treatment thanks to their champions and friends. After all the dust settled, the following had been overlooked or given special attention: Reindeer hunters, chicken farmers, watchmakers, pen manufacturers, ministers, military personnel, timber growers, oil and gas investors, some commodities' investors, low-income housing investors, building rehabilitators, steel manufacturers, tuxedo rental firms, companies with Puerto Rican operations, solid-waste facilities, and tax-exempt bonds from Rhode Island! So, to compensate for dollars that would be lost via the concessions to special interests, the reduction in tax bracket rates, and elimination of tax burden on the lowest wage earners, Congress increased tax burdens on corporations. The impact of these decisions will be recorded and judged in the future.

Meanwhile, in order to balance the credits and debits of the changes, another "tax shelter" came under attack during the simplification effort—the IRA. Proponents of change charged that high salaried employees had been taking unfair advantage of this $2,000 retirement program as a tax shelter. This point was important to the legislators' balancing act because the Treasury is denied the taxes on IRA contributions—until a later date, when the individual retires. Thus, the well-paid worker was painted with the same brush that had been used on the "abusive" raiders of the Treasury. If the facts support this contention, then the well-paid workers should indeed be denied the tax deduction and the IRS should be paid its taxes immediately. But let's look a little closer.

The first question to be asked: Is the IRA a true tax shelter?

In Chapter Five of this book, we will demonstrate that the IRA is not a "tax shelter" similar in any way to those that were the prime targets of reform. Unlike participants in the abusive tax shelters, IRA participants don't get to take advantage of any tax credits, accelerated depreciation schedules, or other bookkeeping gymnastics. The taxes on IRA contributions are not forgiven; rather, they are just deferred—the IRS will eventually collect the original deferred tax dollars, plus accumulated appreciation, at the time of distribution. At the cost of deferring the collection of taxes, the government permitted millions of people the opportunity to increase their chances of attaining financial security when they needed it the most—at retirement. The IRA is a self-help program—*not a giveaway*—in the best tradition of the American way.

But the Congress, in its wish to reduce budget gaps, elected to target the IRA. It preserved eligibility for all and deductibility for most. It eliminated tax deductibility for the higher salaried, pension-covered employees, and reduced tax deductibility for middle income employees on a sliding scale basis; but it preserved deductibility for those not covered by a pension plan and for lower-income employees. (The details are provided in Appendix B of this book.) This "band-aid" maneuver, which the government has undertaken to reduce the deficit, may be justified and may even help some; but why has the IRA been the only program of this type to be so treated?

The tax-deferral provision of the totally deductible IRA is exactly the same as two other popular tax-deferred compensation programs: The 401(k) and the 403(b) programs. The 403(b) is the sole province of the nonprofit organizations—schools, universities, and so on—while any organization so motivated may install the 401(k). Unlike the IRA, these programs involve deferred taxes that are invisible to the IRS because employers reduce the 401(k) participant's earned income by the deferral sum, and report only the *net* income to the IRS. The employee's money (including the IRS' deferred taxes) is deposited with the 401(k) trustee. As with the IRA, the IRS is denied access to the deferred taxes too, until the individual retires and/or his money is distributed to him.

The maximum income on which these deferred compensation participants may defer taxes is now 350% more than the IRA. Until 1987, employees of organizations that adopted a 401(k) program were permitted to defer taxes on income up to $30,000. This maximum was reduced to $7,000. At a 40% tax bracket, these individuals were depriving the IRS of $12,000. With reform, the loss has been cut to $2,310 (33% of $7,000). This compares with a maximum deferred tax of $660 on an IRA.

From the above figures, one can see that if Congress wanted to use the tax reform legislation to retrieve some of the deferred tax dollars the IRS had been missing out on, they targeted the Davids, not the Goliaths!

But the most important issue to all wage earners is: **Does eliminating the tax-deductibility of contributions diminish the value of an IRA?**

The answer to this question depends on what is compared to the IRA. If we balance it against a conventional non-IRA investment, the answer is **NO.** The high salaried earner who cannot take an immediate tax deduction will be treated the same as will the investor in any tax-deferred vehicle: The money will compound tax-free. However, the IRA will permit him to treat *any* investment as tax-deferred—including a bank CD. So even for a high salaried investor, the IRA has advantages.

When we compare non-IRA investors to the IRA participants who qualify to take a full deduction, we see that the IRA has even bigger advantages. In Chapter Five of this book, we demonstrate that their personal money and profits are returned *tax-free*. That's an almost incredible benefit that speaks loudly for the IRA.

Regardless of the individual benefits, Congress's main motivation for squeezing the IRA was the IRS' loss of current revenues. With massive deficits, our legislators can't be faulted for moving in this direction. Along these lines, the ideal plan would have been to:

1. Permit the IRS to collect all of its deferred tax immediately and not have to wait ten, fifteen, or thirty years.
2. Preserve all the tax benefits that the IRA provided for all participants before 1987. This would benefit all.

Sounds great for everyone! Is it possible to keep this large cake and feast on it at the same time? I suggest that the answer is **YES.** I would have advocated a somewhat different approach than the one Congress has actually taken. Here's what I mean.

At present, those taxpayers who qualify for full deductions follow the path that will be discussed in Chapter Five and pictured in Figure 5-6

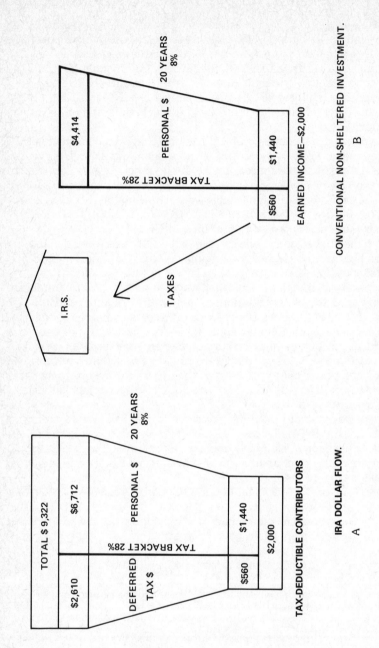

TAX-DEDUCTIBLE CONTRIBUTORS

TOTAL $ 9,322

$6,712

$2,610

PERSONAL $ 20 YEARS
8%

TAX BRACKET 28%

DEFERRED
TAX $

$560

$1,440

$2,000

IRA DOLLAR FLOW.

A

I.R.S.

TAXES

$4,414

PERSONAL $ 20 YEARS
8%

TAX BRACKET 28%

$560

$1,440

EARNED INCOME—$2,000

CONVENTIONAL NON-SHELTERED INVESTMENT.

B

Figure 5-6

4

(reproduced here). The conclusion of that discussion is that, at retirement, the participant will pay the IRS the deferred taxes on all the accumulated tax-deferred income. The remainder—the individual's personal dollars and the appreciation—is distributed to him or her. These dollars are effectively *tax-free*. This is proven in Chapter Five.

The bottom line is that IRA participants will not escape paying sizeable taxes on their tax-deferred dollars unless they are in a reduced tax bracket at retirement. With the lowering of tax brackets and rates, falling into a lower bracket would be tantamount to economic disaster at retirement—an outcome that will be highly improbable if you follow the basic principles and plan outlined in this book. Accepting that truth, we can theoretically conclude that those qualified for full deductions would not be affected if they simply gave the IRS the tax-deferred dollars at time of contribution instead—and then, received their personal money untaxed at retirement. That is precisely what will happen to all the fully deductible IRA participants.

Such is not the case for the partially deductible and non-deductible IRA participants. They have been discriminated against—but that's another issue.

Using this basic analysis, I would have recommended that the IRA's tax-deferred contribution dollars be paid to the IRS up-front, permitting individuals to invest the remaining personal dollars in the IRA. The personal dollars would then grow tax-free and be distributed without any future taxation. Delivery of personal dollars tax-free is exactly what will happen to all IRAs adopted from 1974 to 1987, and to the fully tax-deductible IRAs adopted in the future. Let's use the example discussed in Chapter Five to prove this premise.

In part A of Figure 5-6, the IRA participant deposits a *one-time* contribution of $2,000 which accumulates to $9,322. After paying his taxes of $2,610, he is left with $6,712 of after-tax dollars.

Part B depicts the modification proposed. Our participant pays the $560 tax immediately and deposits the $1,440 in an IRA. After the same holding period and appreciation, the *same* $6,712 is his or hers to have *without taxes*. The end result is the same—$6,712 for each scenario.

However, the advantages are strikingly simple and would result in major cost savings for the government:

1. The IRS would receive its tax money immediately, helping to reduce the deficit.
2. After the *benchmark* age of 59½, the participant could retrieve the IRA dollars at any time and on any schedule.
3. Monitoring by the IRS would be minimal and reduce costs considerably.
4. The present mandatory scheduled withdrawal after age 70½ could be eliminated, probably saving millions of dollars in compliance costs for the IRS.
5. The Treasury would not be raided.

The potential benefits of this proposal should be considerable. In fact, I believe Congress should create a *Super-IRA*, a single vehicle for the IRA plus the other deferred compensation programs—the 401(k) and 403(b) programs mentioned earlier. The deferred allowance for each of these could be added to the present IRA, giving the Super-IRA the following maximum limits:

Present IRA	- $ 2,000
401(k)	- $ 7,000
403(b)	- $ 2,000
Total:	$11,000

With this single vehicle, all qualified individuals could determine their own permitted economic limit, pay the appropriate tax to the IRS and deposit the remaining dollars with an IRA trustee. Penalties for early withdrawal would have to be increased, but at 59½, the funds would be available to the individual tax-free.

The Treasury would be healthier with this Super-IRA. They would collect their money up-front. Of course, the attraction of IRA's "tax *deductibility*" would be lost, but an even better benefit would replace it— *TAX-FREE*.

All this may sound overwhelming; but fear not. You will be in a better position to appreciate these concepts after you have read on. Ideas are advanced here to try to change the perception that the IRA has somehow lost its value with the changes in the law. That supposed outcome is not supported by the facts.

The IRA has a splendid future if all its potential is developed. In fact, it could even be the best ally in the government's push to save the Social Security system. But that's too big a proposal to examine in this book. For now, read on to learn about the real estate IRA, to find out about the HOUSEPOWER plan—a route you can take to gain nearly automatic financial security in retirement. Afterwards, return to this introduction and reexamine the proposed changes. But most important of all, do not lose confidence in the IRA. It is and can be an invaluable tool in achieving retirement security.

ONE

The Role of the Real Estate IRA

This book is about one of the most amazing duos since Katharine Hepburn and Spencer Tracy: A team consisting of real estate investment and the Individual Retirement Account (IRA), which together form a special type of IRA known as the *real estate IRA*. This winning combination is unfamiliar to most Americans, but if you're reading this book, it's obvious that the possibility of merging two of the hottest investment vehicles around has sparked your curiosity.

By itself, a real estate IRA cannot provide retirement security. But it can assuredly help you achieve that security. To make your real estate IRA as effective as possible, you must integrate it into your personal retirement plan. This will help you formulate that plan and put it into action.

The very word *retirement* is one of the most frightening in our dictionary. The young usually overlook it; they feel that their own retirement is too far away to worry about. True, retirement is for the senior citizen. But **RETIREMENT PLANNING** is for everyone. All working people—young and mature alike—must accept this fact and start the planning process immediately. You will more than likely face retirement at age 55, 60 or 65. Why not spend it in affluence, or at least in worry-free stability? Financial security in retirement can be your ultimate reward to yourself.

Fortunately, if you are reading this book you have already shown that you are concerned about your retirement security. By the time you finish the last page, I am confident that you will be on the road to achieving it.

7

HOW TO ACHIEVE A SECURE RETIREMENT: AN OVERVIEW

If you quickly size up the resources you will use in retirement, two types will probably come to mind right away: your company pension and your Social Security benefits. But will these really be sufficient? Very likely not. Social Security offers only a minimum safety net level of support and will be of only slight assistance. A pension may help: If you are covered by a pension plan at work and anticipate staying on the job a long time, you may receive a substantial pension benefit. However, if you're like most Americans, pension checks coupled with Social Security will not fulfill your dream of a worry-free retirement. You will need more resources, and they will have to come from your assets—your savings, and your investments. Most of all, your secure retirement will depend on your determined efforts to achieve it. To guide your efforts, you must have a plan.

Dreams Alone Cannot Give You a Secure Retirement

As a child, you dreamed of all kinds of wealth. Remember Robert Louis Stevenson's *Treasure Island?* Silver, gold, and jewels dazzled your imagination. Or perhaps it was pirate movies that excited you. Fantasy turned dreams into reality for a moment, and that seemed enough.

Then you grew up, and you stopped relying on dreams alone. Remember your first car, your first house, your children's college educations? These milestones in your life were dreams at first, but you ultimately attained them not by childhood fantasy but by adult action. You *worked* for them! Unless you're one of a select few, you didn't make these dreams come true by winning at the track, casino, or in a lottery. It's the same story with your dream of a financially secure retirement. That dream can't be left to your chances at the gaming tables; the price of failure is too high. To succeed, you must take the only feasible option: you must use adult planning and action. You *can* do it.

Consider Mel Fisher. He had a magnificent dream—one many of us may have shared. Perhaps when he was still a boy, he began to dream of his own "Treasure Island"—and in 1985 his dream came true. Fisher located a Spanish galleon that had gone down in a storm forty miles off Key West, Florida, in 1622. Its sunken treasure was valued in excess of $400 million; it was the richest undersea discovery ever made. But luck had nothing to do with Fisher's find. He didn't "stumble" onto the fortune. Nor did he chug out to sea and dispatch divers randomly. No way! He achieved his fabulous booty solely through *planning and determination.*

Years earlier, Fisher had laid the groundwork for his long, persistent quest; months of organized and elaborate research preceded his direct endeavors. He researched Spanish archives, studied centuries-old shipping logs, and traced the history of wrecks around Florida. He put together information from far-flung sources, leaving almost nothing to chance. Only when he had completed his plan was he prepared to go into action to pursue his dream. And though he followed his plan resolutely, he was also careful to adjust it as conditions dictated.

There may only be a few Spanish galleons on the ocean floor. But you can recover an equally important treasure if you follow Mel Fisher's example and set up a plan to make your own financial dream a reality. The bounty you get may not be as impressive as Fisher's; but it is even more critical that you obtain it, since it's your own well-being in retirement that's at stake.

THE TWO BIG OBSTACLES TO YOUR SECURE RETIREMENT

Even with a good plan, your pursuit of financial security in retirement is going to be a challenge. Your voyage will not be short or easy. There will be problems to overcome—obstacles that will make your own personal treasure hunt difficult. The worst of these obstacles will be an ever-present twosome: **Taxes and inflation.** These two enemies may leave you alone for short periods, but they will never disappear. To protect yourself against them, you must take definite action. Token or casual efforts won't do. Throughout this book, you are shown how to battle these enemies. Each one is examined below, and each will be included often in later discussions.

TAXES—AND HOW THE IRA CAN HELP YOU BEAT THEM

Taxes erode your earned and invested dollars without let-up. Even the latest tax reform may not alter the fact that you may have to work for almost four months just to pay a given year's taxes! Of course, the best strategy in the battle is to *avoid taxes legally*.

The IRS allows certain parts of your earned income and yields on certain investments to remain untaxed, and you should take maximum advantage of these breaks. Doing so has been encouraged by the highest court in the country. Early in this century, the famed jurist Learned Hand ruled that, while citizens have an obligation to pay taxes, they have an *even greater* responsibility to keep the taxes they pay to the legal minimum! That people are following Hand's advice is obvious from the increasing numbers of tax accountants, lawyers, and financial planners who now dot our landscape. The tax code has become so complicated that adhering to Hand's dictum requires an army of specialists.

Even such professional assistance brings no guarantee of success. Congress often changes the rules and undermines people's carefully laid plans for lowering their taxes. You may have been among those whose tax strategy was thwarted by the 1986 reforms. Fortunately, there are still government-sponsored and approved programs that ease the tax bite. These include the 403(b) TSA plan for employees of nonprofit organizations (educators, for example) and the 401(k) tax-deferred compensation programs, which are available from employers who institute them.

And there is a third plan that most Americans have the option of adopting. This plan is the Individual Retirement Account, or IRA. The IRA is a retirement-oriented savings and investment program that allows wage earners to postpone IRS tax treatment of income that you set aside in the plan (or, as the IRS says, "contribute" to the plan). It lets that money accumulate interest, and thus grow, on a tax-deferred basis, thereby offering you an opportunity to blunt the tax bite in two ways. It's an invaluable ally in your search for financial security in retirement.

The IRA boasts three big tax benefits:

1. Reduction of taxes: When you open an IRA, most of you may deduct all or part of your contribution from your taxable income, and thus reduce taxes. Your accountant, tax adviser, or financial planner has probably advocated this policy for many years.

2. Long-term tax advantages: The IRA permits all contributions to avoid annual taxation, allowing your funds to grow tax-free. You don't pay the tax until you retire, at which time your tax rate may possibly be reduced.

3. "Millionaire" status: Tax-free compounding generates astonishing numbers, and you may even be able to accumulate a seven-figure fortune. Becoming a "millionaire," even on paper, is intoxicating.

The public has responded to these inducements. Millions of Americans had contributed a cumulative total of $280 billion to IRAs as of 1985.

INFLATION—AND HOW INVESTING IN REAL ESTATE CAN HELP YOU BEAT IT

The IRA is sometimes touted as the total answer to everyone's retirement objective, but it really is only a part of the solution. Because now you must confront your second opponent, *inflation*. You may have won a battle by lowering your taxes, but you can still lose the war, because inflation is the stronger adversary. And you will win or lose your fight on the basis of how your chosen savings and/or investments fare against this nemesis. The real challenge, then, is selecting winning investments from the spectrum of available choices.

You may think that the range of investment possibilities is staggering. Hundreds of banks, security brokerages, and insurance companies all compete fiercely for a share of the multi-million dollar IRA pot, each boasting that its own specific IRA is the best investment choice and the one that offers the greatest retirement benefit. These far-flung claims and the unsettled economy have only increased investor's confusion, making their reasoned selection difficult.

But, despite the flurry of choices you perceive, your investment options are actually fewer than you may think. If you were to prepare a list of investments, you would likely include stocks, bonds, futures, collectibles, real estate, annuities, and bank CDs.

Examining these closely, I suggest that the last two—CDs and fixed annuities—are not really investments. Banks guarantee your principal, but they will only pay you a specified interest regardless of the return *they* get on the use of your dollars. You're *lending* your money to the bank by any definition.

So you can eliminate CDs and fixed annuities from the list—they're loans. That reduces the variety of vehicles that can truly be termed investments. Most investments normally involve some degree of risk, which entitles you to profits. In general, the greater the risk, the higher the potential yield. But if you're an aggressive investor (a euphemistic description of a gambler), you have probably suffered at some point on the roller coaster ride that comes with speculating in stocks, bonds, futures, gold, diamonds, silver, or the like. This is particularly true if you have listened to the doomsday investment pundits who, motivated by fears of runaway inflation and economic collapse, suggest buying precious gems or metals and then heading for the hills. I personally wish these "experts" a speedy and safe journey!

If you're not willing to ride the investment roller coaster but you still want a good chance at whipping inflation, where can you turn? Among the available options, the soundest by far is real estate. You will find that one investment—your *home, condo,* or *co-op*—has out performed all other investments, not by 10% or 25%, but by as much as *100%!* Your home has probably yielded investment returns that have been 400% to 500% *greater* than those of your stocks, bonds, or savings accounts!

Sounds incredible, but it's true. Historically, real estate has produced higher yields than other investments, and its leveraged performance has constantly outpaced long-term inflation. You probably used a leveraged purchase to buy your home. (Leveraging is discussed in Appendix A, if you're unfamiliar with the term.) Not only that. Real estate investment confers unique tax advantages. You can defer taxation of profits when you sell a home and when you sell your principal residence after you reach age 55. An accumulated profit of $125,000 is yours tax-free.

Taking all of these benefits into consideration, you'll see that the return on your house will make all other conventional investments pale by comparison. There's no contest! Real estate roundly trounces both taxation and inflation.

We've seen how real estate constantly beats other investments at overcoming inflation. We've also seen how the IRA lets you save or invest with dollars that will grow tax-deferred. So what happens if they are combined? What happens, in other words, **if our IRA dollars are used to buy real estate?**

THE BEST OF BOTH WORLDS

Buying real estate with your IRA can help defeat both taxation and inflation simultaneously. This sounds too good to be true, you may be saying. You may even be wondering: **Is it legal and within regulations to purchase real estate with the funds in an IRA?**

Wonder no more. The answer is a resounding YES! Not only is it legal, but it makes good sense, too.

Maybe you're still dubious. Well, read on. Because the purpose of this book is to back up this assertion. As the basic intent of the IRA—retirement security—is explored—I will also demonstrate how the real estate IRA can lend a helping hand as you build your retirement nest egg.

This book will answer many questions, including:

1. Which IRAs permit you to purchase real estate?
2. How do they work?
3. What kind of real estate qualifies?
4. How much can you purchase?
5. What is the final payoff?

The book will also reveal and discuss in detail certain distinct advantages of the real estate IRA. For example:

- The real estate IRA can be the key to a substantial pension: Working with your present home, the real estate IRA can help provide you with an additional five-figure income to give you a carefree retirement lifestyle that only a handful of retirees now enjoy.
- The real estate IRA brings relief to renters: A real estate IRA can help liberate renters from constant housing cost increases. In retirement, renters may have to use an ever-greater percentage of their fixed income for shelter, which can have devastating consequences. A real estate IRA can help renters stem this hazardous dollar drain.

Best of all, the real estate IRA is the key to an innovative, fail-safe financial retirement plan, which we will present in this book. This plan is revolutionary in part because it's simple. And it's effective. If you follow it, you *will succeed*. We will show you how the real estate IRA, in conjunction with your existing assets, can:

- Virtually assure your financial security in retirement.
- Eliminate the need for complex financial plans that require a high degree of expertise.
- Enable you to keep the plan under your control.
- Let you outline a plan that is inflation-proof.

This all sounds hard to believe, but as you read on, you'll see it's true. The plan's common sense and logic are unassailable. This book may shake up your beliefs about your present retirement strategy. I hope you'll approach my ideas with an open, questioning mind and I accept the challenge to deliver on my promises.

TWO

Your Plan for a Secure Retirement

Financial security in retirement! This phrase conjures up a different image for everyone. You may envision anything from a modest home with a patch of lawn to a palatial mansion with a view of San Francisco Bay.

Whatever your own personal view, the basic need for financial security in retirement is universal. Equally widespread is the fear of failure to achieve that security. In fact, a recent survey reported:

About four of five (79%) respondents said that their own retirement security is more important than a college education for their children.*

These figures may give the impression that there is plenty of parental neglect, selfishness, and insensitivity out there. Quite the opposite is true, though. Most parents simply don't want to be a burden to their children in their old age.

No matter how much they worry about their retirement, few Americans actually do much to prepare for it. In fact, you'll be amazed to learn that fewer than ten percent of retirees have achieved financial security. This unexpected contradiction forces us to ask: **Why do so many people fail at a task that is so high on their priority list?**

There are four major answers:

- Procrastination
- Inconsistent saving habits

* Source: Responsive Analysis Corp. **USA TODAY,** Gannett Publication, 1986

13

- Poor investment performance
- No clear plan of action

Any one or more of these can cause failure. But the one that will most certainly guarantee failure is the lack of a plan. Even with a plan, you *may* fail because of factors beyond your control. But without a plan, you assuredly *will* fail.

YOU MUST HAVE A PLAN

Only a handful of people have a retirement plan. If you don't have one, you're a member of the majority. Few people really seem to know what a financial plan *is*. There are two common misconceptions. First, most existing plans are ones that have been generated by professionals—accountants, lawyers, bankers, insurance agents, and "financial planners"—who normally cater to higher-income clients. This leads people to think that only the rich need financial planning. Quite the contrary! Actually the rich need less help. They can afford mistakes and losses—others can't. It's ordinary working people who need a good, fail-safe financial plan—a plan that is objective-oriented and workable. It's that simple.

Second, most existing financial "plans" simply concentrate on ways to reduce taxes and manage a client's assets. These strategies may produce more dollars, and may shield more funds from taxes. But do they address specific objectives? Not usually. More dollars alone do not a plan make: your plan needs *direction*.

THE OBJECTIVE OF YOUR PLAN: THE INCOME TRANSFER PROCESS

The main job of your financial retirement plan is to generate income sources that will replace your present income—the earnings from your job. I call this replacement process, or evolution, *the income transfer process*. Only after a successful income transfer process, when replacement sources of income can provide a satisfactory level of support, can you afford to stop working and actually retire.

For years, you've gone to work and exchanged your services for a variety of compensations. The most visible one is your paycheck. With it, you've sustained yourself and your family, paying for the goods and services you use every day and for the big financial commitments you've undertaken along the way—buying your home and sending your kids to college, for instance. With all these expenses, building a nest egg for your retirement may have been the farthest thing from your mind. Or maybe you have said, like Scarlett O'Hara, that you'll think about it tomorrow.

But now you're reading this book, and retirement planning is clearly on your mind. Maybe you're even a little anxious about it and are unsure where to begin. It's not so difficult. If you want to formulate a coherent retirement plan, you must first ask yourself a very basic, concrete question:

How Much do I Need in Retirement?

The only sensible way to answer this crucial question is to determine your *specific* retirement financial needs. Then you can work to build the assets that will fulfill those needs. Sound complicated? It's not, really. It's based on the relationship among five factors:

1. Present salary
2. Inflation
3. Spending patterns while working
4. Projected final career salary
5. Retirement spending patterns

The first factor—your present salary—is your starting point. It reflects or, more accurately, sets your standard of living. Over many years, inflation will increase the cost of living, but your salary should also rise to keep pace with inflation. Hopefully, your raises will keep you ahead of the game.

This process continues until you retire. Then things change dramatically. When you stop working, your income will decrease, but so will your needs. An important finding (discussed in Appendix C) is that once you retire, you will need only 65% of your last working year's income to maintain your pre-retirement standard of living. You can easily apply this formula as a guide for your own situation. (See Appendix C for a discussion of how to determine your own personal retirement need.)

WHERE WILL MY RETIREMENT MONEY COME FROM?

OK, you know you'll need only 65% of your pre-retirement income to get by. But where will that money come from? After all, you won't be drawing a paycheck any more. Fortunately, although you may have neglected actively saving for retirement, other forces have been at work for you. (Remember, your paycheck is only the most *visible* compensation for your services on the job.) Throughout your career, your wages have been augmented by deferred-compensation programs designed to provide retirement income. It is these sources, coupled with any personal assets, that will replace your earned income.

The income transfer process shown in Figure 2-1 depicts the career-long exchange of work for salary. It traces how both you and your employer contribute to your Social Security account. It also shows how, if you're covered by a pension plan, additional dollars are deferred for payments on retirement. Coupled with your own savings and investment programs, these will become your sources of income at retirement.

To summarize, your retirement income will come from three sources:

1. Social Security: All wage earners benefit from this source.
2. Pension Plan: Many workers will receive pension benefits that range from meager to substantial.

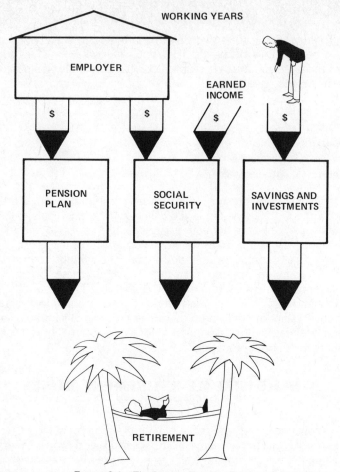

Figure 2-1: The Income Transfer Process

3. Savings and Investments: The impact of this source is variable, depending on personal ability and commitment to save or invest.

Let's examine each component and see how it performs its support role. We'll consider *Social Security* first.

SOCIAL SECURITY

Social Security is a federal program that is funded equally by both you and your employer. Although it is intended to provide only a minimal safety-net support level, it has become important for millions of Americans.

Social Security gives some measure of financial support to everyone. You generate Social Security income automatically, just by working. You don't have to plan or manage it. As you are well aware, you and your employer must contribute to your Social Security account—*it's the law*. Given the choice, you might drop the system and use another means to build a fund. But be that as it may, Social Security provides a significant support for millions of people and will play its role in your life, too.

When Social Security became law in 1935, it was designed to provide basic retirement financial assistance funded by a payroll tax on both employer and employee. Its scope has since been extended to offer financial support to widows and their minor children. In addition, it covers disability and health insurance for 90% of the nation's workers and their families.

Despite its massive growth, Social Security's fundamental objective remains unchanged. You can count on it to deliver benefits upon your retirement, disability, or death. The latter two are helpful programs, but our discussion will address only your future Social Security retirement benefits.

Tracking Your Social Security Account

You are probably painfully aware of how much you pay into the Social Security system. Yet you may have only a vague idea of what your benefits are. Unless you're close to retirement, the exact numbers are not important to you, but to make sure your account is correct, you should first write to the Social Security Administration for a statement of your *earnings record*. Do this every five years, and more frequently as you approach retirement. Address your requests to:

> **Social Security Administration**
> **P. O. Box 57**
> **Baltimore, Maryland 21203**

Calculating Your Benefits

The status of your Social Security account (your earnings record) is useful to know, but there are even more critical aspects of Social Security from the stand point of planning. You must be able to factor these into your transfer process with some accuracy.

First, we must ask how inflation will affect your Social Security benefits. Fortunately, the *true* benefits of Social Security will not be diminished by inflation now or in the future, thanks to annual adjustments using the past year's inflation data. Although the adjustment always comes one year after the fact, it's better than no adjustment at all! These adjustments were instituted in 1977, when Congress overhauled the benefit formulas for people who would reach age 62 after 1978. Our lawmakers adjusted and credited people's base "earnings" by correcting them for inflation and indexing them to keep pace with the cost of goods and services. Therefore, the contribution of Social Security to your retirement income will be **inflation-proof**. This helps to simplify your calculations, because the correction for the unknown but varying inflation rates will be made automatically.

Second, now that we know that our Social Security benefits will be resistant to inflation, we may well ask precisely how substantial they will be. The first step the Social Security Administration will take in determining your initial benefit will be to calculate a figure known as your Average Indexed Monthly Earnings (AIME). The earnings are those on which you paid Social Security taxes over your working years. Unless you've kept excellent records, you are advised to request this information from the Social Security Administration. When you know your AIME, you can establish your *actual* monthly benefit. This is technically called the primary insurance amount (PIA). Plainly, it is the amount of money you'll receive each month.

Here's the procedure for finding your PIA: If you become 62 in 1986 and intend to retire in 1989, take the total amount of your *total AIME* and multiply the:

- first $297 by .90 (90%)
- next $1,493 by .32 (32%)
- excess of $1,790 by .15 (15%)

Let's say your total AIME is $1,030. Your PIA will be:

$$\begin{array}{l} \$297 \times .9 = \$267.30 \\ \$733 \times .32 = \underline{\$234.56} \\ \$501.86 \end{array}$$

Third, having established the dollar value of our projected Social Security benefits, we must now think of their worth in *relative* terms. In other words, how do Social Security benefits affect people at different income levels?

What will happen, for instance, if your salary shoots way up—let's say, so high that your AIME doubles? The PIA doesn't go up in the same proportion. The new amount will be $689.48—only $212.56 more for *doubling* your contributions to the system! This is comforting if you're at a *lower* salary scale—because a greater percentage of your income is returned to you in benefits—but not if you're at a higher point. This is consistent with the basic purpose of the program—to provide a safety net level of support. Social Security certainly cannot be characterized as an investment program. If it were, it would be a disaster! But lower percentages for top wage earners make sense because high-income people are better able to take care of themselves financially.

For those of you curious about what is presently the most you could receive from Social Security, we show the example herein. If you earned the maximum taxable income all your working years and you were age 62 in 1986, intending to retire in 1989, your AIME would be $2179. Your monthly PIA on that maximum AIME will be:

$$\begin{array}{l} \$297 \times .9 = \$267.30 \\ \$1493 \times .32 = \$477.76 \\ \$389 \times .15 = \underline{\$58.35} \\ \text{Total:} \quad \$2179 = \$803.41 \end{array}$$

A review of the benefit schedule for the whole earnings range of participants (see Table 1-1) will give you the information needed to find your own future

TABLE 1.1 Social Security Benefits For Person Retiring At Age 65 In 1989
Benefit Table

1	2	3	4	5	6	7	8
Soc. Sec. Wage			42000		Max AIME	2179	
		Computing the Personal Income Amount					
% of Std	Salary	AIME	(90% × 297.00	(32% × 1493.00	(15% of excess)	PIA	Percent of Sal
300	126000	2179	267.30	477.76	58.35	803.41	8
290	121800	2179	267.30	477.76	58.35	803.41	8
280	117600	2179	267.30	477.76	58.35	803.41	8
270	113400	2179	267.30	477.76	58.35	803.41	9
260	109200	2179	267.30	477.76	58.35	803.41	9
250	105000	2179	267.30	477.76	58.35	803.41	9
240	100800	2179	267.30	477.76	58.35	803.41	10
230	96600	2179	267.30	477.76	58.35	803.41	10
220	92400	2179	267.30	477.76	58.35	803.41	10
210	88200	2179	267.30	477.76	58.35	803.41	11
200	84000	2179	267.30	477.76	58.35	803.41	11
190	79800	2179	267.30	477.76	58.35	803.41	12
180	75600	2179	267.30	477.76	58.35	803.41	13
170	71400	2179	267.30	477.76	58.35	803.41	14
160	67200	2179	267.30	477.76	58.35	803.41	14
150	63000	2179	267.30	477.76	58.35	803.41	15
140	58800	2179	267.30	477.76	58.35	803.41	16
130	54600	2179	267.30	477.76	58.35	803.41	18
120	50400	2179	267.30	477.76	58.35	803.41	19
110	46200	2179	267.30	477.76	58.35	803.41	21
std	42000	2179	267.30	477.76	58.35	803.41	23
90	37800	1961	267.30	477.76	25.67	770.73	24
80	33600	1743	267.30	477.76	.00	745.06	27
70	29400	1525	267.30	393.06	.00	660.36	27
60	25200	1307	267.30	323.33	.00	590.63	28
50	21000	1090	267.30	253.60	.00	520.90	30
40	16800	872	267.30	183.87	.00	451.17	32
30	12600	654	267.30	114.14	.00	381.44	36
20	8400	436	267.30	44.42	.00	311.72	45
10	4200	218	196.11		.00	170.80	49

support from Social Security. Column 2 of Table 1.1 shows earnings from $4,200 to over $126,000. Note that Column 1 lists the percent above or below $42,000, which was the maximum taxable wage level in 1986. For earnings in excess of $42,000 in that year, no additional Social Security taxes were imposed. But no more benefits will accrue either, as shown in Columns 3 through 7—the AIME and PIA amounts.

A most useful piece of information is shown in Column 8—the benefit as a *percent* of wages or salary. If you earned the maximum Social Security

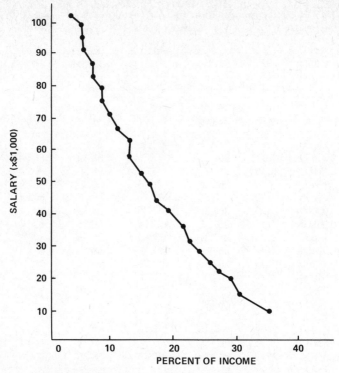

Figure 2-2: Social Security Benefit as a Percent of Income

taxable salary all your working career, your benefit will be $803.41 per month, or 23% of your salary.

If you earned more than the maximum taxable salary, you would not pay any more into Social Security. Your benefit would also top out at the maximum level determined earlier. As a percentage of your greater earned income, the Social Security benefit will decrease. If your income were $60,000, for example, you would still receive $803.41 per month, but the percent of support would drop to 16%. This shows that at wages below maximum, the dollar value of Social Security benefits is lower, but the percentage of support is higher. This pattern is demonstrated in Figure 2-2.

What Changes are in Store for Social Security?

One modification in the Social Security system will affect you strongly if you were born after 1935. Starting in the year 2000, the minimum age for collecting full retirement benefits will rise two months yearly from 65 to 66 by 2005. Ten years later, it will begin to extend two months yearly again until age 67 by 2022. People born before 1935 will continue to receive full benefits at age 65.

Future changes will also see fewer people collecting benefits prior to age 65. A 62-year-old retiree now receives 80% of his or her full benefit. By the year 2000, such inducements to retire will shrink. By 2022, a retiring 62-year-old will receive only 70% of his or her full benefit.

What Role Will Your Social Security Benefits Play in Your Retirement?

While it may bring you a relatively small monthly check if you're a three-source retiree, Social Security remains important. It will be there for most of today's workers, despite some dire forecasts to the contrary. As mentioned before, the program is inflation-proof through your working career. And your benefit expressed as a percentage of your income will be relatively fixed.

For this benchmark exercise, we conservatively estimate that Social Security will provide ten percent of your last working year's salary. The balance of your retirement income must come from other transfer components. One of them is your *pension plan* that is discussed next.

PENSION PLANS

Whether private or public, pension plans are a valuable income source for those whom they cover. These plans offer support that ranges from weak to significant. In any case, they are a generous benefit since the employer, not you, funds them. The popularity of pension plans has grown steadily since the 1950s.

If you have a pension plan, its value has escalated since key revisions were initiated under the sweeping Employee Retirement Income Security Act of 1974 (ERISA). ERISA regulates rules that govern eligibility, vesting (ownership of accrued benefits), funding of plans, and operations of plans. Further improvements were made by the Tax Equity and Fiscal Responsibility Act of 1982 (TEFRA).

If you are covered by a pension plan, your benefits are controlled by the written plan, which federal regulators had to approve before your company adopted it. Vested pension benefits are your property. They are extremely valuable assets that you should monitor. Your employer's benefit officer in charge of your plan is legally required to disclose full information about the plan to you and all covered employees.

Types of Pension Plans

Three types of general plans qualify under ERISA rules. They are:

1. Defined Benefit Plans: These plans are set up to guarantee you a specific retirement *benefit*. They are calculated by a formula that factors in your age, your length of service, and your salary. Since your benefit is contractually assured, your employer *must* contribute sufficient funds to your pension plan to give you that benefit when you retire.

2. Defined Contribution Plans: In this type of plan, the company guarantees only its contribution to the plan, not the size of your retirement check. The contributed

amount is either a percentage of your earnings or a flat dollar sum. Your benefits will depend on both the *dollars contributed* and how much the invested contributions have earned.

3. Profit Sharing Plans: In these plans, the company contributes a certain percentage of its *profits* to your retirement fund. Since they are profit-sensitive, these plans are less reliable, and, therefore, so is your pension benefit.

Because the government approves pension plans, it also supplies guidelines for compliance with them. The first condition that affects you in any type of pension is eligibility.

Eligibility

Regulations insist that no plan may discriminate, thus protecting your right to be covered under your company's plan. Prior to 1986, your participation could have been denied if you were under 25 years of age or had not completed one year of service, whichever came later. And some plans that vested you fully after three years of service could have required you to wait to participate until after that period. The only time you could have been denied participation is if you were hired within five years of the retirement age specified in the company's defined benefit plan.

Present regulations provide that a plan may not withhold eligibility longer than two years. If you must wait for two years, the plan must provide that you own (or be vested) 100% of your pension assets, at that time.

Year of Service

The term "year of service" is important to eligibility. Technically, a year of service consists of a twelve-month period in which you work 1,000 hours. These 1,000 hours can be accumulated in any manner—40 hours for 25 weeks, for example, or 20 hours for 50 weeks.

Vesting

Once you become eligible, you should learn about *ownership* of both the funds contributed and the accrued benefits. The process by which *you* acquire ownership of your pension plan from your employer is called *vesting*. ERISA insisted that a specific vesting or ownership formula be established in each pension plan. Accordingly, the IRS accepted a variety of schedules but demanded that they all conform to certain fair guidelines. A few of the acceptable and approved alternatives included:

1. Five & Fifteen Year Rule: This rule required that you be 25% vested (own 25% of the cumulative benefits) after five years of service. At the end of fifteen years, you were 100% (fully) vested.

2. Ten-year Rule: This rule simply meant you would be 100% vested after ten years of service. Generally, you would accrue ten% ownership after each year of qualified employment. ERISA did not insist on a specific rate of increase, however.

3. Rule of 45: Under this rule, after you've been employed five years, you were 50% vested, if the sum of your age and years of service totals 45. From then on, your vesting continued at a ten% annual pace for the next five years.

Congress improved the vesting requirements in 1986, mandating that pension plans conform with one of the following two options:

1. The "cliff" type, which says you must "hang in" until you complete five years of employment. There is no ownership or vesting until then. At that time, you will be 100% vested.
2. The "step" type, in which you become vested gradually over a period of seven years:

Year:	1	2	3	4	5	6	7
Vesting Percentage:	0	0	20	40	60	80	100

You must be 100% vested in two years if the plan contains a two-year eligibility provision, as discussed earlier.

The Keogh Plan

The pensions discussed above pertain to employees who work for someone else. But there is a vast army of *self-employed* people for whom another program is designed.

Rules and regulations governing types of Keogh plan benefits, contributions, vesting, eligibility, and distribution have been modified over the years. They now basically conform to corporate pension plans, and they function in a largely similar way.

How Sizable Will Your Pension Benefits Be?

Pension benefits can be the largest component in your income transfer process. Whether you have a corporate plan or a Keogh, if you track your pension benefits, you can project their value and how much support they will give you in retirement. Fortunately, the dollars from a **defined benefit plan** are inflation-proof, just like Social Security. Such plans typically average your last three years' salary, into which inflation is factored. This relieves you of any worry about tracking these dollars against cost-of-living increases.

Our discussion of pensions has just been a brief introduction to the subject. However, it can make you knowledgeable enough to ask the right questions. The answers you receive will give you a good handle on the value of your future retirement benefits. To really get to know more about your pension, you should use the guidelines and sample questions listed in Figure 2-3.

Figure 2-3: Is the Plan Under Which You Are Covered:

Corporate _____ Keogh _____ Public _____
Defined Benefit _____Defined Contribution _____
Profit Sharing _____

ELIGIBILITY

How many years' service qualify you for coverage? _____
What minimum age must you be to qualify? _____
What maximum age can you be to qualify? _____

CONTRIBUTIONS

If the plan is *profit sharing*, what is:
Contribution formula _____
If your plan is *defined contribution*, what is:
Contribution formula _____
If your plan is *defined benefit*, what is:
Benefit formula _____
Inflation index of benefit, if any _____
Return benefits—what are payment options? _____

VESTING

What vesting formula below are you under:
Immediate _____ 10-Yr. Rule _____ 5 & 10 Yr. Rule _____
Rule of 45 _____ Other _____
Accrued Vesting Percentage _____

BENEFITS

Present Account Value _____
Benefit at Retirement _____
At what age is early retirement available? _____
At what age does regular retirement begin? _____
At what age is the latest retirement allowed? _____
What is the benefit schedule or percent for early retirement? _____
Describe your survivor benefits: _____
_____

What are the lump sum rollover provisions? _____

If you are disabled before normal retirement, what are your benefits? _____
May you take a loan against pension assets? _____
If so, what are the conditions and amount limits? _____
_____

MISCELLANEOUS

Who are the trustees—the body which holds and invests the funds of your pension? _____
Is your pension integrated with Social Security? _____

24

What Role Will Your Pension Play in Retirement?

The question remains: what proportion of your retirement needs will your pension fill? We indicated earlier that the range of pension payments is wide, but we must establish a working reference level or percentage. After reviewing many plans, we estimate the average anticipated support from pensions is 30% of pre-retirement income. If yours is *less*, you will have to make up in the difference from your savings and investments.

Combined with Social Security's 10%, you can see that your two "automatic" sources—Social Security and your pension—will probably give you 40% of your last working year's salary in retirement. You're aiming at a target of 65% to maintain your standard of living. So you will have to get the *remaining 25%* from the last source—*savings and investments* (S & I). These

Figure 2-4: The Income Transfer Process

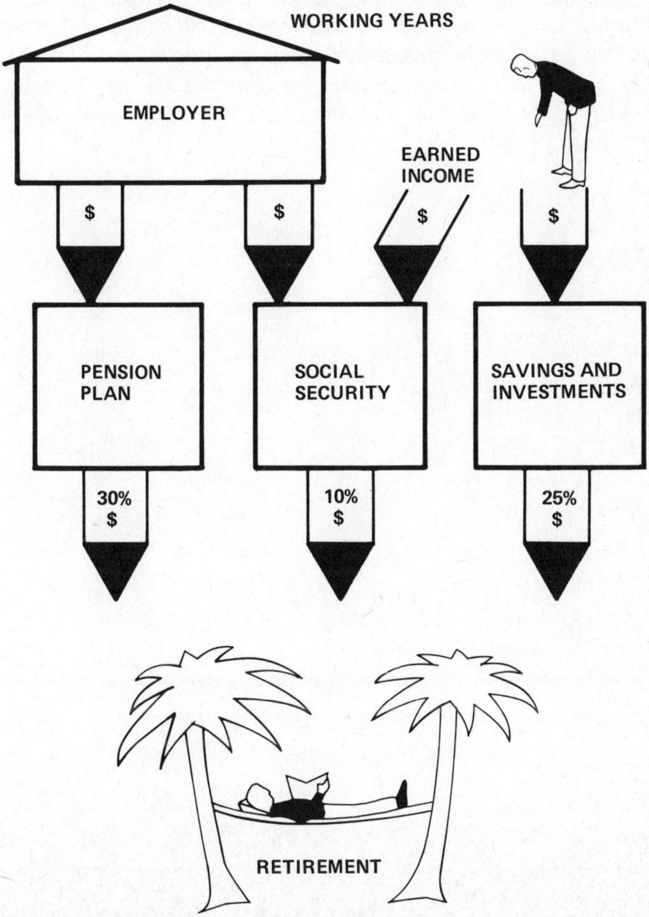

benchmark targets have been assigned to the three transfer process sources as shown in Figure 2-4.

SAVINGS AND INVESTMENTS

Unlike your participation in Social Security and pension plans, your commitment to S&I is voluntary. Accumulating S&I may be difficult, because to do so you must use "extra" dollars left over from your income. These will normally be already-taxed dollars whose growth will be taxed *again!* In addition, inflation will erode them further. You can begin to see the problems you must overcome to make your savings and investments pay off.

Your S&I won't grow as routinely or effortlessly as your Social Security account or your pension fund. Instead, you will have to apply your personal knowledge, and become involved if you want to see these funds grow. You will have to make decision upon decision in your search for the best investment choices. You have no guarantees in S&I participation; you can succeed or fall flat on your face. Your S&I goals will challenge you at all times.

Because savings and investments require special attention, they must be addressed separately. Their strong performance is so essential to your retirement security that we will devote all of the next chapter to an understanding of them.

THREE

Savings and Investments

Your impossible dream is slowly becoming reality, and so far fantasy has had nothing to do with it. You're on the way to being the next Mel Fisher! When you first assessed your chances of accurately calculating how much income you'd need in retirement, you probably felt like Don Quixote tilting at windmills! Your target was elusive, and your weapons seemed ineffective. Victory seemed impossible.

By now you've made significant progress—more than you could have expected before you picked up this book. Let's review the building blocks you now have in place.

You've determined the level of financial support you'll need in retirement—65% of your final working year's salary. And when you add your Social Security checks to your pension benefits, you know you have already secured about 40% of your pre-retirement income. And you've accomplished all this with *no expert financial planning!* In addition, you can bask in the knowledge that these two transfer elements grow automatically and are inflation-proof, too!

Up to now, it's been easy. But the honeymoon is over. Because now it's time to address the last of the three transfer sources—your *savings and investments* (S&I). This is where you will win or lose the game. There's nothing routine or automatic about S&I. Their growth and performance depend completely on your active efforts, and on your sound investment decisions.

RETIREMENT INCOME AND SPENDING: THE
BOUNCE PROCESS

S&I must provide the difference between your overall objective and the combination of your Social Security and pension benefits. Remember, the latter two combined will probably deliver 40% of your final working year's salary. But since you will need 65% of pre-retirement earnings as retirement income, S&I will have to yield the last 25%—a tall order!

The process of using invested funds to sustain future needs is shown in Figure 3-1. I call this the *bounce process*. The term seems appropriate since money put into savings and investments must "bounce" out to enable us to pay for goods and services. Whatever investment option you select, you must retrieve dollars from it to buy something later.

In retirement, purchasing *items*, not accumulating *dollars*, is your real objective. The items you will buy include the basic goods and services— including shelter, food, transportation, and so on—that are your needs now and will be your needs in retirement, too. The quantities and ratios may change, (see Appendix C for an analysis of your retirement needs) but the basic needs will not. You must pay for these needs with dollars from your pension plan, Social Security, your savings, and investments.

Figure 3-1: The Bounce Process

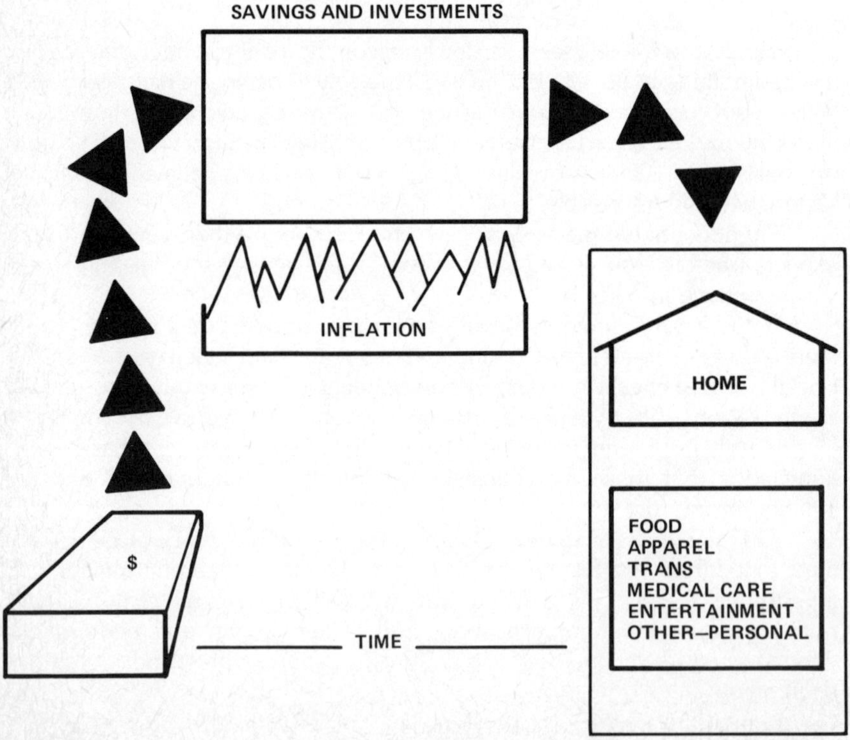

SAVINGS AND INVESTMENTS

INFLATION

$

HOME

FOOD
APPAREL
TRANS
MEDICAL CARE
ENTERTAINMENT
OTHER—PERSONAL

TIME

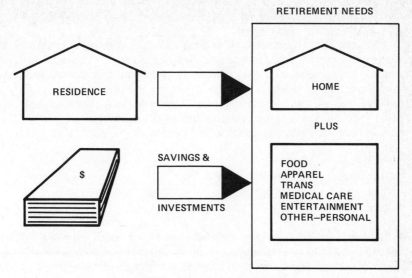

Figure 3-2: Conventional Planning

If you own your home, you probably expect to have paid it off entirely by the time you retire. This is conventional planning (see Figure 3-2) and is a situation we will address later in this chapter. On the other hand, your ability to purchase food, clothing, transportation and the like will depend on your retirement dollars. As we've seen, S&I must provide 25% out of a total of 65% of these dollars.

Many hurdles confront you in amassing a S&I portfolio that will give you adequate "bounced" dollars in retirement. For one thing, you probably know how hard it is during your working year to save any of your discretionary dollars. You have all too few dollars left to put aside after you pay for all the goods and services you need now. And even if you are disciplined enough to save and invest, our two by now familiar enemies— taxes and inflation—are just waiting to bedevil your efforts.

Taxes are immediate and visible; they nibble at your paycheck before you even receive it. Your other nemesis, inflation, is silent, almost invisible, and thus more treacherous. Its low profile lulls you into complacency. And when you least suspect, it will intercept your "bounce" with full force. But since taxes affect you first, let us consider them first.

THE IMMEDIATE PROBLEM—TAXES

The first thing that hits you about taxes is the alarming realization that your *earned* dollars are quite different from your spendable or *discretionary* ones. You work hard for your earned income. But before it reaches your hands, the IRS and Social Security wield their computerized axes to hack their share from your paycheck. You may get some kind of refund from these latter-day

Paul Bunyans. But, like a tree that is felled, your income-tax dollars, for the most part, can never grow again.

This tax drain fluctuates. Congress changes the rules often. Until recently, tax brackets were as high as 50%, as noted in Appendix A. The recent tax-reform legislation may actually work in your favor; it has reduced both the number of brackets and the rates that individuals are required to pay. Nevertheless, the tax bite still runs counter to your efforts to build up your S&I. The IRS will demand the following shares of your income so you can work only with the resultant diminished dollars:

Income: $100

Tax Bracket	15%	28%
Tax	$15	$28
Net	$85	$72

Like the rest of us, you pay your bills with what's left and hope a few dollars remain. If you do have any left, you look to launch them somewhere in the vast sea of savings and investment alternatives. Yet almost every option will result in a *secondary* tax on any yield on the sum you have invested—which, as you will recall, had already been taxed before you invested it.

Let's see what happens to your money when you invest it in two conventional savings products: A bank instrument and an insurance company annuity.

Investing in a Bank Instrument. Say you select a 36-month CD that pays a locked-in interest rate of 8%. You have been advised that while the money will be committed for three years, your loss of liquidity will be offset by the bigger-than-average yield. However, your expectations are soon shaken. When the bank notifies the IRS of your earnings, you are reminded that you must pay income taxes on the yield. If you're in a 28% bracket, Uncle Sam takes 28% of the 8% profit, leaving you only 5.76%. Every $1,000 you earn is taxed in a similar fashion:

Earned income	$1,000.00
Income tax (28%)	280.00
Net investment amount	720.00
CD yield (8%)	57.60
Tax on yield (28%)	16.13
Yield *after* tax	41.47
After-tax balance	$ 761.47

And here's the *really* scary part. Suppose you decide to invest $1,000 of your pretax earned income every year for 10 years ($10,000 total). From the process outlined above, you'll have a total of only *$9,924* after 10 years of savings. In other words, you'll have actually accumulated *less* than the pretax earnings you started with. Can you think of a more frustrating way to be in the red?

To avoid this exasperation, you try another savings vehicle that temporarily shields you from the double jeopardy just described. Let's look at what happens when you put your money into an insurance company's annuity:

Investing in an Annuity. Let's say an annuity will give you a return of 8%, too. Fortunately, you will not be taxed yearly on the yield, as you would with a bank CD; because of favorable tax-code provisions, the accumulated interest is not taxable until you ultimately receive the money. This allows your savings to grow tax-free. And, as you probably know, the difference between taxed and tax-free accumulation is significant. With all that going for you, you expect that the annuity will be a winner over savings. Maybe a *big* winner.

Well, let's trace the same $1,000 of annual earnings in an annuity after 10 years and see:

Earned income	$ 1,000.00
Income tax	280.00
Net investment amount	720.00
Future value (10 yrs. 8%)	11,264.75
Pretax return	4,064.75
Tax on gain ($4,064 × 28%)	1,138.00
After-tax balance	$10,126.00

Surprised? Well, it is *better*, but only slightly. And it too produces about the same $10,000 you started with. The tax-deferred annuity delivers only a few more after-tax dollars than the annually taxed bank CD. The much touted tax-deferred advantages of annuities are insignificant and can only help if you plan to be in a reduced tax bracket when you withdraw funds. I hope you're more financially successful than that!

This comparison conveys two powerful messages:

1. **Tax obligations thwart capital accumulation.**
2. **Significant after-tax yields are essential for asset development.**

This situation has you and millions of other investors gritting your teeth. You have struggled to set aside what little you can, and you find yourself a victim of the double taxation that erodes whatever real gain you attain.

Happily, relief is in sight. Surprisingly, it comes from the same source that caused your original problem—Congress. Our legislators have been enlightened (*pressured* is a better word) and have enacted programs that postpone regular taxation (on some of our gains, at any rate) right up to the time you retire. There are generous gifts that offer most of us an excellent opportunity to reduce our tax problems. This is "an offer you can't refuse." As shown in Figure 3-3, you have the option to save or invest with tax-free or after-tax dollars. There are no other choices.

Among the available tax-deferred programs is one that all qualified wage earners can use—**the IRA.** This instrument enables most people to contribute up to $2,000 each year and allows this money to grow in a tax-free environment. Clearly, the IRA is a valuable S&I tool for building your assets

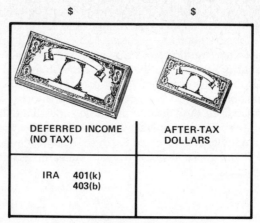

Figure 3-3: Savings & Investments

as part of the overall transfer process. (Appendix B tells in more detail how the IRA actually works.)

But before you close this book and blithely conclude that *any* IRA will provide the needed 25% of your last working year's salary, we must advise you that there are many different types of IRAs and that, to paraphrase George Orwell, some IRAs are more equal than others. The differences among them involve how they respond to your other adversary—inflation.

THE LONG-TERM PROBLEM—INFLATION

Even with an IRA, you cannot guarantee that S&I will produce 25% of your pre-retirement income. It can be jeopardized by *inflation* that counteracts some of the gains made by any long-term savings and investment program. In fact, as we noted earlier, inflation casts a more frightening pall over S&I than taxes do. It is an erosive force that is time-dependent but whose rate is impossible to forecast with any precision. Although inflation rates have cooled down recently, double-digit levels could return. If the inflation rates of the next 40 years are like those of the past 40, the prices that you will pay even for common staples may be mind-boggling.

The *bounce process* requires you to select carefully from a host of S&I choices. If your investment portfolio turns to ashes in the flames of inflation, you will be unable to buy the goods and services you'll need in retirement. Therefore, it is imperative that your investment yields *exceed* the rate of inflation. You must search out and select the *best possible investment*. That's your only chance to survive the destructive effects of this insatiable blaze.

Your S&I options include bank CDs, government securities, stocks, bonds, annuities, and mutual funds, to name just a few. Their promised yields may indeed compound, as we saw earlier in this chapter, but the tax drain on your efforts is constant. And what taxes don't drain away, inflation usually

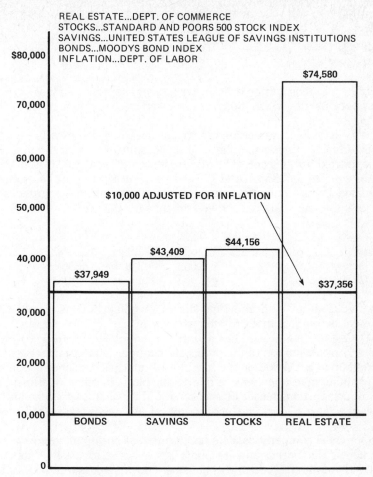

Figure 3-4: Investment Comparisons 1960–1985

burns up. So what is your best investment choice? When all is said and done, the most outstanding—and also the most dependable—investment is **REAL ESTATE**. There is no contest! Investment data reveal that your residence has far surpassed other investment choices.

We can prove this claim by comparing the performance of real estate with that of other vehicles over the past 25 years (see Figure 3-4). These data track the performance of a $10,000 sum invested in each of four vehicles— stocks, bonds, savings, and a personal residence—in the year 1960. (The real estate investment presupposes that you paid in full for a $10,000 house. Most probably, you, like millions of Americans, purchased your house with a small down payment.)

Ignoring the effects of secondary taxation, the total accumulated in each $10,000 investment by the year 1985 follows:

Stocks	—	$44,156
Savings	—	43,409
Bonds	—	37,949
Personal residence	—	74,580

The results for the first three vehicles are not very impressive. However, look at your personal residence. It has far surpassed its closest rival by more than $30,000, or 75%.

We advised you earlier in this chapter that when you measure returns, you should bear in mind that the only significant yields are those that have been corrected for inflation. On that basis, the original $10,000 in 1960 dollars is equal to $37,356 in 1985. There is no *real* increase in value until the appreciated value of the investment exceeds that inflation-adjusted sum. Therefore, the real value of each investment's *net gain* was:

Stocks	—	$ 6,800	(44,156 − 37,356)
Bonds	—	$ 593	(37,949 − 37,356)
Savings	—	$ 6,053	(43,409 − 37,356)
Personal residence	—	$37,224	(74,580 − 37,356)

These results shout loud and clear that your home has been your finest investment by far. But that's not the whole story.

Your home investment has had the benefit of tax-deferred growth. In addition, a major portion of the profits are tax-free. After you reach age 55, any profit up to $125,000 on the sale of your principal residence is untaxed.

No other investment enjoys this double plus. No other investment can boast of such uncharacteristic IRS generosity. This makes your home the best source of after-tax, one-time tax-free gift of any investment. And there's more.

Our initial comparisons were based on an *all-cash* purchase of various investments. But hardly anyone purchases a home for cash. When you purchased your home, you probably made a down payment of 20% or less. In 1960, $10,000 would thus have purchased five $10,000 homes, each for a down payment of $2,000. Instead of one home, you would have had five homes in your investment portfolio. In this leveraged pattern, the $10,000 would have risen in value to $372,900 by 1986. It's almost unbelievable! And when you correct that total for inflation, the original $10,000 investment would still have returned an amazing $335,544 in real dollars. (See Figure 3-5.) Real dollars, of course, are the only figures to watch for.

At this point you may be wondering, "Is there a catch to this?" And some proponents of other investments may say there is. They may argue that real estate requires continued support dollars, and that the down payment is not the only investment you'll have to make. They'll suggest that after the closing costs, you must pay the mortgage, heating bills, taxes, and other expenses. But this argument doesn't wash. First, those additional or monthly expenses are *not* investment costs. They're the price of *living* in the house. If you didn't buy the home, you would have to *rent* it or find some other home or apartment; the down payment is the *only dollar investment* in your home.

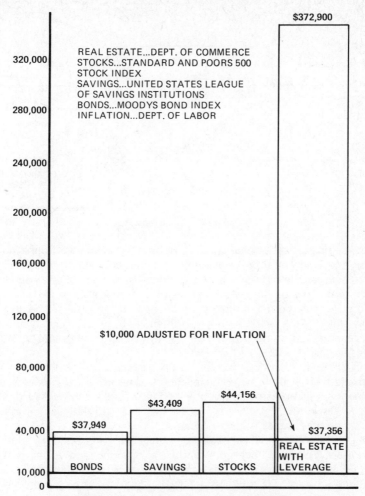

Figure 3-5: Investment Comparisons 1960–1985

And second, if you bought the house purely as an investment, the monthly expenses would be paid by the person who occupies the house—the renter, whose plight we examine in Chapter Twelve.

Now you know what you may have suspected all along—your home is your best investment by far. Having settled this matter, let's now consider the roles your residence can play in your retirement plan.

WHAT TO DO WITH YOUR HOUSE WHEN YOU RETIRE: A DILEMMA

When you retire, you'll need two things: A place to live in, and money to live on. More precisely, you'll require a home for shelter and the money to purchase all the other goods and services that the CPI lists. If you're like

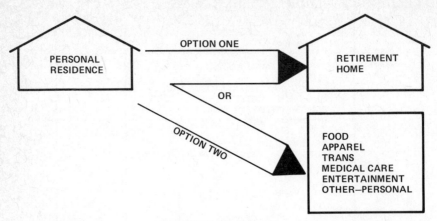

Figure 3-6:   The Dilemma

millions of others, as we noted earlier, you expect to own your house free and clear by the time you retire, leaving your retirement income to pay all your other expenses. The residence in question may be the only home you've ever lived in or it could be the last of a series of homes you've owned. You may elect to use it as your retirement home, or you may sell it and move to another state. In any event, securing a retirement house becomes a sure thing if you're already a homeowner. You don't need any investment strategy or expertise to assist you.

On the other hand, as we've just established, when you search for the investment that will best overcome inflation and furnish enough dollars to buy retirement goods and services, you will find it in your own backyard. That's right, it's your residence again. As we saw earlier, that same residence outpaces all other types of investments.

So now you face a real dilemma. Equity has been building up in your largest asset. You may have up to $200,000 or more lying dormant in your home. All that money is just sitting there. You know it can give you a terrific additional income if you could just tap it. What to do? Figure 3-6 presents the problem and shows you the two options that your home offers you. It can guarantee a debt-free retirement home, or it can provide cash for retirement goods and services.

You are comforted that your house can perform either of these vital functions for you. But your house *can't do both* simultaneously. You can't have your cake and eat it, too.

At retirement, you will have to make a choice between these two alternatives. But don't worry unduly. This is not a case of win or lose; rather, it's an issue of which is the *better* choice for you. Neither is wrong nor harmful, but one will resolve your financial retirement objectives while the other will not. So it is critical to study each in detail.

Option 1: Real Estate as a Residence

Option 1 is a familiar one. Millions of people stay on in their homes when they retire. They view their home only as a *residence* both through their working years and into retirement. These people see a house as having no other particular benefit.

Let's say you *do* decide to stay in your home at retirement. You've satisfied your shelter requirement. But in so doing, you've foregone use of the best investment dollars you've ever developed. These could have given you substantial retirement cash for all your other needs.

The good part of this option is that you will have virtually no mortgage expenses in your golden years. The bad part is that you will have to depend on S&I for the cash to buy retirement goods and services. The unpredictable, long-term effects of inflation can jeopardize your S&I's capacity to give you the remaining 25% of pre-retirement income.

With this risk clouding option 1, let's look closely at option 2.

Option 2: Real Estate as an Investment

Option 2 asks you to visualize your home as a future money-tree. However appealing this may sound, it may go against your grain. You probably have had a love affair with your house and are strongly attached to it. You've beautified it and babied it. The improvements you've made reflect your own tastes and personality. In light of these feelings, it's difficult to think of using your house as a bank! Yet, this is how your house can repay you for all the tender love and care you have given it. We'll look at this "bank" and see the superlative value it holds beyond the shelter it has so ably rendered.

Reluctant as you might be, you should consider the ultimate sale of your house to get hold of its huge equity. Let's think for a minute about how you accumulated this great profit. This powerful equity has grown without trauma or wheeling and dealing. None of the "60 point drops" or "market corrections" that plague the stock market were involved, nor was any world crisis that precipitated a rush on precious metals.

Instead, the growth of your home equity began with your dream of a white picket fence, a suburban lawn, or a split-level home. Whatever induced you to buy your first home, it was a step you took with great exhilaration—and trepidation. Remember when you moved into your first house? You were so happy, but you also worried how you could meet the mortgage payments. But within a year, the tax advantages made themselves felt and gave you some relief. Then you got a raise, and soon it didn't seem so difficult for you to keep up with the payments. In fact, they became easier every year. And the value of your house grew yearly.

All around you, neighbors who moved away boasted how much they sold their homes for. You were impressed, but you went on silently amassing more profit every year you lived in your house. Best of all, you didn't have to pay an annual tax on your gain. With any other investment the IRS would have knocked at your door each year for its share. You enjoyed the benefit of deferring taxes indefinitely.

Soon you decided you needed a bigger home for a growing family. Or perhaps your company transferred you. For whatever reasons, you decided to move. Figure 3-7 follows this process through the sequential purchase and sale of your home. The original home **A** had been purchased with a small

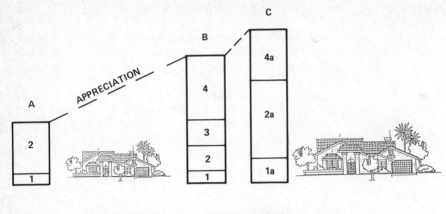

1. DOWN PAYMENT   1a. DOWN PAYMENT
2. MORTGAGE   2a. PLUS 4a EQUALS MORTGAGE
3. IMPROVEMENTS   4a. DEFERRED PROFIT
4. PROFIT

Figure 3-7: Sale of Residence

down payment, 1, and a mortgage, 2. The increase in value is shown by the height of the bar **B**. This includes:

1. The original down payment
2. The reduced mortgage
3. Improvements
4. The taxable profit

If you decide not to purchase another home and rent, you pay the mortgage (2), the tax on the profit (4), and keep the balance of the monies. But you bought "up." Using the untaxed increased equity from your first home you were able to make a big down payment on a more expensive one. You were able to put more down because Uncle Sam didn't tax the gain. He said, in effect, "Don't worry, pay it later." Thus you got a great break via the tax deferral allowed on your profit. And by taking advantage of it, you started off at a higher base of worth than you could afford with your own resources alone. That's some uncle!

But don't forget, although the purchase price was the total height of **C**, the IRS reduces this by the deferred profit, 4, and will base its future calculations of taxable profit on this second home—based on 1a + 2a not on the purchase price, 1a, 2a, and 4a. Your uncle is deferring—not forgiving. Because your second home was more expensive, it appreciated faster than the first. And your equity racked up fatter totals each year. If you were to buy a third house, this growth would only continue. This use of deferred taxes on profits from previous home sales is an incredible estate builder for you. Coupled with the favorable benefits of a leveraged purchase itself, this is the finest environment for an investment you could find anywhere.

This outline may help you realize how your home equity will mount up over 20 or 30 years. The simple act of buying your first house set it all in motion.

WHY YOUR HOUSE IS THE ONLY INVESTMENT YOU REALLY NEED

Eventually you will be 55 and may begin to consider retirement. By that time, you will have amassed tremendous equity in your final home. If you have owned several homes, it is likely that your last home is more expensive than that of the person who has only owned one.

And you'll be richer, too, because next comes the real bonanza. You decide to sell after age 55. Uncle Sam again plays Santa Claus! He gives you the right to claim a one-time exemption on all tax-deferred dollars due on up to $125,000 profit from the sale of your principal residence. How much nicer could he be? First he has put off collecting your taxes, which you have used for down payments. Then he *forgives* most of these taxes forever. No other investment enjoys any such breaks! This is an unparalleled windfall.

To give you a better handle on the numbers and how they amount, consider the following typical scenario: You buy your first home in 1970 for $30,000. At 10% appreciation, it is worth $80,000 in 1980, when you sell it for that sum. You immediately buy your second home for $110,000. That home will be worth $200,000 by 1988 at the same 10% annual appreciation. It is easy to see how quickly your initial investment can grow—a typical experience for a long-term homeowner.

Besides your $125,000 tax-free profit, you also receive tax exemption on the original price of the house and all improvements you've made to your house(s) over the years. These alterations not only increase your tax exemption but also make your house more valuable. This exemption usually brings the total untaxed sum to about $200,000 when you sell at 55 or older.

Now, if you sell your house and invest that $200,000 at 10%, you will have a supplemental $20,000 annual income—a sizable pension plan sum. Indeed, this income source can quite simply be viewed as a pension of substantial proportions. Let's review the significance of this extra "pension."

Let's say you have lived in your home(s) and worked for one company for 25 or 35 years. You expect and receive a reasonable pension from your company. Now look what happens with your house. You have lived in it, enjoyed it, and found it a source of refuge and joy. So what does the house do? Instead of *charging* you for satisfying you so much, it turns around and hands you an excellent pension, maybe even better than the one you worked so hard for all your career! The house actually *rewards* you with a tremendous pension for the pleasure and pride of having owned it. Now that's a friend everyone should have!

If your pre-retirement income is $80,000, a $20,000 supplemental pension from a $200,000 tax-free equity represents 25% of that income—the exact percentage of S&I you need to retire successfully. If you earn less, you'll be even better off in retirement. For example, for someone earning $40,000 yearly, the house "pension" is 50% of pre-retirement income, far exceeding target goals.

Mere home ownership has almost magically bestowed a pension big enough to fulfill your total objective of retirement income success. This *single* element of your S&I portfolio will satisfy the 25% need by itself. All your other S&I assets are just icing on the cake!

The amazing reality is how easy it's been to accomplish this. It has taken place automatically. No planning has been necessary. No involvement. No decisions. No worry.

Let's summarize what has happened. At the outset of our discussion, we established that the income-transfer process is the mechanism by which you will achieve your target retirement income. We set that objective at 65% of pre-retirement income, regardless of your salary. This 65% is being delivered by your pension plan (30%), Social Security (10%), and house "pension" (25%). These are all automatic, requiring no expertise or action at all on your part. Best of all, they are all inflation-resistant. All you had to do was work for a company with a pension plan and own your house. Could you have believed all you had to do to achieve fiscal security in retirement was work and live in your house?

Our goal here has been to deliver you the 65%, and we have done exactly that. But in attaining this ideal plan, you have had to give up the functional possession of shelter. Your house has been redirected to a better purpose—the completion of your income transfer process. Therefore, you now have before you the only real task you must undertake to put the finishing touch on this plan: You need to acquire a *debt-free replacement home* to live in when you retire.

We will now proceed to a discussion of how to secure a paid-up retirement house. There are many ways to achieve this objective.

FOUR

The Debt-Free Replacement House

By now, you may be in a state of disbelief. You were convinced you'd never get something for nothing. And yet, placed neatly in your lap, with "no strings," are the funds you need in retirement. You didn't have to do very much to get them.

Work for an organization that has a good pension program, comply with the Social Security laws and take care of your house—that's all. This almost automatic plan for financial security in retirement is dependent upon all of the transfer sources, including the funds from your savings and investments.

And it is an almost incredible demonstration of the power inherent in your house. In fact, the material discussed in the previous two chapters is the essence of the retirement phase of a total life-cycle program based on the potential of your home, that I call HOUSEPOWER.

HOUSEPOWER is a simple, logical, self-fulfilling plan that goes "back to the basics" and uses your home to achieve financial objectives and security. It works at many levels in your life, eventually providing all the means for ultimate economic independence in retirement by simply owning your principal residence. It is a diverse and dynamic lifelong strategy. Because of its many aspects and ramifications, only the retirement phase of HOUSEPOWER is touched on by this book. A subsequent book will be published that covers HOUSEPOWER in its entirety—from the first home purchase to the end of your career. The book on HOUSEPOWER will demonstrate how you can use the capacity of a personally owned residence to enable you to satisfy all your biggest lifetime responsibilities.

Meanwhile, we will now dwell only on the retirement reward of

41

HOUSEPOWER. As noted, your *house* is what has created this bonanza of funds. After having supplied your functional need for shelter through your working years, it now offers you the means to pursue a financially stable lifestyle. You are truly free to enjoy your golden years.

But where will you enjoy them? Remember, you've sold your house to complete your income transfer process. Now you must find other shelter, and it must be clear of debt. Only when you have secured somewhere to live in retirement will you be able to sell your principal residence and become financially independent. As noted at the end of the last chapter, you must now secure:

A DEBT-FREE REPLACEMENT HOUSE

You should understand one point clearly before we proceed. While you will pay for your replacement home with dollars, your primary reward from this replacement home will *not* be financial gain. You shouldn't expect to derive profit from this house. Instead, your paramount concern should be its *function* as a suitable retirement dwelling for you. Any profits and income it may generate are secondary bonuses.

You may be among the many people who have bought a second home or condo as a weekend or vacation getaway. Or perhaps you have bought a second home as a rental property, a type of investment. You may not vacation there, but you'll earn return on your investment. In either case, your second home can eventually become your functional shelter. Your purchase will have given you a place to live in retirement, completing your retirement plan.

Since you can eventually use it as a retirement home, you should not be reluctant to buy a second home of any type. The sooner you do so the better. In fact, because prices are rising faster than the average person's capacity to save for a down payment, you may never get a second home if you wait.

The locations and types of replacement residences are as diverse as people. No two purchases are ever exactly alike. When house hunting, you should look for what reflects you, your personality, your lifestyle. You have to be comfortable with the home you choose. Particularly popular categories include:

- A beach house
- A mountain cabin
- A lakefront house
- A two-family house
- A single-family house

Regardless of which you prefer, remember that you can use any of the above type homes to satisfy your functional requirement for later shelter—either directly, or by selling the property and buying one you want to live in for retirement.

While we urge you to buy now if you haven't already done so, you may

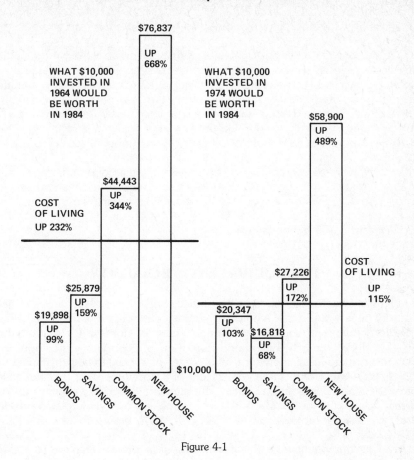

WHAT $10,000
INVESTED IN
1964 WOULD
BE WORTH
IN 1984

WHAT $10,000
INVESTED IN
1974 WOULD
BE WORTH
IN 1984

$76,837
UP
668%

$58,900
UP
489%

$44,443
UP
344%

COST
OF LIVING
UP 232%

COST
OF LIVING
UP
115%

$27,226
UP
172%

$25,879
UP
159%

$20,347
UP
103%

$19,898
UP
99%

$16,818
UP
68%

$10,000

BONDS   SAVINGS   COMMON STOCK   NEW HOUSE

BONDS   SAVINGS   COMMON STOCK   NEW HOUSE

Figure 4-1

resist this suggestion. The hard reality is that most homeowners do not own a second home. Many people don't know where they want to spend their retirement. They quite naturally hesitate to buy just anywhere. Others don't see how a second home can become a replacement home. Still others simply procrastinate. People really sit on buying *another* property. It's a scary purchase for many of us.

Many buyers delay because they wonder whether it's better to buy the home now or wait until retirement. They prefer to save and invest in other vehicles and use those funds to buy the home later. But that route is very risky. If you look at Figure 4-1, you see all the ladders that represent the different investment choices. You can see that the clear performer in the future is the home. The other selections offer little hope of raising enough money for a replacement home. Also, if you go any route except the immediate home purchase, you will be compromising your easy plan and its

* Source: *U.S. News & World Report*

chances of success. Clearly your best path is to stick to the plan and buy the home—and soon.

The best reason to buy right away is that real estate is the only valuable item you can buy today and not use until years later. (True, you could buy a 1986 car, seal it up somewhere for 25 years, and then unveil it as an antique in mint condition; but that would be about the only other item to have a comparable increased value, and some use, later.) Furthermore, you can't buy at *today's* prices the costs of tomorrow's labor, material, and financing for building a home. In the future, you'll only be able to buy these components at inflated prices.

OK, perhaps you agree that you should buy a second home now. But perhaps you still won't actually do it for one very good reason: *You simply can't afford it.* Otherwise, you would gladly follow our plan and buy the replacement home. You and millions of others are in the same boat. But don't despair. **We have a solution.**

THE EQUIVALENCY SOLUTION

I call the answer to your dilemma the *equivalency solution*. This plan does *not* involve buying portions of a house or putting your house together piecemeal. We don't intend for you to buy roofing supplies or storm windows bit by bit whenever you can afford them and store them in your garage until you can pay someone to install them (at a future date you'd have to pay inflated labor costs, anyway). There is *one* component of a house that you *can* purchase now at *today's* prices and use later. This element is a perfect alternative to a direct home purchase, and it is the key to making our whole plan work. In fact, it is the very foundation of HOUSEPOWER, both literally and figuratively.

The component we speak of is the *homesite*, or a lot—a piece of land—to build the house on. It is the one major part of a house that you can buy now and store with no inconvenience until you are ready to use it at a later time. We recommend that if you can, you ultimately buy four homesites—not just one. Why?

Figure 4-2 shows the cost components of a finished home. The chart indicates that the most recent cost of a homesite averages 25% of the cost of the total home. So, by mathematical logic, it follows that if you own four homesites, you will have the full equivalent (100%) of a house. Buying four homesites is the equivalency solution. This route to home ownership offers you the best way to reach your objective of a debt-free replacement home, because you can buy as little as one-fourth (25%) of a house at a time—a much more affordable strategy than buying a whole house. We call this the "four-lot concept."

The Rising Costs of Land

The equivalency solution utilizes the fastest inflating component in real estate—the homesite. It is steadily appreciating more rapidly than other home

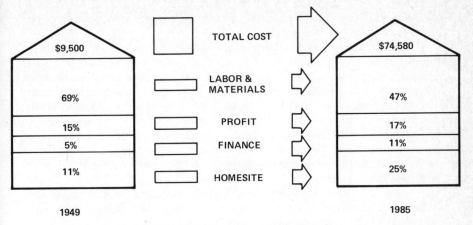

Figure 4-2: Cost Components of a Typical Home

elements, as shown in Figure 4-2. It has continued to spiral steadily as a percent of costs since World War II. In 1949, for example, an average house cost only $9,500, and the lot comprised only 11% of the cost, or $1,045. By 1985, a typical house cost $74,580 and the land had climbed to $18,650, or 25% of the total price.

Other related statistics are equally revealing. The nonland costs of an average house rose from $9,500 in 1949 to $74,580 in 1985; that's a 685% increase, or an annual average of 19%. But, meanwhile, in the same period, the value of the homesite soared from $1,045 to $18,650—a resounding 1,685%! That's an amazing average of 47% per year!

And that's only the *average*. Land costs can reach 50% of total residence costs in attractive, prestigious or otherwise sought-after communities—notably in prized resort or vacation spots, but also in less celebrated beachfront and waterfront properties as well.

These staggering statistics send a clear signal about homesites. Homesites have risen in value almost two and one half times faster than other real estate components, all of which have enjoyed healthy gains. To use investment jargon, this phenomenal performance can only be described as "going through the roof."

Because land is inflating quickly, investors' interest in homesites has been leaping. It's the "hot" choice among investment options in the overall area of real estate—already the outstanding performer, as we have seen.

Why have homesites accelerated so much in value, and why do they continue to do so? One reason is the universal desire of a growing population to own land. More homeowners than ever want and are buying second homes or properties. And lifelong renters are looking for a first house as a retirement home.

Then, too, "they're not making any more." Quite simply, there is *less* residentially usable land left every time a development is started or completed. Furthermore, as more homes are erected in a desirable area, the developable pool of homesites shrinks, raising the costs of preparing an area for homes. Costs are not the only factors responsible for the decreasing number of buildable homesites.

Infrastructure problems are also involved. A mounting number of municipalities will no longer support unbridled growth. Taxpayer resistance is intensifying against enlarging school, police, fire, and public-works systems to accommodate large influxes of new residents. Sewage systems are operating at capacity, with few communities eager to expand them. Most critically, potable water supplies are shrinking dramatically as a consequence of environmental pollution and other ecological factors. Acid rain and other contaminants have threatened development in many areas. Shortages of available drinking water may well become the most salient obstacle to homesite development.

All these factors highlight the increasing importance of the homesite in a real estate purchase. We hope you can see the irrefutable logic behind the equivalency solution to owning a debt-free replacement home.

WHY THE EQUIVALENCY SOLUTION WORKS

You can reap the benefits of the equivalency solution by eventually selling three of your four homesites and using the cash to build your debt-free replacement home on the homesite that remains. There are many variations on this simple idea, which we will discuss shortly; first, let's review what the four-lot approach accomplishes.

In essence, the four lots deliver the biggest need in retirement housing. They consequently liberate typically up to $200,000 equity from the sale of your principal residence. By investing that large sum in a 10% return product, we have secured an extra $20,000 pension.

Because homesites appreciate well ahead of inflation and even ahead of other housing costs, there is no way you can fail to achieve your debt-free retirement home, regardless of how severe inflation may be. In fact, given rapidly inflating land costs, obtaining four lots assures that you may even have far more in your pocket than just the cost of your replacement home.

One of the best examples of this startling success may be my own. My story really points up all the great things that can happen when you implement the four-lot strategy. In fact, part of the reason I'm writing this book is my amazing good fortune in buying lots. I was inspired to formulate my plan largely because I could see, from my own profitable acquisitions, that its appeal and application are universal.

I bought four lots in 1972 for a total of $26,000 cash. The area where I purchased the lots developed steadily and satisfactorily for all concerned. Right now, my homesites are surrounded by lovely lived-in homes on more than half the neighboring properties, all of which were homesites when I first bought. I just put the four lots "away"—in storage, as it were. But I didn't want to trade them in, realizing I'd be selling off a future master bedroom or some other valuable home component. It seemed to me that holding on to the lots would assist me later, although I could have made some profit by selling them. And here's what happened as a result of holding on to them.

In 1986, a local appraiser valued my four lots at $210,000. My appreciation had averaged 15% per year. Try to get that return regularly from any other investment! Yet my experience is not uncommon. It is the *rule* in desirable areas—and in some areas the percentage of appreciation is even higher.

Let's look at my options. I can do any number of things with the lots, or do nothing at all. By selling three of the lots, I can build my dream house on the fourth one now and use it later. In the meantime, I can rent the house out. But handling landlord/tenant problems is not my idea of happy home ownership, nor do I want various repair or maintenance headaches before I take occupancy myself. So I "rent" my four lots to the birds, the bees and the squirrels.

You don't have to follow my example. My decision not to build now or rent is a purely personal one. But in my case, I can postpone my choice of what type of home to build and where to build it until I'm ready to retire. I know that, whatever else happens, my four lots will pay for the house I want.

Of course, by delaying the construction of my replacement house, I do face the forces of inflation. No doubt about that. The house will cost more later, true. But if you recall the *bounce process*, you know that direct ownership of a desired object negates any effects of inflation. Well, I've got the home equivalency in my four lots. If I build now, I'll have a $210,000 (ignoring taxes) house after selling my four lots. If I hold on to the lots for eight more years, and if today's $210,000 house will then cost $430,000 (10% annual appreciation), I will still have the cost covered because the *lots will rise in value over the years*. My four lots are the world's best inflation beater. They will always be equivalent to a house in any economic climate, because the homesite price is inextricably tied to the house price.

Let me reiterate where I stand by owning four lots:

- I am assured of my retirement home, regardless of its price.
- When I feel like retiring, I just sell my three lots and build my house on the fourth.
- Under no circumstances can any stockbroker, banker, or investment counselor call me to announce that I've lost my living room or patio. No market drops or plunging investment values will take away my third bedroom. I'm taking no chance that conventional financial planners can get me my house. My dream house could shrink to a doghouse in their hands.

I hope you are convinced by now that the equivalency solution is the ideal way to guarantee your eventual replacement house. Four homesites are more affordable than one house because you can buy them one at a time. Of course, you must carefully choose where you buy your homesites and what kind you select. This issue will be discussed in Chapter Eight.

How to Buy Your Replacement Home

The most important point to emerge from this discussion is that you can begin *now* to consider buying a single lot. This is the real payoff; you can buy all or a part of your equivalent home, in the form of a homesite, with your *real estate IRA*.

Your options within this general framework are interesting and varied. You will be able to use your IRA and/or your spouse's, to acquire anywhere from one to four lots. In fact, you need not purchase all four to attain your objectives, although four is ideal. Even a three-lot owner will come out on top, for two reasons. First, we have established that the value of homesites is escalating rapidly. If current trends continue, an investor will soon need only *three* lots to complete his or her full home equivalency. This is a distinct possibility, given that the value of the homesite as a percentage of total home cost has soared from 11% to 25% in three decades. Second, the three-lot owner can always sell off these properties and buy his or her replacement house in a less expensive community.

Even two-lot and single-lot owners have good reason to be optimistic. While they have a higher mountain to climb, their lot ownership has put them well on the way to attaining a retirement home. They are still in a far better position than if they had invested comparable sums in competitive instruments.

Because you will ultimately be buying your replacement house through the purchase of individual homesites, we will examine the ramifications of this activity in more detail in later chapters. And since you will be using the *real estate IRA* to acquire your homesites, we will also look carefully at exactly what the IRA is and what it isn't. This federal investment vehicle is not well understood by the general public, and what we have to say about it may surprise you.

A better grasp of the IRA will enable you to get more out of it. So let's proceed to examine the IRA and its restrictions in order to learn the true advantages as well as disadvantages of this working person's "tax shelter."

FIVE

The IRA: What It Is and What It Isn't

The initials I-R-A have not always been associated with a federal tax shelter. From 1974 to 1981, if you saw these letters, you might well have connected them with the Irish Republican Army and the troubles in Ulster. During that time, you weren't qualified for an IRA if you had a pension plan at work, so you paid little attention to the new federal program.

But in 1982, *all* wage earners became eligible for the Individual Retirement Account, and you could no longer ignore the blizzard of messages about it. For most Americans, the initials I-R-A suddenly took on a new meaning—a way to create a fund for retirement.

While 120 million citizens became eligible to open an IRA in 1982, only 30%, or 36 million, had done so by 1985. This might seem to you a sign of neglect or lack of interest; yet as Congress learned recently during its tax-reform deliberations, the IRA enjoys strong support among the American public, who clamored against changes in it. The IRA was, of course, modified (see Appendix A), but its basic characteristics were left intact.

What advantages of the IRA make it so popular? How can the IRA fit into your retirement plan for financial security? To find out, you will have to learn far more than the fact that the initials I-R-A no longer identify only the Irish Republican Army.

WHAT DO YOU REALLY KNOW ABOUT THE IRA?

You have probably learned about the IRA from print advertisements, radio and TV commercials, or brochures put out by sponsoring institutions. Unfortunately, these sources are often less than candid or thorough. They are

49

designed to *sell* (not inform), and to lure your dollars to the sponsor's own particular IRAs. With this single objective in mind, each sponsor makes sure that the information its messages convey is slanted or biased to its best interests. And this approach has been extremely successful.

Bank propaganda has been so extensive and effective that many Americans simply equate an IRA with a CD and believe that the IRA is a sales vehicle for banks. Nothing could be farther from the truth! You can use your IRA to buy *dozens* of other financial products. If you have been lulled by bank advertising, wake up! Sure, the banks couldn't be happier for you to keep making your IRA deposits with them for the immediate "tax savings" they promise. But do you know what's *really* happening to your assets?

You may pay dearly if you keep your IRA eggs in the bank basket. Let's discuss what we mean. As we do so, we may shatter your notions about what the IRA can and can't do. We will expose the realities, limitations, and advantages of the IRA, so that you will be able to use it for your optimal gain.

Exactly what are the claims that blitz the public from January until the April 15 tax deadline? The promises are many. Collectively, they tell you that an IRA will give you the following benefits:

- Immediate tax savings
- Long-term tax advantages
- Use of Uncle Sam's money for retirement
- Benefits of lower tax rates
- IRA "millionaire" status
- Miraculous tax-free compounding
- Early contribution bonus

You may recall hearing or reading these contentions in one form or another. They have been reported so often since 1975 that they're widely accepted as fact. Intensive repetition of a statement, regardless of how true or false, verifies it for many people. It is a strategy you must be alerted to in all forms of persuasion.

ARE YOU STILL ELIGIBLE FOR AN IRA?

Prior to 1987, all wage earners were eligible to adopt an IRA. The tax reforms enacted by Congress in 1986 did not change eligibility requirements. Everyone who has earned income can still take advantage of the tax-free environment of the IRA. However, Congress separated individuals into three distinct groups based on their existing pension coverage and income. The purpose of this change was to deny some the ability to deduct all or part of their contribution from taxable income. These changes are discussed in Appendix B, which visualizes the three groups entering the IRA fortress through three doors, as shown in Figure 5-1.

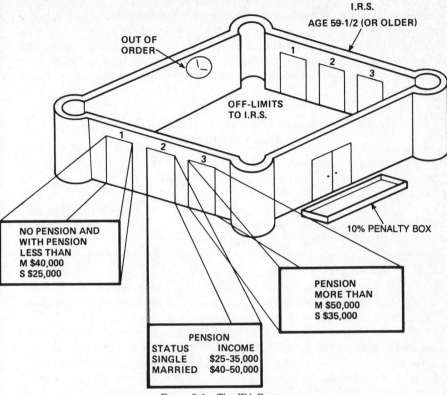

Figure 5-1: The IRA Fortress

Gate 1: These individuals are permitted to take a tax deduction for the total contribution.
Gate 2: These individuals can only take a partial deduction for their contribution.
Gate 3: These individuals cannot deduct their contributions. They must contribute after-tax dollars to their IRA.

It would appear that those qualified for gate 1 benefit from the tax deduction while those going through 2 and 3 benefit partially or not at all. It also follows that the issue of tax reduction is obvious for the first group, questionable for the second and moot for the third.

But not everything is what it appears to be, and to accept the "obvious" without question can sometimes be misleading. Because the issue is so important, we ask:

Will an IRA Reduce Your Taxes Immediately?

Have the new regulations deprived the IRA advertisers of the powerful appeal of tax reduction? The IRS people know you can't resist the temptation to pay less taxes. Avoiding taxes is as American as apple pie. Our founding fathers started this tradition when they dumped tea into the Boston harbor to protest paying more than their share of import duties.

It would appear that the tax reduction has been preserved only for all

wage earners *not* covered by a pension plan or for those pension-covered
married couples earning less than $40,000 and single persons covered by a
pension but earning $25,000 or less. This is certainly the perception
conveyed by the reports that focused on the loss of the tax deduction enacted
by Congress. But you're in for a surprise. For it turns out that. . . .

There is no Immediate Reduction in Taxes for an IRA Participant

Has Uncle Sam really become Santa Claus? Does he let some of you put
$2,000 in an IRA where the money can grow tax-free, and then foot
one-third of the cost?

One should *always* question surprise "gifts" from anyone—particularly
the IRS. To put it bluntly, there is no such thing as a free lunch! If you think
that immediate tax advantages come to you merely by your opening an IRA,
you have been misled. The IRS has only *delayed* tax treatment of your
money. You are permitted only to defer the tax due on the amount of income
contributed to your IRA. There is no gift or reduction of taxes at the moment
of contribution; there is only a *postponement* of taxation until distribution.
The easiest way to prove this point is by example:

Mr. Smith prepared and filed his federal taxes on January 10th. A few
weeks later he saw an advertised claim about a tax refund he could get by
simply opening an IRA. Rather than put $2,000 into the IRA immediately, Mr.
Smith opted to claim an IRA deduction of $2,000 and retrieve the taxes he
had already paid on $2,000 of income. Then he contributed $2,000 to his
IRA before the April 15 deadline.

Figure 5-2 depicts what took place. First, Mr. Smith filed an amended

Figure 5-2: The Deferral Process

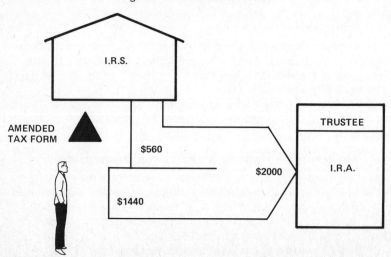

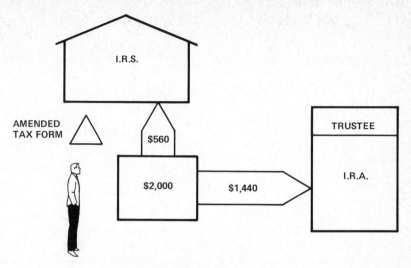

Figure 5-3: The Non-Deferral Process

tax form with the IRS, claiming an IRA contribution of $2,000. Since his taxable income was reduced by the total of the IRA contribution, he qualified for a refund of $560 (28% of $2,000). The IRS sent him the refund in the first week of April. To fulfill his IRA commitment, Mr. Smith added $1,440 of his personal funds to his $560 refund and contributed the total $2,000 to his IRA. Note—Mr. Smith was not able to keep the $560 refund! Whichever option he exercised, this sum would always be sent elsewhere. Without an IRA, it goes to the IRS. With an IRA, it ends up with the sponsoring institution. The participant never keeps it. From a tax perspective, nothing has happened. No tax savings has occurred. What took place was a simple deferral of tax action by the IRS until much later.

The question of tax savings will be resolved when the IRA money is distributed. At that time, the IRS will calculate whether the IRA holder has actually saved any tax dollars. Only time will tell.

The only sure "reduction" is in the amount of "deferred taxes" that the IRS does not collect when it should. In our example, the $560 contributed to Mr. Smith's IRA trustee is revenue *denied* Uncle Sam. The government is shorted.

On the other hand, those who enter the IRA Fortress through gate 3 do not have the deferral option. They must pay their taxes immediately and contribute only "after-tax" dollars to the IRA. This is shown in Figure 5-3.

There is no immediate tax savings for gate 3 contributors, but neither is there an immediate savings for those who can take the full or partial deduction. The tax advantage can only be assessed at distribution time. Only then can we determine which is the most advantageous gate 1, 2, or 3. Only time will tell.

WHAT ABOUT MIRACULOUS TAX-FREE COMPOUNDING?

Another well-publicized claim by IRA sponsors:

Tax-Free Compounding Works Miracles

This advantage is a real one, and it is true for money contributed to any IRA. Actually, no miracles are involved; what happens is just compounding at work (see Appendix A). The only miracle is that the IRS has been neutralized and cannot get at your money until distribution. The greatest boon to an investment is tax-free growth. The enormous difference in accumulation between a tax-treated and tax-free environment is shown in Table 1.2.

These advertised accumulations are impressive and may well have enticed you to contribute to an IRA, as they were designed to do. But although the numbers are accurate, they do not tell the whole truth. The tax-free advantage works on *all* the money contributed—both the government's tax-deferred dollars *and* your personal funds. The tax-deferred dollars that have grown and compounded will have to be paid to the IRS. This will diminish the advertised totals considerably, although tax-free compounding will nonetheless help your personal funds grow.

WHAT ARE THE ADVANTAGES OF EARLY CONTRIBUTIONS?

Yet another touted plus of the IRA is the clearcut advantage of contributing early, which promises:

A Bonus of Thousands for Early Contributions

This is a valid claim, but it is not unique to IRAs. Compounding, whether in an IRA or not, depends on time to work its mathematical magic. If you make contributions earlier, this simple factor will give your IRA a substantial bonus. For instance, if you make your deposits on January 1 of the tax year rather than at the tax deadline—April 15 of the next year—the 15½ months time difference will affect your accumulations significantly (see Table 1.3).

Your dollar bonus on retirement will be large, just for being an "early bird." In fact, you may even want to borrow the money for your early IRA contribution. Your tax refund will pay for the loan and the cost of borrowing *may* be tax-deductible.

However, for those of you who can deduct all or part of your contribution, a more prudent approach would be to increase the number of dependents you list with your employer. The dollar value of your IRA contribution and the dollar amount of your extra dependent deductions should be compatible. If they are, you will get your tax overpayment back sooner, making it possible to accelerate payments into your IRA. This strategy will pay off handsomely.

TABLE 1.2 Accumulation of $1000 at 8%

Year	Tax Free	After Tax 15%	After Tax 28%
1	1080	1068	1058
2	1166	1141	1119
3	1260	1218	1183
4	1360	1301	1251
5	1469	1389	1323
6	1587	1484	1399
7	1714	1585	1480
8	1851	1693	1565
9	1999	1808	1655
10	2159	1931	1751
11	2332	2062	1852
12	2518	2202	1958
13	2720	2352	2071
14	2937	2512	2190
15	3172	2683	2316
16	3426	2865	2450
17	3700	3060	2591
18	3996	3268	2740
19	4316	3490	2898
20	4661	3728	3065
21	5034	3981	3242
22	5437	4252	3428
23	5871	4541	3626
24	6341	4850	3835
25	6848	5179	4055
26	7396	5532	4289
27	7988	5908	4536
28	8627	6310	4797
29	9317	6739	5074
30	10063	7197	5366
31	10868	7686	5675
32	11737	8209	6002
33	12676	8767	6348
34	13690	9363	6713
35	14785	10000	7100
36	15968	10680	7509
37	17246	11406	7941
38	18625	12182	8399
39	20115	13010	8883
40	21725	13895	9394

TABLE 1.3 Prompt Funding Advantage.
Yearly Contribution: $2,000 Yield: 10% (Pretax Balance)

Years	Start of Year	End of Year	Cumulative Difference
5	13,431	12,210	1,221
10	35,062	38,874	3,188
15	69,900	63,555	6,345
20	126,000	114,550	11,450
25	216,363	196,694	19,669
30	328,988	361,887	32,899
35	596,254	542,048	54,206
40	973,703	885,185	88,518

DOES AN IRA GIVE YOU LONG-TERM TAX ADVANTAGES?

Another common claim is that investing with the total "tax-deductible" IRA dollars is more effective than investing with after-tax non-IRA dollars. Is this just hype, or can it be true? This alleged advantage of the IRA is *not* only advertising talk. It's true. In fact, this is the best of all the advantages. The personal funds you deposit in an IRA are delivered to you at retirement *tax-free.*

We can demonstrate the truth of this claim by examining what will happen to your IRA dollars as you contribute them, watch them grow tax-free, and then withdraw them as shown in Figure 5-4. Our example is based on a *fully* deductible contribution.

To keep this demonstration clear, we will assume that you make only one $2,000 contribution to your IRA. As we noted earlier, your contribution consists of two components—the deferred taxes which belong to the IRS, *and* your personal dollars. It is important to keep this distinction in mind.

The $2,000 contribution will grow in value, as the increasing width of the truncated cone shows. The total growth consists of both the tax-deferred and personal portions. These two components, which grow at the same rate, are separated in the cone by the vertical line that represents your marginal tax bracket. We assume this bracket will remain unchanged until distribution, despite a perception that most people will enter a lower tax bracket when they retire. With a constant tax bracket, the number of dollars in both segments increases, but the *percentage* does not. On distribution, the original deferred dollars are finally payable to the IRS, and so is the *appreciation* of those dollars. None of these tax-deferred monies or their appreciation *ever* accrue to you. These funds were always government property and will be delivered to the IRS on distribution. However, *the compounded personal dollars are yours tax-free.*

This fact warrants emphasis, so let's look at an example that uses numbers. Let's talk about a hypothetical IRA participant, Ms. Roberts.

Say Ms. Roberts puts only one $2,000 deposit in her IRA and allows

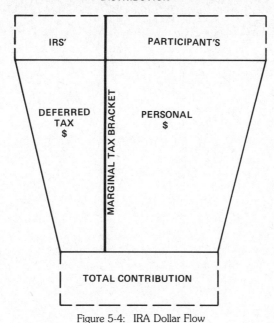

Figure 5-4: IRA Dollar Flow

it to grow for the next twenty years. In addition, suppose Ms. Roberts has successfully built a substantial retirement income that has kept her in the 28% tax bracket throughout the 20-year period and into retirement.

In the 28% tax bracket, Ms. Roberts' $2,000 contribution consists of $560 in tax-deferred money and $1,440 in personal dollars. At an 8% rate of return, these two components will compound to a total of $9,322 in twenty years. At age sixty, Ms. Roberts elects to have all the funds distributed again, to keep the example easy. Her tax burden will be $2,610—28% of $9,322, or the compounded sum of the tax-deferred $560 of her original contribution. Ms. Roberts will keep $6,712. This sum is the compounded value of her $1,440 personal dollars.

The proof that the IRA will deliver more personal dollars to you by allowing you to invest them tax-free is substantiated when we examine the performance of these same "personal" dollars outside the IRA's protective envelope. The comparison is shown in Figure 5-6. The performance of the IRA investors is repeated in Part *A* of this figure. The conventional non-IRA investor's results are shown in Part *B* of the same figure. Starting with the same $2,000 of earned income, the *B* investor paid $560 in taxes to the IRS and invested the balance $1,440 in a conventional nonsheltered vehicle yielding 8%. Because the yield was taxable each year, the 8% is reduced to 5.76% (at a 28% tax rate). At the end of twenty years, the total after-tax yield accumulation is $4,414.

In contrast, the IRA delivered a net of $6,712 after paying the IRS its

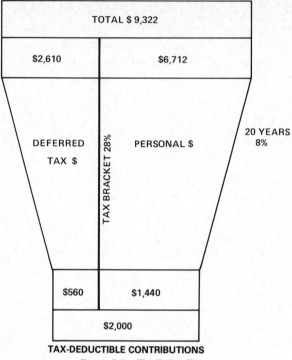

TAX-DEDUCTIBLE CONTRIBUTIONS
Figure 5-5: IRA Dollar Flow

due. Therefore, we can conclude: **The IRA Eliminates Secondary Tax Treatment of Your Personal Dollars and Delivers Their Accumulated Total Tax-Free.**

A critical question that must be addressed in light of the new regulations is:

DOES THE NON-TAX-DEDUCTIBLE IRA RETAIN ITS ADVANTAGES OVER CONVENTIONAL INVESTING?

The answer to this issue is contained in a comparison of the plots shown in Figure 5-7. Our conventional investor's performance is repeated from Figure 5-6(A). The net return is $4,414. The non-tax-deductible IRA participant (B) pays the 28% tax on $2,000 ($560) and elects to put the remainder $1,440 into the IRA. Both A and B start with the same number of dollars—$1,440. However, the tax-sheltered environment of the IRA permits its $1,440 to grow tax-free to $6,712, the same as the personal dollars in the basic IRA in Figure 5-6. When distributed, the tax on this accumulation will be:

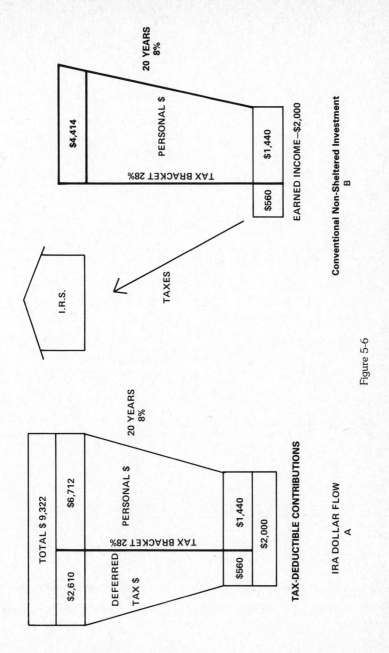

TAX-DEDUCTIBLE CONTRIBUTIONS

TOTAL $ 9,322

$6,712

$2,610

PERSONAL $

DEFERRED
TAX $

TAX BRACKET 28%

20 YEARS
8%

$1,440

$560

$2,000

IRA DOLLAR FLOW
A

I.R.S.

TAXES

$4,414

PERSONAL $

TAX BRACKET 28%

20 YEARS
8%

$560

$1,440

EARNED INCOME—$2,000

Conventional Non-Sheltered Investment
B

Figure 5-6

59

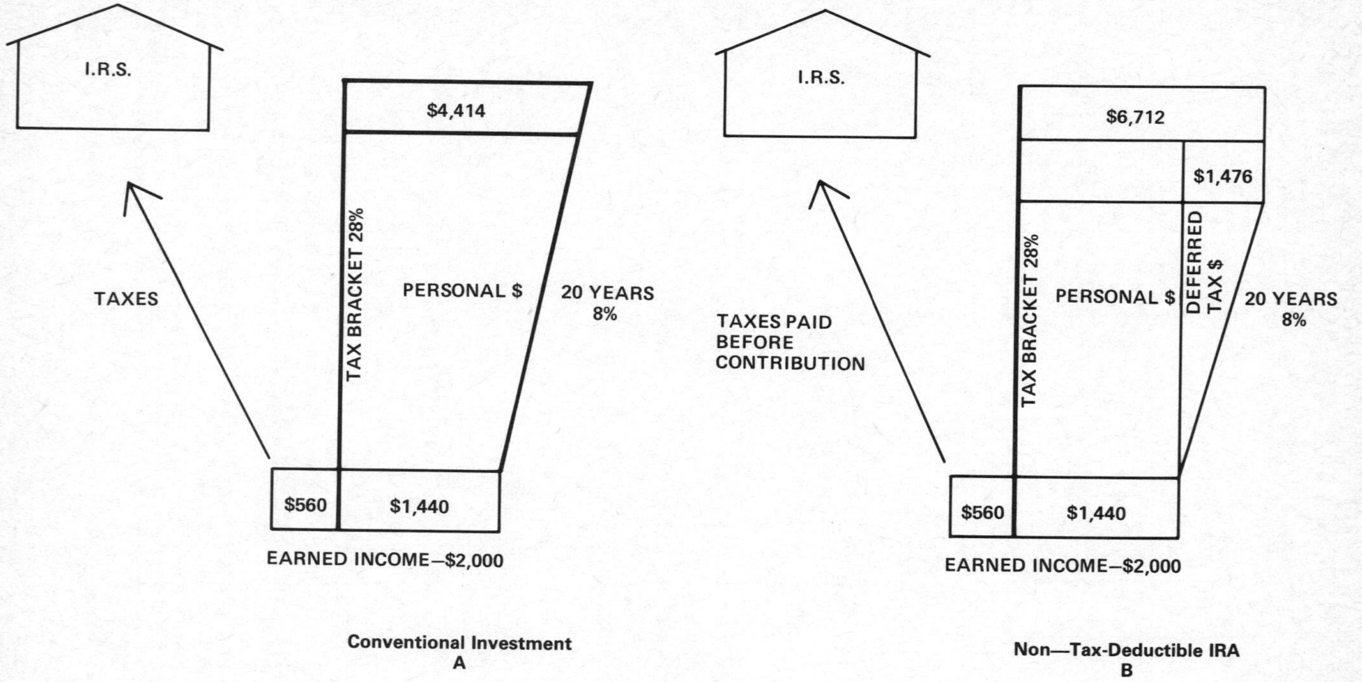

Non—Tax-Deductible IRA
B

$6,712

$1,476

DEFERRED TAX $

PERSONAL $

20 YEARS
8%

TAX BRACKET 28%

$560 | $1,440

EARNED INCOME—$2,000

I.R.S.

TAXES PAID
BEFORE
CONTRIBUTION

Conventional Investment
A

$4,414

PERSONAL $

20 YEARS
8%

TAX BRACKET 28%

$560 | $1,440

EARNED INCOME—$2,000

I.R.S.

TAXES

Figure 5-7

Total dollars	$6,712
Original taxed dollars	− $1,440
Taxable yield	$5,272
Tax at 28%	$1,476
Net =	($6,712 − $1,476) = $5,236

This result is $822 greater than the conventional option. Bearing this in mind, you can safely say: **The IRA is Still the Better Option and does Provide Clear Advantages for all Wage Earners.**

WILL YOU ENJOY THE BENEFITS OF LOWER TAXES WHEN YOU CASH IN YOUR IRA?

According to the ads and promotional literature, distribution time holds another pleasant treat in store for you. You can hope to win the tax game with an IRA, you are told, because at retirement you will be in a lower tax bracket and will pay less taxes, making you an IRA winner.

This must be modified for those whose IRA contributions were made with all-taxed or partially-taxed dollars. However, there is still the issue of the final tax at distribution. The answer can be approximated by examining the case of the totally deductible IRA.

Let's think about what the projection actually says. It can bode ill for you. It suggests that your financial status in retirement will be lower than it is now. That may in fact occur, but it's certainly not something you should *plan* for! Who plans for failure, especially at the most vulnerable period of life? If I had advisers who proposed such a scenario, I'd fire them!

To get a better perspective of the final scenario, we can say that in the IRA: **Winners Will be Retirement Losers and Losers Will be Retirement Winners.** Sound contradictory? Let's reflect together.

Remember, retirees count on income from pension plans, Social Security payments, personal savings, and investments. If they are financially successful, these individuals will receive monies from *all* these sources, making them "winners" in the retirement quest. Those who *fail* to build an adequate retirement income from any or all of these sources must be judged retirement "losers."

The "winners," those with a substantial retirement income, will be at or near their pre-retirement tax bracket. Conversely, the retirement "losers" will slip into a *lower* tax bracket. Now, adding your IRA distributions to your income, your base retirement tax bracket can only rise. So, the "winners" will "lose" on distribution because they will pay a greater percentage of taxes than when the funds were originally contributed. Conversely, the "losers" at substantial retirement income are winners when they withdraw their IRA because of the reverse effect. Let's illustrate this paradoxical phenomenon.

Let's say Ms. Roberts, a 28% taxpayer, makes a one-time contribution of $2,000 to her IRA—$560 in deferred tax money and $1,440 in personal

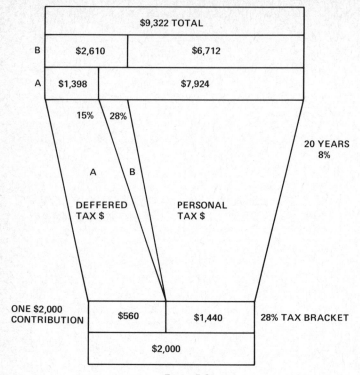

Figure 5-8

funds. At 8%, her total contribution will grow to $9,322 in twenty years, as shown in Figure 5-8.

If Ms. Roberts fails to develop substantial sources of retirement income, she will become a retirement "loser." Her income will be substandard and taxable at lower rates. This is shown in the 15% "A" line in Figure 5-10.

The ultimate tax obligation for a person in the 15% bracket decreases to only $1,398. Compared to the higher "B" lane, Ms. Roberts has thus come out $932 ahead ($2,610 - $1,398) in terms of what she would have owed the IRS. In losing the war of financial security, Ms. Roberts has actually won the IRA battle, although her victory is very hollow.

On the other hand, let's assume that Ms. Roberts was very successful in her career and in building up her three components of retirement income. In this case, let's say she started in the 15% bracket and climbed to the 28% rate at retirement. The same $9,322 accumulates, but she would come out losing $932. The winner or loser status depends on the starting and ending tax brackets for the funds. And, factoring in a number of future simplifications by Congress, the end game is certainly not predictable. However, today's strategy dictates using the IRA route. The chances are you'll be a winner.

WILL AN IRA MAKE YOU A MILLIONAIRE?

The most appealing promise of all about the IRA is the one that may fulfill your fondest dream: **"Become a Millionaire with an IRA."**

If this claim is true, the IRA is certainly the retirement bonanza to beat all. The mere suggestion of becoming a millionaire conjures up images of security and perpetual freedom from money worries. This is the "good news" that has attracted millions of people and billions of dollars.

But the bad news is that although you may accumulate millions in your IRA, you won't be able to live like one of the millionaires of today.

This can't be true, you may protest. After all, you say, the computers show that a twenty-five-year old worker can accumulate $1 million or more in his or her IRA by age sixty-five. And to confirm your belief, you produce a chart much like the one shown in Figure 5-9 that plots this growth at various interest rates.

These eye-popping totals are not incorrect. The mathematics are undeniable. Then, you ask, why won't you be able to live like a millionaire? Let's examine the reality beneath the dazzling numbers.

If you contribute $2,000 a year to an IRA for forty years at a yield of 12%, tax-free compounding will swell your account to $1,718,285. But you will *not* be a millionaire in terms of your ability to purchase goods and services. Remember the two enemies, taxes and inflation? Well, I'm afraid they will eat into the true value of your IRA account.

Figure 5-10 examines what will actually happen to your ostensible accumulation of $1,718,285. The first shock is the blow struck by the IRS's ax: In the 28% tax bracket, this would be:

$$28\% \times \$1,718,285 = \$481,120$$

After Uncle Sam hacks away his share, then you can claim $1,237,164. This loss is simple and understandable under tax law. Not so easily recognized is the damaging, invisible erosion of dollar value caused by that more insidious force, *inflation*.

Inflation is the major deterrent to true wealth and you must overcome it if you're to succeed in this or any long-term investment program. Inflation is the real reason why amassing $1 million many years from today will not enable you to live like a millionaire. We have only to look at the escalating costs of goods and services to grasp this unpleasant truth. Consider how staggeringly expensive the following staple items will be in 40 years at an annual inflation rate of just 8%:

	1986	2026
Hamburger	$2	$43
Breakfast	$3	$65
House	$90,000	$1,954,800
Loaf of bread	$1	$22
Apartment rent	$700	$15,218
Movie ticket	$5	$109
Automobile	$12,000	$260,880

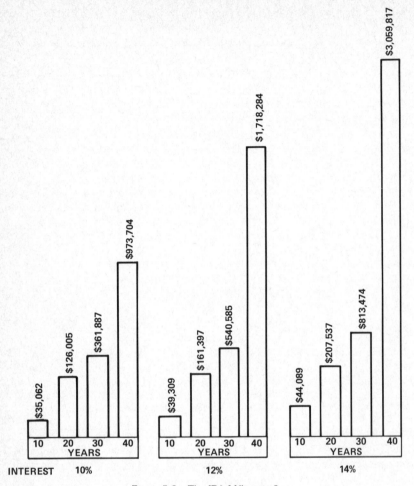

Figure 5-9: The IRA Millionaire?

Are these forty-year projections farfetched? Hardly! Not when you compare a movie ticket today with one forty years ago. Many people in their fifties recall going to the movies for a quarter. If you were under age twelve, admission was only a dime or fifteen cents. Not only that, for your quarter, you got a double feature, and often cartoons, serials, and newsreels. Today's $5.00 movie costs twenty times more than it would have forty years ago, and in most theaters the double feature is a thing of the past; you're lucky if you get coming attractions. If inflation escalates at the same rate over the next forty years, the cost of seeing a film will exceed $100.

    You may take some comfort in the speculation that movie theaters will have been rendered obsolete by home VCRs by 2020, but you'll still have to deal with the vastly inflated prices everywhere else you go. To buy four

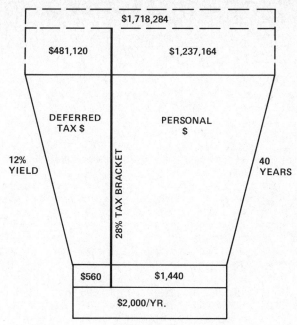

Figure 5-10

Plymouths, for example, or one top-of-the-line Mercedes, you will need $1 million.

In light of these statistics, you begin to see what your IRA "millions" will really be worth. Let's examine their value more closely. As seen in Figure 5-10, you amassed $1,718,284 in your IRA and after taxes you were left with $1,237,164.

To translate the value of these future dollars into today's terms, we use the concepts of future and present values discussed in Appendix A. Using the chart in Table 1.4, we can determine the future value of $1 at various inflation rates for various lengths of time. For instance, $1 will only be equivalent to 10¢ (.0994 from chart) in thirty years. Put another way, thirty years from now $1 will only have the purchasing power that 10¢ has today if inflation is 8% a year during that time.

Using the appropriate factor (.0460) from Table 1.4, we can see that at an inflation rate of 8%, one dollar will only be worth 4½ cents in forty years. Therefore, the real value in today's dollars of our future accumulation will be:

$$(\$1,237,164 \times .0460) = \$56,910$$

If we are lucky and our current low inflation persists—say, at a constant rate of 5%—$1 million will be worth:

$$(\$1,237,164 \times .1420) = \$175,677$$

Sadly, our hopeful "millionaire" will scarcely be able to live like one.

TABLE 1.4 Present Value of One Dollar

	Annual Rate of Return										
Year	5	6	7	8	9	10	11	12	13	14	15
1	.9524	.9434	.9346	.9259	.9174	.9091	.9009	.8929	.8850	.8772	.8696
2	.9070	.8900	.8734	.8573	.8417	.8264	.8116	.7972	.7831	.7695	.7561
3	.8638	.8396	.8163	.7938	.7722	.7513	.7312	.7118	.6931	.6750	.6575
4	.8227	.7921	.7629	.7350	.7084	.6830	.6587	.6355	.6133	.5921	.5718
5	.7835	.7473	.7130	.6806	.6499	.6209	.5935	.5674	.5428	.5194	.4972
6	.7462	.7050	.6663	.6302	.5963	.5645	.5346	.5066	.4803	.4556	.4323
7	.7107	.6651	.6227	.5835	.5470	.5132	.4817	.4523	.4251	.3996	.3759
8	.6768	.6274	.5820	.5403	.5019	.4665	.4339	.4039	.3762	.3506	.3269
9	.6446	.5919	.5439	.5002	.4604	.4241	.3909	.3606	.3329	.3075	.2843
10	.6139	.5584	.5083	.4632	.4224	.3855	.3522	.3220	.2946	.2697	.2472
11	.5847	.5268	.4751	.4289	.3875	.3505	.3173	.2875	.2607	.2366	.2149
12	.5568	.4970	.4440	.3971	.3555	.3168	.2858	.2567	.2307	.2076	.1869
13	.5303	.4688	.4150	.3677	.3262	.2897	.2575	.2292	.2042	.1821	.1625
14	.5051	.4423	.3878	.3405	.2992	.2633	.2320	.2046	.1807	.1597	.1413
15	.4810	.4173	.3624	.3152	.2745	.2394	.2090	.1827	.1599	.1401	.1229
16	.4581	.3936	.3387	.2919	.2519	.2176	.1883	.1631	.1415	.1229	.1069
17	.4363	.3714	.3166	.2703	.2311	.1978	.1696	.1456	.1252	.1078	.0929
18	.4155	.3503	.2959	.2502	.2120	.1799	.1528	.1300	.1108	.0946	.0808
19	.3957	.3305	.2765	.2317	.1945	.1635	.1377	.1161	.0981	.0829	.0703
20	.3769	.3118	.2584	.2145	.1784	.1486	.1240	.1037	.0868	.0728	.0611
21	.3589	.2942	.2415	.1987	.1637	.1351	.1117	.0926	.0768	.0638	.0531
22	.3418	.2775	.2257	.1839	.1502	.1228	.1007	.0826	.0680	.0560	.0462
23	.3256	.2618	.2109	.1703	.1378	.1117	.0907	.0738	.0601	.0491	.0402
24	.3101	.2470	.1971	.1577	.1264	.1015	.0817	.0659	.0532	.0431	.0349
25	.2953	.2330	.1842	.1460	.1160	.0923	.0736	.0588	.0471	.0378	.0304
26	.2812	.2198	.1722	.1352	.1064	.0839	.0663	.0525	.0417	.0331	.0264
27	.2678	.2074	.1609	.1252	.0976	.0763	.0597	.0469	.0369	.0291	.0230
28	.2551	.1956	.1504	.1159	.0895	.0693	.0538	.0419	.0326	.0255	.0200
29	.2429	.1846	.1406	.1073	.0822	.0630	.0485	.0374	.0289	.0224	.0174
30	.2314	.1741	.1314	.0994	.0754	.0573	.0437	.0334	.0256	.0196	.0151
31	.2204	.1643	.1228	.0920	.0691	.0521	.0394	.0298	.0226	.0172	.0131
32	.2099	.1550	.1147	.0852	.0634	.0474	.0355	.0266	.0200	.0151	.0114
33	.1999	.1462	.1072	.0789	.0582	.0431	.0319	.0238	.0177	.0132	.0099
34	.1904	.1379	.1002	.0730	.0534	.0391	.0288	.0212	.0157	.0116	.0086
35	.1813	.1301	.0937	.0676	.0490	.0356	.0259	.0189	.0139	.0102	.0075
36	.1727	.1227	.0875	.0626	.0449	.0323	.0234	.0169	.0123	.0089	.0065
37	.1644	.1158	.0818	.0580	.0412	.0294	.0210	.0151	.0109	.0078	.0057
38	.1566	.1092	.0765	.0537	.0378	.0267	.0190	.0135	.0096	.0069	.0049
39	.1491	.1031	.0715	.0497	.0347	.0243	.0171	.0120	.0085	.0060	.0043
40	.1420	.0972	.0668	.0460	.0318	.0221	.0154	.0107	.0075	.0053	.0037

This cruel example points out the truly devastating effects of inflation. It is this little-recognized phenomenon that should command your attention and care. If you ignore it, you may suffer real *losses*.

To sum up this chapter so far, we have established that the IRA is the best tax shelter of all because:

- Personal dollars within fully-deductible tax contributions are delivered tax-free.
- If you are in a lower tax bracket at retirement, some of the IRS' tax-deferred dollars in your IRA will be returned to you.
- Early contribution into the IRA's tax-free environment works wonders.

However, we have also established that the single most important consideration you must bear in mind when looking at various kinds of IRAs is not taxes but inflation. Therefore, the ultimate value of your IRA lies in the *quality* of the investment you select. The savings and/or investment vehicles you choose *must* perform at rates that exceed those of inflation to win at the IRA game.

CAN AN IRA EVER BEAT INFLATION, THEN?

This challenge is not unfamiliar. We discussed it in Chapter Three, where we saw inflation handily defeated by one investment alone—real estate. It is logical that real estate is the best investment vehicle for your IRA dollars.

This statement may surprise you; you probably have not heard of a real estate IRA or, more accurately, an IRA that permits you to buy real estate. There is a good reason for this. Banks use the IRA to sell you CDs or their other products. They don't let you purchase real estate with their IRAs because *banks don't sell real estate.*

What would happen if you went to a local restaurant and asked to buy a Queen Anne chair? Or, conversely, if you went into a furniture store and ordered a "ham on rye to go, hold the mustard?" It's the same situation with banks and real estate. Banks do not sell real estate because real estate is not their business.

Where, then, do you go to open an IRA that allows you to buy real estate? This is the question we answer in the next chapter.

SIX

The Self-Directed IRA

When Congress legislated the IRA into existence in 1974, it uncharacteristically left investment decisions up to the participants. It is this fact that enables you to purchase real estate, along with other savings and investments, with your IRA dollars. An IRA in which you, rather than a trustee institution, have control of your own investments is called a *self-directed* IRA.

The fact that an IRA is self-directed does not imply that the IRS relinquishes all control of it. It doesn't. In fact, all IRAs are rigidly controlled and monitored by government agencies and must comply with universal rules and regulations about qualifications, penalties, and taxation. These conditions are outlined in Appendix B. We urge you to become acquainted with them to prevent any problem or misunderstanding.

Appendix B makes an important distinction between what goes on outside versus inside the IRA. To help you understand these differences, I have envisioned the IRA as a fortress. The rules and regulations that affect everyone who has an IRA lie *outside* the fortress. They are set and monitored by the IRS. When you adopt an IRA, you must comply with these external "do's and don'ts" or be subject to penalties and even possible disqualification.

Within the fortress, however, investment decisions are left up to you. Except for a few specific investment prohibitions, that we shall discuss below, the IRS does *not* interfere with any of your IRA savings and investment activities. Note that this observation runs counter to what many people think—that IRA investment options are restricted to savings products such as a bank CD. Actually, a wide variety of investments is possible. We'll look at them briefly below.

WHAT INVESTMENTS ARE PERMITTED IN AN IRA?

The investments permitted in an IRA include virtually every financial product or vehicle on the market. You have the right and responsibility to select the one that best suits you. To clarify the IRS's position and your own role in your investment decisions more fully, let's review the appropriate regulations.

In 1962, when the Keogh plan was introduced, Congress legislated a list of "permissible" Keogh savings and investment vehicles. This list prevailed until 1974, when the Employee Retirement Income Security Act (ERISA) was enacted, primarily to correct serious abuses in the pension field. This sweeping legislation, also known as the Pension Reform Act, not only introduced a new program—the Individual Retirement Account (IRA)—but also rejected the use of a "permissible investment" list. Instead, a covenant, or warning, was issued to purveyors of all pension programs, including IRAs. This congressional covenant became known as the *Prudent Man Rule.* It requires all parties associated with pension programs to act in a prudent manner and exercise good judgment. Otherwise, the parties in question may be held responsible for any improper or unethical transactions.

Simultaneously, ERISA banned IRA participants from purchasing life insurance with IRA funds. This was not done as an indictment of life insurance, but rather to protect the government's interest. You see, the IRS intends to collect the tax-deferred portion of your IRA funds—increased by compounding—on distribution. But if you were to purchase a term insurance policy, the IRS couldn't collect anything. The IRS will lose even with cash value policies that are a mix of pure insurance and a savings account. At distribution time, the portion of funds used to pay for insurance would have been expended. Since there are no funds to distribute, the resulting deferred tax on these dollars would be zero.

In 1982, legislation known as the Tax Equity Fiscal Responsibility Act (TEFRA) added "collectibles"—that include gold, silver, coins, art, antiques, stamps, diamonds, and gemstones—to the list of investments that cannot be purchased with IRA dollars. However, the tax bill of 1986 opened the door slightly. It qualified certain silver and gold coins for IRA investment. And guess whose coins—the U.S. government's, of course!

The IRS has ruled that investment in collectibles constitutes a distribution of IRA funds. This ruling subjects such an investment to the 10% penalty before you reach age 59½, and you must also pay normal income tax on your earnings. This regulation is not an arbitrary one. It was passed largely because no regulatory agency comparable to those that monitor banking, securities, or real estate transactions keeps an eye on dealings in collectibles.

Except for the specifically excluded items mentioned above, however, the range of financial products that you can purchase with IRA funds is all-inclusive. And that, incidentally—to jump ahead for a moment—means you *can* invest in real estate with your IRA funds. During my experience, there have been isolated occasions when real estate has been identified with collectibles as an excluded product. But those have stemmed from a misunderstanding of the IRS's definition of collectibles. The originators of this misinformation should examine the regulations more carefully. Their opinions are erroneous and unfounded.

But before we talk more about real estate IRAs, it will be helpful to continue with our discussion of how IRAs work.

Types of Sponsored IRAs

When the IRA was introduced, organizations that market investment products saw the immense promise of this new vehicle. Anxious for a share of this potential billion-dollar market, thousands of banks, insurance companies, and brokerage houses rushed to have their IRAs approved by the IRS.

ERISA requires all sponsors of IRAs to submit a plan for review by the IRS. Each must satisfy the same operating regulations to gain approval. Since the IRS does not advocate any specific investments as being better then others (except for those that it explicitly excludes from the IRA), the only difference among the plans the various sponsoring organizations offer is the *type* of investments. Consequently, an IRA is identified according to the product line of investments its sponsor markets. A typical lineup of IRAs would include:

- Bank IRAs: These permit investment in passbook accounts, certificates of deposit, and other bank products.
- Insurance company IRAs: These offer mutual funds and annuities, which are basically savings accounts.
- Brokerage house IRAs: These allow investment in stocks, bonds and mutual funds.

The above are the three most prevalent types of IRA. Figure 6-1 shows the IRA fortresses with the gates to each of these options. The choice of which door to enter is yours. While the same tax-neutral conditions apply in each of the fortresses, other variables do not. Your choice should therefore be influenced by the *quality* of the savings and investment offering.

Bank IRAs

In a typical bank IRA, your savings options may be restricted to a choice between an 18-month or a 36-month CD. Such an IRA, therefore, lacks flexibility. Nonetheless, it is simple to implement and doesn't need management. All you have to do is to monitor the current yield periodically to compare it with the inflation rate.

Banks and thrifts do not normally charge trustee fees for servicing your IRA. There's no need for them to do so, as they more than recover their costs. They profit handsomely from the difference between the fixed return they pay on your IRA and the yield they receive by lending your money to others, or even to you.

Banks normally impose penalties for premature termination of CDs. They impose a penalty of three months' interest for one-year certificates and

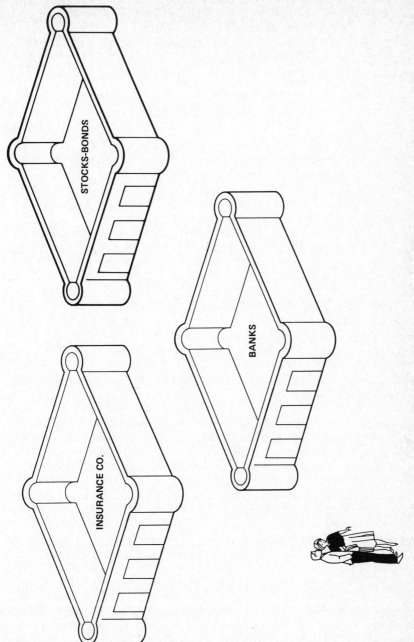

STOCKS-BONDS

INSURANCE CO.

BANKS

Figure 6-1: The Traditional Choices

71

at least six months' interest for longer-term maturities. These penalties could significantly hurt you if you had to liquidate a CD inside an IRA prematurely for any reason. To guard against excessive penalties, your best bet would be to distribute these assets among many small CDs rather than just one or two larger ones. This point holds true for non-IRA accounts, too.

IRA Involving Annuities

Although insurance companies are not permitted to sell life insurance within the IRA, they do offer annuity savings and/or investment plans. An *annuity* is an agreement whereby an insurance company pays an "annuitized" income at a future date based on the accumulated sum of money in the annuity. The amounts distributed will depend on your life expectancy, the amount you've invested, and the payment option you select. Note that the word "annuity" describes a procedure that involves the withdrawal of money over an extended period of time. Your accumulation may never be distributed periodically or "annuitized" should you elect to withdraw the funds in a lump sum.

There are two major types of annuities. With one type, the *fixed annuity*, insurance companies are responding to the popularity of bank CDs among IRA participants; a fixed annuity will pay a periodically fixed return on invested dollars, and can basically be described as a savings account with an insurance company. Like bank interest, the yields are fixed for a specific period, but, unlike bank interest, they may fluctuate from year to year relative to a basic financial instrument, such as government bonds. Both fixed annuities and CDs offer current yields and guaranteed basic floor yields. Normally, although the base returns do not fluctuate, the current yields do—and thus warrant monitoring.

In response to an inflation-sensitive climate, insurance companies have also designed the *variable annuity* to lure securities-oriented prospects. The adjective "variable" refers to the flexible investment return of the contract. This feature would appeal to an IRA investor who seeks a higher return than the locked-in return a fixed annuity promises. A variable annuity buys into either mutual funds, a fund of municipals, or a choice of government securities. Since these markets fluctuate, so will the return on the investment. Rather than guaranteeing a *fixed* rate, the variable annuity presents a *hope* of beating the inflation spiral through high yields—the ideal goal of any IRA investment portfolio, as noted. In reality, however, the gain is unpredictable and uncertain. Consequently, this option offers the choice to annuitize, at withdrawal, only whatever funds have accumulated in the account.

When evaluating annuities, you should be careful to consider their potential or hidden costs. These costs include administrative expenses and commission expenses, both of which are assessed to the buyer. In the "front-loaded" type of annuity, which is the less desirable, the invested monies are diminished by the cost of commissions and "up-front" expenses, leaving a reduced amount within the annuity to earn interest for you.

In response to negative client reaction to "front-loaded" annuity costs, insurance companies have also designed a "back-loaded" instrument. In this type of annuity, costs are deducted only if the money is distributed *before* maturity. This early distribution penalty is comparable to the one that banks impose on CDs. The costs are normally spread over a period of years and diminish to zero when the insurance company's yield is sufficient to absorb them. These impact of loads, front or back, must be weighed in your investment decision.

Bonds in an IRA

Another major category of IRA investment is bonds. These include units issued by corporations, municipalities, and the federal government. Such instruments are basically loans on which the issuing agencies promise to pay a specific rate of interest.

The attraction of bonds for investors is the potentially high yield. The greater the real or perceived risk, the higher the yield; conversely, the more solid the guarantees, the lower the yield. Within acceptable risk limits, the yield becomes the paramount basis for choice.

All types of bonds are available in the variable annuity programs that insurance companies offer. Securities and brokerage houses also include them in the smorgasbord of investments that their IRA includes.

Should Stocks be Included in an IRA?

The stock market is a complicated entity, and people who don't have an extensive knowledge of its workings are at a disadvantage if they choose to play it. The selection of specific stocks should be left to professionals, who study the myriad factors that affect the market and are expected to know how to cut their clients' losses. The best technique for laypersons in this game is to entrust their money to the pros.

The need for professional management and market expertise has given impetus to the formation of mutual fund investment organizations, which have become popular. The managers of a fund act for the mutual gain of all investors in that particular group. The fund's portfolio may include a family of stocks, bonds, or money instruments in any combination. Investors make no decisions except to buy or sell their interest in the fund.

Wall Street's long-term performance has not been very favorable for the small investor. Admittedly, it can occasionally produce startling results; you should be sure to note that for every winner in securities, there must be a corresponding loser. Except for initial offerings, sales in the stock market are "secondary" trades between buyers and sellers and the same security, rather than directly between the buyer and the corporation. Everytime a sale is made, there is the implication that the seller has lost confidence in the investments, but the buyer is betting that the seller is wrong. *Someone* has to be wrong and become the loser.

Discussing the intricacies of the stock market properly is an overwhelming task that does not fit into the design of this book. Suffice it to say that few people, even among the pros, really understand the stock market. If you disagree, then ask yourself one question: How do the "experts" fail to anticipate a one-day, 60-point drop in the Dow Jones average? Unless you can accept large losses in your IRA, investing in the stock market is not recommended. The securities industry itself gives you the same warning.

WHAT IS THE BEST INVESTMENT FOR YOUR IRA DOLLARS?

In our search for handsome corrected-for-inflation yields, we must overcome many hurdles. For example, we must steer a course between safety and risk. We may get high yields if we take risks that prove successful; we will normally get lower yields with more secure investments. IRA investments should not pose high risks, because their basic purpose is to provide financial support in retirement. Nevertheless, a reasonable balance ought to be struck between low-yielding safety and high-yielding risk.

Amid these treacherous waters, one investment stands out like a welcoming beacon year after year—real estate. Few would dispute its excellent track record—certainly not the millions who have owned the most common real estate investment of all, a personal residence. The value of residential homes has consistently risen. Appreciation has delivered a quiet, steady reward for homeowners, as well as the pleasures of a residence.

The appreciation of real estate has been spectacular at times. But mostly, its performance has been like that of the legendary tortoise when he raced with the hare. In that contest, the hare alternated between bursts of energy and periods of distraction when he forgot to be concerned about his slower rival. Meanwhile, the tortoise forged ahead—and his less dramatic, quiet steadfastness ultimately won the race. Real estate appreciates with the same deliberation and constancy. The erratic performance of the hare is best left to the thrill seeker or gambler.

Investing IRA dollars in real estate is not only sensible, but it's legal. This ideal investment has been as firmly approved by legislation as CDs, stocks, or bonds. They are all notable for their absence from the short list of *prohibited* investments—life insurance and most collectibles. However, while CDs, stocks, and bonds can be handled by sponsoring institutions, a real-estate IRA must be created through adoption of a *self-directed plan*.

THE SELF-DIRECTED IRA

Unlike conventional IRAs, that allow you access to only one chamber of the IRA fortress, as shown in Figure 6-1, the self-directed IRA opens up the entire fortress and *all* qualified investment modes to its user, as seen in Figure 6-2.

Self-directed IRAs are offered by trust companies that are not linked to any particular investment vehicle. These trust companies sell no insurance, stocks, bonds, annuities, or any other financial product. They have the option of designing their own self-directed plan, or they can obtain approval to use a plan designed by the IRS. This obviously preapproved plan is described and

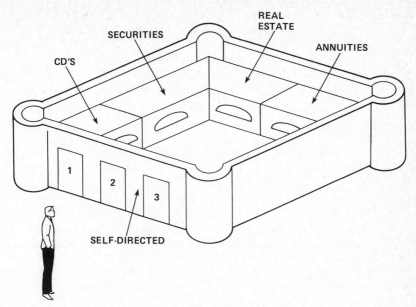

Figure 6-2: The Self-Directed IRA

explained in IRS Form 5305. Figure 6-3 reproduces this document in its entirety.

One word of caution here: In addition to these truly self-directed IRAs, you'll find that the term "self-directed" has been erroneously used to describe a number of other IRA plans. A number of organizations and a few books claim, essentially, that a self-directed IRA is one that allows you to select from a variety of stocks, bonds, or mutual funds. True, the range of investments these plans offer may indeed be greater than that offered to, say, a bank IRA participant. Regardless of the scope they offer, these plans are *not* really totally self-directed. An analogy may help you understand this point: The legendary automaker Henry Ford offered his customers any color car they required, so long as it was black. The restrictions on these allegedly "self-directed" IRAs may not be as severe as Mr. Ford's, but they still limit your choices.

Trustees of truly self-directed plans, by contrast, do *not* provide financial advice, nor will they invest funds until they receive precise investment instructions from *you*. This is the real meaning of "self-directed." Once you adopt such a plan, the trustee *acts only on your instructions and handles investment transactions on your behalf*. The true self-directed IRA plan has three special advantages:

- Full Investment Options: The choices are yours. You can purchase any available investment product except life insurance and collectibles (apart from U.S. gold and silver coins, now approved). You thus have access to the best inflation hedge of all—real estate.

Form **5305**		
(Rev. November1983) Department of the Treasury Internal Revenue Service	**Individual Retirement Trust Account** (Under Section 408(a) of the Internal Revenue Code)	OMB No. 1545-0365 **Do NOT File with Internal Revenue Service**

State of ▶ .... } SS ☐ Amendment

County of ▶ ....

Grantor's name .... Grantor's date of birth .... Grantor's social
security number .... Grantor's address ....
Trustee's name   Retirement Accounts, Inc.   Trustee's address or principal place of business ....
                 663 N. Harold Avenue, P.O. Box 3017, Winter Park, FL 37290

The Grantor whose name appears above is establishing an individual retirement account (under section 408(a) of the Internal Revenue Code) to provide for his or her retirement and for the support of his or her beneficiaries after death.

The Trustee named above has given the Grantor the disclosure statement required under the Income Tax Regulations under section 408(i) of the Code.

The Grantor has assigned the trust .... dollars ($ ....) in cash.

The Grantor and the Trustee make the following agreement:

Article I

The Trustee may accept additional cash contributions on behalf of the Grantor for a tax year of the Grantor. The total cash contributions are limited to $2,000 for the tax year unless the contribution is a rollover contribution described in section 402(a)(5), 402(a)(7), 403(a)(4), 403(b)(8), 405(d)(3), 408(d)(3), or 409(b)(3)(C) of the Code or an employer contribution to a simplified employee pension plan as described in section 408(k).

Article II

The Grantor's interest in the balance in the trust account is nonforfeitable.

Article III

1.   No part of the trust funds may be invested in life insurance contracts, nor may the assets of the trust account be commingled with other property except in a common trust fund or common investment fund (within the meaning of section 408(a)(5) of the Code).

2.   No part of the trust funds may be invested in collectibles (within the meaning of section 408(m) of the Code).

Article IV

1.   The Grantor's entire interest in the trust account must be, or begin to be, distributed before the end of the tax year in which the Grantor reaches age 70½. By the end of that tax year, the Grantor may elect, in a manner acceptable to the trustee, to have the balance in the trust account distributed in:

(a)   A single sum payment.

(b)   An annuity contract that provides equal or substantially equal monthly, quarterly, or annual payments over the life of the Grantor. The payments must begin by the end of that tax year.

(c)   An annuity contract that provides equal or substantially equal monthly, quarterly, or annual payments over the joint and last survivor lives of the Grantor and his or her spouse. The payments must begin by the end of the tax year.

(d)   Equal or substantially equal monthly, quarterly, or annual payments over a specified period that may not be longer than the Grantor's life expectancy.

(e)   Equal or substantially equal monthly, quarterly, or annual payments over a specified period that may not be longer than the joint life and last survivor expectancy of the Grantor and his or her spouse.

Even if distributions have begun to be made under option (d) or (e), the Grantor may receive a distribution of the balance in the trust account at any time by giving written notice to the trustee. If the grantor does not choose any of the methods of distribution described above by the end of the tax year in which he or she reaches age 70½, distribution to the Grantor will be made before the end of that tax year by a single sum payment. If the Grantor elects as a means of distribution (b) or (c) above, the annuity contract must satisfy the requirements of section 408(b)(1), (3), (4), and (5) of the Code. If the Grantor elects as a means of distribution (d) or (e) above, figure the payments made in tax years beginning in the tax year the Grantor reaches age 70½ as follows:

(i)   For the minimum annual payment, divide the Grantor's entire interest in the trust account at the beginning of each year by the life expectancy of the Grantor (or the joint life and last survivor expectancy of the Grantor and his or her spouse, or the period specified under (d) or (e), whichever applies). Determine the life expectancy in either case on the date the Grantor reaches 70½ minus the number of whole years passed since the Grantor became 70½.

(ii)   For the minimum monthly payment, divide the result in (i) above by 12.

(iii)   For the minimum quarterly payment, divide the result in (i) above by 4.

2.   If the Grantor dies before his or her entire interest in the account is distributed to him or her, or if distribution is being made as provided in (e) above to his or her surviving spouse, and the surviving spouse dies before the entire interest is distributed, the entire remaining undistributed interest will, within 5 years after the Grantor's death or the death of the surviving spouse, be distributed to the beneficiary or beneficiaries of the Grantor or the Grantor's surviving spouse. However, the preceding distribution is not required if distributions over a specified term began before the death of the Grantor and the term is for a period permitted under (d) or (e) above and distributions continue over that period.

If the Grantor dies before his or her entire interest has been distributed and if the beneficiary is other than the surviving spouse, no additional cash contributions or rollover contributions may be accepted in the account.

Article V

Unless the Grantor dies, is disabled (as defined in section 72(m) of the Code), or reaches age 59½ before any amount is distributed from the trust account, the Trustee must receive from the Grantor a statement explaining how he or she intends to dispose of the amount distributed.

For Paperwork Reduction Act Notice, see back of this form.   Form **5305** (Rev. 11–83)

FIG 6.3

Article VI

1. The Grantor agrees to provide the Trustee with information necessary for the Trustee to prepare any reports required under section 408(i) of the Code and related regulations.

2. The Trustee agrees to submit reports to the Internal Revenue Service and the Grantor as prescribed by the Internal Revenue Service.

Article VII

Notwithstanding any other articles which may be added or incorporated, the provisions of Articles I through III and this sentence will be controlling. Any additional articles that are not consistent with section 408(a) of the Code and related regulations will be invalid.

Article VIII

This agreement will be amended from time to time to comply with the provisions of the Code and related regulations. Other amendments may be made with the consent of the persons whose signatures appear below.

Note: *The following space (Article IX) may be used for any other provisions you wish to add. If you do not wish to add any other provisions, draw a line through this space. If you add provisions, they must comply with applicable requirements of State law and the Internal Revenue Code.*

Article IX

Contributions to the trust and any earnings therefrom may be directed, in accordance with your instructions, into any lawful investment acceptable to us. Cash balances not otherwise invested will be placed in interest bearing accounts at our discretion.

We may resign by giving 30 days written notice to you or may be removed by your giving us such notice. A successor Trustee may be appointed by you or us.

In consideration for our services under this Agreement, we shall receive the fees specified on the applicable fee schedule included with this package. We may substitute a different fee schedule at any time on thirty (30) days written notice to you. Fees may be paid by you directly or we may deduct them from your account.

In the absence of cash or money market shares within your account, we may liquidate any interest required to pay fees. In such event, we shall liquidate the last interest purchased under the account. Further liquidations, if required, will be done in reverse order of purchase.

An annual maintenance fee will be charged for any calendar year or portion of any calendar year during which you have an account with us. We may charge you for any reasonable administrative expenses arising from unforeseen situations (e.g. legal expenses in defense of your interests, etc.).

Termination fees are charged when your account is closed whether the funds are distributed to you or to a successor custodian or trustee. Termination fees are not charged when the termination of the Account is attendant to the payment of regular distributions after participant reaches age 59-1/2, total disability or death of participant.

The amount of any liability for unrelated business income taxes incurred by the trust account shall be paid out of funds in the trust account or, if account funds are insufficient, we shall be authorized to liquidate assets of the trust account or cease reinvesting assets of the trust account in order to pay such liability.

We shall furnish reports to you setting forth receipts, investments, disbursement, and other transactions required to be performed hereunder. We shall not, except as directed in writing by you, vote proxies.

Notwithstanding the terms contained in Article I, we may accept direct transfers exceeding $2,000 for the tax year.

We shall have no liability or responsibility for transactions reported on any statements unless question or objection is raised thereto within 30 days of mailing of the statement.

Grantor's signature _____

Trustee's signature _____
AUTHORIZED SIGNER

Date _____

Witness _____
(Use only if signature of the Grantor or the Trustee is required to be witnessed.)

Instructions

(Section references are to the Internal Revenue Code unless otherwise noted.)

Paperwork Reduction Act Notice

The Paperwork Reduction Act of 1980 says that we must tell you why we are collecting this information, how it is to be used, and whether you have to give it to us. The information is used to determine if you are entitled to a deduction for contributions to this trust. Your completing this information is only required if you want a qualified individual retirement account.

Purpose of Form

This model trust may be used by an individual who wishes to adopt an individual retirement account under section 408(a). When fully executed by the Grantor and the Trustee not later than the time prescribed by law for filing the Federal income tax return for the Grantor's tax year (including any extensions thereof), an individual will have an individual retirement account (IRA) trust which meets the requirements of section 408(a). This trust must be created in the United States for the exclusive benefit of the Grantor or his/her beneficiaries.

Definitions

Trustee.—The trustee must be a bank or savings and loan asociation, as defined in section 408(n), or other person who has the approval of the Internal Revenue Service to act as trustee.

Grantor.—The grantor is the person who establishes the trust account.

IRA for Non-Working Spouse

Contributions to an IRA trust account for a non-working spouse must be made to a separate IRA trust account established by the non-working spouse.

This form may be used to establish the IRA trust for the non-working spouse.

An employee's social security number will serve as the identification number of his or her individual retirement account. An employer identification number is not required for each individual retirement account, nor for a common fund created for individual retirement accounts.

For more information, get a copy of the required disclosure statement from your trustee or get **Publication 590,** Individual Retirement Arrangements (IRA's).

Specific Instructions

Article IV.—Distributions made under this Article may be made in a single sum, periodic payment, or a combination of both. The distribution option should be reviewed in the year the Grantor reaches age 70½ to make sure the requirements of section 408(a)(6) have been met. For example, if a Grantor elects distributions over a period permitted in (d) or (e) of Article IV, the period may not extend beyond the life expectancy of the Grantor at age 70½ (under option (d)) or the joint life and last survivor expectancy of the Grantor (at age 70½) and the Grantor's spouse (under option (e)). For this purpose, life expectancies must be determined by using the expected return multiples in section 1.72-9 of the Income Tax Regulations (26 CFR Part 1). The balance in the account as of the beginning of each tax year beginning on or after the Grantor reaches age 70½ will be used in computing the payments described in (d) and (e) of Article IV. Article IV does not preclude a mode of distribution different from those described in (a) through (e) of Article IV prior to the close of the tax year of the Grantor in which he/she reaches age 70½.

Article IX.—This Article and any that follow it may incorporate additional provisions that are agreed upon by the grantor and trustee to complete the agreement. These may include, for example: definitions, investment powers, voting rights, exculpatory provisions, amendment and termination, removal of trustee, trustee's fees, State law requirements, beginning date of distributions, accepting only cash, treatment of excess contributions, prohibited transactions with the grantor, etc. Use additional pages if necessary and attach them to this form.

Note: *This form may be reproduced and reduced in size for adoption to passbook or card purposes.*

6.3 CON'T

GENERAL

The following information is being provided in accordance with the requirements of the Internal Revenue Service. Individual Retirement Accounts, or "IRA's", were established under the Employee Retirement Income Security Act of 1974. Under the provisions of the Act, contributions and any earnings on the IRA assets are not subject to federal income tax until you actually begin to receive distributions from your account. The state income tax treatment of your IRA may differ and details should be available from your state taxing authority or your own tax advisor.   does not act as your tax, legal, or investment adviser for this IRA.

RIGHT OF REVOCATION

You are entitled to revoke this account within seven days from the date you adopt the Trust. Upon revocation, the entire account plus the establishment fee will be returned. The notice of revocation shall be in writing. The written notification of revocation may be mailed or hand delivered to us on or before seven days after the date you adopted the Trust.

In the event that the written notification is mailed, it shall be deemed to be mailed on the date of the postmark, or if sent by certified or registered mail, it shall be deemed to be mailed as of the date of certification or registration. If mailed, the written notice of revocation shall be mailed in the United States in an envelope or other appropriate wrapper, and it is to be mailed by first class mail with the postage prepaid, and is to be addressed to:

STATUTORY REQUIREMENTS

The statutory requirements with respect to your account as described in Section 408(a) of the Internal Revenue Code are as follows:

1. Except in the case of a rollover contribution, no contribution will be accepted unless it is in cash, and contributions will not be accepted for the taxable year in excess of $2,000.00 (or such limit as may be prescribed by law) on behalf of any individual.

2. No part of the trust funds may be invested in life insurance.

3. Your entire account balance is non-forfeitable.

4. The assets of your account may not be commingled and for that reason you must have a separate individual account.

5. The entire interest of your individual retirement trust must be distributed not later than April 1 following the end of your taxable year in which you attain age 70-1/2 or it may be distributed, commencing before the close of such taxable year, over your life expectancy or the lives of yourself and your spouse or a period of time not extending beyond the life expectancy of yourself or the life expectancy of yourself and your spouse. Your distributions, whether in some type of periodic payment or in a lump sum, are taxed as ordinary income. If the distribution selected does not equal or surpass IRS minimums, a non-deductible excise tax of 50% will be imposed upon the difference between the amount required and the amount distributed.

6. If you should die before the entire interest has been distributed to you or if distribution has commenced as provided above in #5 to your surviving spouse and such surviving spouse dies before the entire amount has been distributed to such spouse, the entire interest (or the remaining part of such interest if distribution has already begun) must, within five years of your death (or the death of your surviving spouse), be distributed. However, the preceding distribution is not required if distributions over a specified term began before your death and the term is for a period permitted under the plan and distributions continue over that period.

CONTRIBUTIONS

Contributions to the Trust may be either "rollover" contributions or personal contributions. Personal contributions must be made in cash or cash equivalents (i.e., a check).

Rollover contributions (may be of any amount) are eligible lump-sum distributions received by you from another tax-qualified retirement plan or another IRA. Money, property, or proceeds from the bona fide sale of property so distributed must be contributed within 60 days of receipt. Property rolled over must be the same property distributed. Rollover contributions may consist of all, or as little as 50%, of a lump sum distribution from a tax qualified retirement plan.

Contributions which are not rollovers cannot exceed the maximum amount allowed as a deduction under the Internal Revenue Code. This amount varies, depending on whether the contribution is to your IRA under a Simplified Employee Pension plan or a personal IRA contribution. Personal contributions cannot exceed $2,000.00 or 100% of compensation, whichever is less, per year. The $2,000.00 limit is increased to $2,250.00 if contributions are made to an IRA established for the benefit of a non-employed spouse. If your non-employed spouse is included, two separate accounts must be established, but the contributions need not be equally divided. However, the contribution to either IRA cannot exceed $2,000.00. Such contributions to an IRA can be made even if you are an active participant in a qualified plan or a Simplified Employee Pension Plan. Also, contributions on behalf of a non-employed spouse to an IRA are allowable if your employer is contributing to your IRA account under a Simplified Employee Pension Plan. If contributions are being made to your IRA account under your employer's Simplified Employee Pension Plan, the maximum contribution limit is increased to the lesser of $30,000.00 or 15% of your compensation in addition to personal IRA contributions.

Because the IRS does not allow deductions for any personal contributions for the taxable year in which you reach age 70-1/2, the IRA trust agreement provides that no cash contributions may be made to your account for that or any following taxable year. Rollover contributions, however, can be made at any time. Contributions made on your behalf to your IRA under a Simplified Employee Pension Plan may be made after you attain age 70-1/2. Also, contributions can be made on behalf of the non-working spouse (if under age 70-1/2) even if the working spouse is 70-1/2 or older.

The maximum amount that an individual can contribute to a   IRA for a tax year is reduced by any contributions that the individual makes to another IRA, and by any voluntary tax deductible employee contributions the individual makes to his or her employer's retirement plan for that year.

Except for rollover contributions, establishment of and personal contributions to your IRA for a taxable year may be made up through the due date (excluding extensions) for that year's federal income tax return. You may claim the deduction and file your income tax return before you actually make the contribution, but remember, the contribution must be made by the original due date of the federal income tax return. Because of this time flexibility, you should advise us of the taxable year to which each of your contributions applies. If no indication is made with respect to the tax year for which the contribution is to apply, we will assume it to be made the year in which it is actually received.

If your contributions for any taxable year are greater than the maximum deductible amount, no deduction will be allowed for the excess. The amount of the excess will also be subject to an annual 6% excise tax. This excise tax is not deductible. However, this tax can be avoided if you withdraw the excess contribution and any earnings attributable to it before the due date of your Federal tax return for the year in which the excess contribution is made, and you were not allowed a deduction for the excess amount. The withdrawn earnings, if any, must be included in income for the tax year in which the excess contribution is made.

DEDUCTIBILITY OF CONTRIBUTION

Cash contributions are deductible from gross income on your federal tax return and may be taken whether or not you itemize your deductions. The maximum amount deductible under your IRA is the lesser of $2,000.00 or 100% of your compensation. The deductible dollar limit if your spouse has no compensation from personal services in a given tax year is increased to $2,250.00. If contributions are being made to your IRA by your employer under the terms of a Simplified Employee Pension Plan, the maximum amount deductible is the amount contributed, which may not exceed the lesser of $30,000.00 or 15% of your compensation.

Deductions for your personal contributions to your IRA are allowed even if you participate in certain employee benefit plans.

No deduction, however, will be allowed for the taxable year in which you reach age 70-1/2 or for any succeeding year (except if pursuant to a Simplified Employee Pension Plan).

Rollover contributions, if properly made, are not included in your gross income and therefore are not deductible from it.

TRANSFER AND ROLLOVER CONTRIBUTIONS

In addition to current year contributions, you may fund an IRA with transfer or rollover contributions.

A transfer contribution is one in which assets are forwarded directly to this IRA from another IRA custodian or trustee. There is no restriction on the number of times that transfer contributions may be made.

A rollover contribution is one in which assets distributed to you from any of the following sources are contributed by you to this IRA within sixty days after you receive them from: 1) a qualified corporate plan 2) a Keogh plan 3) a 403(b) tax-deferred retirement plan 4) a qualified bond purchase plan 5) a deceased spouse's IRA or 6) another IRA maintained by you.

Rollover contributions may consist of all, or as little as 50%, of a lump sum distribution from a tax qualified retirement plan. The distribution from a qualified employer plan must be a lump sum distribution as defined in Section 402(e) of the Internal Revenue Code or a total distribution resulting from a plan termination. The rollover amount may not include nondeductible employee contributions to the employer's qualified plan. If you maintain assets that you have rolled over from a qualified plan in a separate IRA and do not commingle them with the assets of an IRA to which you make current-year contributions, you are permitted to rollover the assets in such a "conduit" IRA back to a qualified plan. You may not roll rollover assets from one IRA to another more often than once in a twelve-month period.

There is no maximum dollar amount or age limit with respect to either transfer or rollover contributions and such contributions may be in cash or in kind.

6.3 CON'T

STRIBUTIONS

You must begin to receive distributions from your IRA trust account no later than April 1 following the end of your taxable year in which you reach age 70-1/2. You must choose have your IRA trust account distributed to you in a lump sum or in a series of monthly, quarterly or annual payments over a period of years. After age 70-1/2. the period can be longer than your lifetime, the lifetime of you and your spouse or any period of years which does not exceed your life expectancy or the life expectancy of you and your spouse.

If you make no choice of the method of distribution before the 30th day preceding the end of your taxable year in which you reach age 70-1/2, we will make a lump-sum distribution you as of the end of that taxable year.

The methods of distribution which are available under your IRA trust account are designed so that you will be withdrawing the required amount of money when the required time mes. However, if for any reason you or your beneficiary do not withdraw the amount required by law, you or your beneficiary must pay a non-deductible tax equal to 50% of the uired amount not withdrawn.

Amounts distributed to you are includable in your gross income in the taxable year in which you receive them and are taxable as ordinary income. Optional ten-year forward averaging treatment that is available to certain lump-sum distributions from qualified plans is not available for IRA distributions. Normal five-year income averaging, however, may be available.

IRA's are intended to be used for income during retirement years. Therefore, early withdrawal of money from your IRA trust is subject to a federal penalty tax. The tax is 10% of amount withdrawn. The amount withdrawn will also be included in your income for the tax year in which it is withdrawn. There is no penalty tax if a withdrawal is made:

- after reaching age 59-1/2,
- because of death or disability at any age,
- to effect a rollover within 60 days to another IRA or Qualified Plan,
- to correct an excess contribution before the due date of your tax return, or
- to correct an excess rollover contribution which was caused by erroneous tax information supplied by your employer on which you reasonably relied.

ROHIBITED TRANSACTIONS

An IRA can lose its exemption from federal income tax if the individual establishing the IRA or the beneficiary engages in so-called 'prohibited transactions'. Prohibited transactions ude any direct or indirect:

Sale, exchange or lease of any property between the IRA and a disqualified person;
Lending of money or any other extension of credit between the IRA and a disqualified person;
Furnishing of goods, services or facilities between the IRA and a disqualified person;
Transfer to or use for the benefit of a disqualified person of the income or assets of the IRA;
Act by a disqualified person who is a fiduciary whereby he or she deals with the income or assets of the IRA in his or her own interest or for his or her own account; and
Receipt of any consideration for the personal account of any disqualified person who is a fiduciary dealing with the IRA in connection with a transaction involving the income or assets f the IRA.

In general, the term "disqualified person" includes the individual establishing the IRA, any designated beneficiary of the IRA, and any person who is a fiduciary or who provides services the IRA.

If the IRA loses its tax exemption, the fair market value of the IRA's assets must be included in your gross income for the taxable year in which the loss of exemption occurs. An itional tax of 10% of the amount included in gross income as a result of such loss of exemption will be levied if the IRA is disqualified before you attain age 59-1/2. addition, if you pledge all or a portion of the assets of your IRA as a security for a loan, that part of the IRA assets pledged shall be treated as a distribution and taxed accordingly, ., subject to premature distribution tax if distribution occurs prior to age 59-I/2.

DERAL GIFT TAX AND ESTATE TAX

The participant's designation of a Beneficiary for his IRA account does not constitute a gift for federal gift tax purposes. However, a participant's contributions under a spousal IRA the separate account of the participant's nonworking spouse is a present interest gift under the federal gift tax law. The making of a contribution under a spousal IRA does not require filing of a federal gift tax return nor the paying of any federal gift tax.

SCELLANEOUS INFORMATION

Form 5329.
You need not file IRS Form 5329 for each taxable year during which your IRA is maintained. However, you must file IRS Form 5329 for any tax year for which a tax is due because of an excess contribution, a premature distribution, or an excess accumulation.

Unrelated Business Taxable Income.
There is an exception to the generally tax-exempt status of investments within your IRA when you invest in a limited partnership interest in a partnership which is debt-financed or which actively conducts a trade or business rather than passively receiving income.

a. Income from the active conduct of a trade or business of the partnership or debt-financed income may generate unrelated Business Income which may be taxable to the Custodial Account if it exceeds $1,000.00 on an annual basis.
b. These taxes are an expense of the Account and should be paid by the Account.
c. We may, at our sole discretion, liquidate any assets in the Account to satisfy such taxes. We will liquidate assets in reverse order of purchase.
d. If you wish to send funds to the Trust to pay these taxes in order to avoid liquidation of an asset, these funds must be included as a contribution for the taxable year in which such funds are sent. Attention should be given to the possibility of an excess contribution resulting from this procedure.
e. If any allowable investment generates Unrelated Business Taxable Income, loss or gain, you must agree to prepare or have prepared on your behalf any necessary forms including Form 990-T, "Exempt Organization Business Income Tax Return ," if required, and return the Form 990-T signed by yourself (as "preparer" only) along with an authorization for the Custodian to pay any tax due out of the assets of the account.

Financial Disclosure.
Because the investment of the assets of your IRA is self-directed by you, it is impossible to guarantee the growth in value thereof. The value of your IRA will increase depending upon the amount of your contributions, the length of time over which you contribute and the performance of the investments you make.

IRS Approval
The   IRA has been approved as to form by the Internal Revenue Service. Because Internal Revenue Service approval is a determination as to form only, it does not represent a determination of the merits of the   IRA.

Account Termination.
You may terminate the IRA at any time after its establishment by sending a written notice of such termination, which is signed by you and includes the account number of your IRA, to:

our IRA will terminate upon the first to occur of the following:
a. the date your written notice of termination (as described above) is received by   or, if later, the termination date specified in the notice;
b. the date all assets in your IRA have been distributed; or
c. the date the IRA ceases to qualify under Section 408(a) of the Internal Revenue Code.

Additional Information.
You may obtain additional information about IRAs in general from any district office of the Internal Revenue Service.

Figure 6-3: Form 5305 Individual Retirement Account Disclosure Statement

- Total Investment Control: Only *you*, not a financial institution, choose the investments and decide if and when to sell or buy. What's more, you initiate the investment decisions whenever you wish. You have total control.
- Flexibility: The above two advantages combine to give you unparalleled flexibility. You are not locked into a bank's instruments or a broker's offerings. You have a complete range of investment choices, and you can act whenever you are inclined. The procedure to change investments is simple. You merely request the trustee to make the switch. Remember, the trust company has no financial interest in the product; it does not reap any "inside" harvest from the use of your money. But it does charge fees for its services. These charges are its only source of earnings. The trustee will bill you for three basic services:

1. Establishing the plan
2. Annual maintenance
3. Termination

A typical set-up charge ranges from $25 to $50; it is a one-time fee that covers the costs of establishing your account. An average maintenance fee is $50 or $75 per year. This covers the administration of your account: Accepting and distributing contributions and periodically reporting to you and the IRS. You may be allowed up to five transactions yearly as part of normal maintenance. Additional transactions can incur extra expenses. The termination fee is for closing your account and final reporting to the IRS. It can run approximately $100. These trustee fees are reasonable in light of the personal control, range of investment options, and flexibility you gain.

Including Real Estate in Your Self-Directed IRA

Since the self-directed IRA enables you to choose from the total spectrum of legal investment options, you can—as we have noted—include real estate in your plan. Combining this top inflation-beater with the tax-deferred IRA will give you a powerful financial edge. But don't forget: While you'll have the privilege of taking charge of your own financial destiny, you'll also have a big responsibility. Although the trustee of your self-directed IRA will execute your orders to buy or sell, *you* must select the real estate that will assure your financial security in retirement. It's your plan, your investment, and your future.

To help you make sound decisions in this challenging process, we must address the following questions:

- What are the basic advantages of conventional real estate investment?
- Do these advantages change when you invest in real estate with IRA dollars?
- What real estate investments are practical or compatible with the IRA environment?
- What are the potential rewards?

In the chapters that follow, we will look into these questions and see how the real estate IRA will specifically contribute to your retirement security.

SEVEN

The Compatibility of Real Estate and the IRA

You now see that the combination that seemed "too good to be true" is possible, thanks to a truly self-directed IRA. This type of IRA provides the same tax benefits available in any other IRA. But more important, it lets you invest in real estate—enabling you to out distance inflation by several laps.

But there are two conditions that will have a major impact on your decision to purchase real estate with your IRA dollars:

1. The tax-free environment in which your IRA is sheltered.
2. The funding ceiling on your annual contribution.

We must examine these two issues in order to determine whether the real estate IRA will still be as ideal an investment as we think it will be. Before we go on to address these matters, though, we should think for a minute about what real estate really is.

THE COMPONENTS OF REAL ESTATE

Many fortunes in real estate have been amassed by individuals whose personal expertise (or lack of it) often had little to do with their success. For example, no special foresight led anyone to settle in Kissimmee, Florida, before Mickey Mouse decided to construct an East Coast home to rival his California spread; but as Disney World was built, local residents for miles around benefited from skyrocketing property values. And elsewhere across

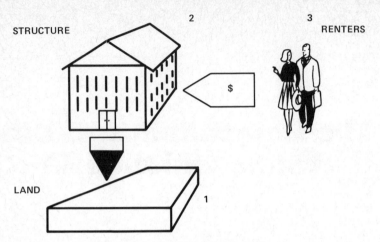

Figure 7-1: Real Estate Components

the nation, developers who have built successful shopping malls, housing complexes, and even entire cities have driven nearby property values way up.

In spite of tales of such unexpected windfalls, though, ignorance is *not* bliss when it comes to real estate—or any other investment. The more you know about it, the better equipped you will be to make sound investment decisions.

Real estate is not a simple entity like a share of stock or a bank CD. On the contrary, real estate consists of several basic components. You can invest in a total package of three components—or in only one or some of them. Different investment principles govern the different components. Furthermore, the various elements involve different tax considerations that further influence your selection.

Figure 7-1 depicts the three main components of real estate. Let's examine each of them:

1. Land: This is the universal and essential ingredient in real estate. Every real estate project must be anchored to terra firma. Regardless of the type of structure—home, apartment house, shopping center, or hotel—construction cannot proceed until the developer has control or ownership of the land. For example, a small, $40,000 single-family home in Atlantic City happened to be located in the planned construction zone of a gambling casino. The negotiations escalated to an asking price in excess of $1 million. Unfortunately, the transaction was eventually aborted because of the homeowner's greed and obstinacy. Outcome: The casino abandoned its original plans, redesigned the project, and will build around the home.

There are different categories of land, based on the land's use. Raw land, or property in its natural, undeveloped state, has relatively little value. If the land has potential utility, then it becomes valuable to developers and/or builders. But only when the developers or builders go ahead and make the property usable—with improvements such as sewers, water and streets—will the land begin to have any real worth. When such services are in place, you've got the beginning of a homesite. The distinction between land and homesites will be part of our focus in Chapter Eight.

Projecting the future value of developed land requires some expertise, but none is needed simply to hold or own it. You do not need the management skills that would be required if you owned a rental property, nor do you have as much responsibility. Furthermore, the only investment value of this component of real estate is its potential for appreciation. Interestingly, even the air above a plot of land is considered to belong to the property. It cannot legally be invaded or utilized without the owner's approval.

2. Structure: This component consists of anything built on land, including personal residences, multi-family homes, apartment houses, shopping centers, and commercial buildings. A structure demands maintenance and repair to prevent deterioration and subsequent depreciation of value. And any building you erect must have economic value to make your investment pay off.

A structure should be built with the intention of attaining maximum economic use. A shopping center in a thinly populated area will fail. Yet you couldn't attribute the failure to the land or structure itself—only to the judgment of the investors who conceived the project. I include this example to show that as the investment becomes more complicated, you need more expertise to make the decisions critical for success.

3. Rental: The third component of real estate is fundamentally different from the land and from the building's bricks and mortar. Rental income is *not* generated by the land, nor by the structure itself. Your profit will come from the business activity that goes on in the building.

A conventional investment approach would be to purchase all three components in one package. Each component performs a different but important function in the whole, as follows:

The *land* is essential since nothing can exist without its acquisition. It is the most indispensable component of the total investment. When a building is erected on it, land remains passive. It can in itself produce no income or tax advantage. Nor can it be depreciated.

On the other hand, the *structure* can be depreciated, thus producing excellent tax benefits. Also, it will—in all probability—appreciate in value.

The *rental* component does not partake in this rather friendly investment condition. Here failure is more likely to result not from the real estate but from the human factor. When considering a rental investment, it is crucial that you investigate the management even more thoroughly and carefully than the real estate itself.

Keeping the three components of real estate in mind, let's now turn to the two questions about the real estate IRA that we asked at the beginning of this chapter.

HOW DOES REAL ESTATE FARE WITHIN THE IRA FORTRESS?

Under normal conditions, certain outstanding characteristics of real estate make it an investment surpassing its competitors. These qualities are:

1. Appreciation
2. Leveraged purchase
3. Tax-favored treatment of expenses

But when we move real estate or a home into a tax-immune environment of the IRA, we must analyze what will happen to each of these advantages.

The first advantage—appreciation—is not altered by the IRA; its potential remains intact. Nor is *leverage* affected. This is a matter of purchase terms and cash flow. (This benefit is important, and I refer to you to detailed discussion of it in Appendix A.) The "no tax" climate has no influence in either of these key spheres.

Because the IRS has no presence within the IRA fortress (see Appendix B), and the tax clock does not tick there, many of the tax advantages we commonly associate with real estate investment disappear. Any expenses you may incur in connection with your property cannot be written off as they could with a real estate investment outside the IRA; nor can you write off any interest you pay on mortgage. To sum up: The marvelous deductibility of real estate expenses—so essential in conventional planning—vanishes within the IRA. Specifically:

- Interest payments *cannot* be deducted.
- Real estate taxes are *no longer* deductible.
- Expenses such as maintenance and insurance, are non-tax-deductible.

Furthermore, since no tax clock ticks, the most favorable "non-cost" time-sensitive expense of all—*depreciation*—cannot exist. This is a big loss. Any profits you earn on the real estate you have bought with IRA dollars are *not* taxed, so long as the sale is made and the proceeds are retained within the IRA. Your money is taxed only when you withdraw it, and you will then pay ordinary income tax on it. If the real estate is sold within the IRA fortress, the profit is not taxed at all. All IRA funds are treated as ordinary income and taxed only on distribution.

Of course, the IRA environment has a neutralizing effect on many tax considerations connected with *other* types of investments, too. For example, bank CDs moved behind the walls of the IRA fortress are not taxed yearly, and they could thus be said to perform like tax-free municipals. The same is true of annuities, bonds and even stocks. This taxless condition makes the IRA the grand equalizer of all investment modes with respect to the effect of taxation. The one characteristic that is *not* affected by taxes—and this is your only basic yardstick for selecting an investment vehicle for your IRA—is *appreciation*, or growth.

As we saw in Figure 4-1, real estate averaged a 33⅓% annual appreciation over twenty years, nearly twice the 17% gain rate of its nearest competitor, stocks. The other two modes—savings and bonds—failed even to match the rate of inflation. So you can see why real estate has paramount appeal as an outstanding investment. But you can also see that the nondeductibility of operating expenses and of depreciation will *reduce* the performance of your investment because real estate relies strongly on such tax breaks to enhance its value, particularly in the early years of ownership. In light of these apparent setbacks, we must seriously ask: **Does the loss of tax breaks disqualify real estate as an investment vehicle for tax-sheltered IRA funds?**

The response is a resounding—NO. We say this because for IRA purposes, we can direct our attention to the real estate component that's *least* affected by the tax-neutral environment of the IRA. This component is the *land*. In no real estate investment does land qualify for any depreciation deduction that the IRS allows. Land simply does not *depreciate*; it can only *appreciate*. Therefore, moving land into an IRA (or any other pension plan) does *not* change its treatment. Of course, land does bear some carrying expenses (property taxes, for example), but these are relatively small and are more than compensated for the investment's strong growth through its leveraged appreciation. So land can indeed help us to realize the promise of our real estate IRA. Thus the IRA's tax-free environment is *not* an impediment to our objective. Rather, it is ideal for it.

HOW CAN THE ANNUAL IRA FUNDING CEILING ALLOW US TO BUY REAL ESTATE?

The tax issue is not the only issue we need to resolve. Another IRA compatibility question involves the funding ceiling. You must certainly be wondering how you can possibly afford real estate with an outlay of only $2,000 per year in payments. You can do it!

To understand how, we must examine the methods by which you can own real estate. These range from simple, direct ownership all the way to owning a small "piece of the action" in a large complex. All types of ownership in this spectrum are compatible with your real estate IRA purchase. We will consider these types here:

1. Limited partnership: In this type of ownership, IRA and Keogh investors can buy small unit interests in large real estate complexes (Figure 7-2). This approach can be likened to owning shares in General Motors. The limited partnership is attractive because investors can at worst lose only their cash investment. They have no personal extended liability. In exchange, a limited partner relinquishes control of the investment to the general partner (GP), who alone is empowered to make operational decisions. The success of the venture will depend on the GP's performance. His or her personal failure can have disastrous results.

Remember, you are technically investing in the *management* of the partnership, not in the real estate itself. Therefore, before you invest, you must be careful to ascertain the credentials of the GP and the details of the real estate. Moreover,

Figure 7-2: Limited Partnership
ORGANIZATION

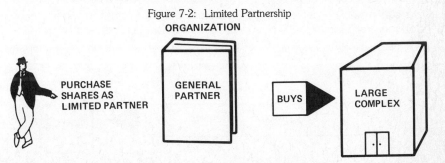

PURCHASE SHARES AS LIMITED PARTNER   GENERAL PARTNER   BUYS   LARGE COMPLEX

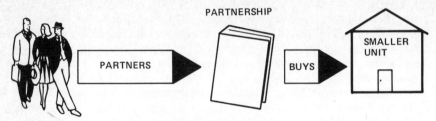

Figure 7-3:   General Partners

because tax-deductibility of operating expenses and carrying charges are critical to support the investment performance of these large complexes, their potential in a tax-free environment is questionable.

2. General Partnership: You can also purchase a small portion of a single real estate complex via a *general partnership*, as shown in Figure 7-3. In this type of multiple ownership, all the partners share the benefits, authority, and responsibilities for the venture. Two or more persons can launch a general partnership, and they may own equal or unequal shares in the real estate. Small apartment houses or multi-family dwellings (2-4 units) are the properties most typically associated with this form of ownership. Since several people share the ownership and the financial obligations on the property, the acquisition becomes financially viable. Each owner will own and control his or her portion of the partnership, and sell it. This is defined as owning the property in common with the other partners. Again, this type of investment may be somewhat dubious because its performance will depend on the management skills of the partners.

3. Individual Ownership: The most common type of purchase—and the one we advocate for your real estate IRA—is *individual ownership*, a category that encompasses all individuals who have purchased their own home, condo, or land (see Figure 7-4). A joint purchase by a husband and wife is a special type of individual ownership. It's called joint ownership with right of survivorship. In these cases, the surviving spouse will automatically be entitled to the whole property.

The big advantage of individual ownership over the other two types of ownership we've discussed is that it enables you to buy land—which, as we've seen, is the one component of real estate whose tax treatment does not suffer within the IRA fortress—and simply let it appreciate in value. You don't have to worry about anyone else's business judgment or management skills.

Now You Know How to Invest Your IRA Dollars

You can now see that either by increasing the number of investors or by reducing the price of the property, a real estate IRA investment is probably

Figure 7-4:   Individual Owner

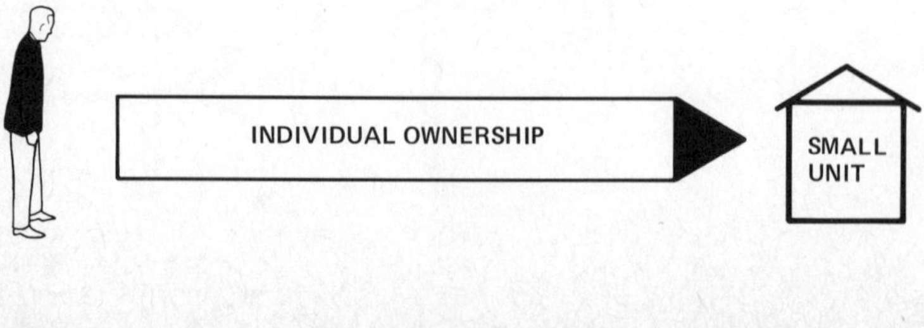

INDIVIDUAL OWNERSHIP

SMALL UNIT

within your grasp, and that the best approach for most people is to buy small tracts of developed land privately. Since the funds in your IRA are restricted, you will be able only to spend a correspondingly limited amount if you opt for individual ownership. But don't forget: The least expensive component of a total real estate package is the *land*. So we can direct our attention to this element, to come to grips with the issue of price compatibility with the IRA's funding limitations. In particular, you should try to invest in just one of the components of a viable real estate package—*developed* land. We will delay our specific discussion of the price and funding of this investment until Chapter Ten so that we can first study land and all of its ramifications.

With the course of your IRA investment set, let's now examine the issues connected with land quality and standards, since you will need to buy an excellent property. If you make a poor choice, you could doom your retirement plan to failure. On the other hand, a prudent selection will help safeguard your objective.

EIGHT

The Selection Process: Homesite vs. Land

By this point, we have learned that the most productive investment vehicle for our IRA funds is real estate. This investment is sanctioned under a self-directed IRA. We have also discovered that it is logical and practical to purchase a replacement house at retirement so as to free up most of our accumulated profits from our principal residence, and we saw how we can use the four-lot equivalency concept, that is highly adaptable to the IRA, to do this. Now we're ready to start thinking about selecting the lots we want to buy.

While seeking out property is an exciting prospect, you may be puzzled and uncertain about what kind of land to buy and where you should buy it. These questions will be the focus of this chapter. We will compare the differences between desirable and undesirable sites, and we will study standards, protective regulations, and buying procedures.

THE "MERCEDES MIRAGE"

Surely, it is foolish to suggest that the purchase of just *any* piece of land will automatically lead to financial stability. People have made disastrous mistakes by responding hastily and without research to "buy before they're gone" sales pitches. We cannot warn you too strongly that disappointment can befall any careless spur-of-the-moment buyer of land. Our purpose here is to spotlight this issue so you can learn how to protect yourself to the fullest as a potential buyer.

As you may be aware, chicanery and trickery have hounded real estate advertising and sales. We can summarize these practices with an allegory I call the "Mercedes Mirage":

A man shops around for the best deal on a luxurious Mercedes-Benz. He searches until he hears of one at a very low price. He rushes to see it and admires it longingly. The model is a shimmering beauty—handsome lines, sparkling finish, lush interior. It has all the distinctive marks and trimmings of a Mercedes. He quickly signs a contract to buy because of the attractive price. After he takes possession, he discovers that the car won't start. Worse yet, there is no motor under the hood and none can be installed. Without an engine, the purchase is useless. The man has bought a worthless item that won't work. He can touch it and admire it, but it is valueless.

History is replete with inequitable and fraudulent real estate transactions that call the "Mercedes Mirage" to mind. But perhaps not until the 1960s and early 1970s was the peak of misrepresentation reached. This was a period of maximum sales exaggeration and buyer exasperation. Countless buyers were woefully deceived.

Some of the most flagrant abuses were in the sale of land for retirement or vacation homes. These lots were advertised as Shangri-las, and developers promised everything but eternal youth. The appeals were inviting and compelling, and attractive financial terms induced prospects to "buy now" so that they could "save later." The time was ripe for ensnaring gullible buyers. The economy was booming, and spiralling homesite costs and home values quickly convinced people that nothing would stop the roll that real estate was enjoying. The heady climate sent second-property demand through the roof. But by the early 1970s, a litany of horror stories circulated. Consider the following disasters:

A Minnesota resident paid $7,500 for one-fourth acre in New Mexico. He failed to read a statement by the sales company that said that the seller "did not promise in writing to install a water line." The embittered buyer learned that *he* had to install his own water line over fifteen miles of barren land.

Another man bought a $9,000 lot and paid $16,000 with interest, taxes, survey costs, and so on. He got a deed he never examined. Too bad. When he was about to retire, he found that he needed a swamp buggy, since his land could be measured by the gallon, not the acre.

Early owner-residents in a large Pennsylvania development were similarly fleeced. While their land offered a beautiful view, it was ugly underneath; its clay and limestone soil was incapable of absorbing waste. Individual septic tanks don't work in such poor soil, so raw sewage seeped and bubbled down the lovely hillsides. The stench was unbearable for miles. Long court action suits and countersuits ensued. Result: The developer was found guilty. The developer, marketing under interstate regulations, had failed to reveal information about the soil condition and the potential sewage problem. Had he included this information in the property report, he'd have been in no trouble with the federal or state authorities.

Sadly, the common thread that runs through these stories is that the developers delivered what their sales documents contended. The core of the problem involved the very real differences between land and homesites. Had they been aware of this distinction, millions of Americans would have been spared disappointment and financial losses. To understand this point, we examine the various types of land that we can buy.

Types of Land

Land can be divided into three basic types, each with a vastly different value.

1. Raw Land: is the most abundant type of land. It is land in its natural, untouched state. Its major worth probably lies in its scenic value or its recreational attractiveness; such land can be very useful as a place in the country to drive to and pitch a tent. Except for sports enthusiasts and campers, raw land possesses little basic value. Unless it is improved, it will have limited future worth. While raw land is able to support plant and animal life, it does not possess the services necessary to accommodate civilized human existence.

2. Farmland: is an important and popular kind of land. It is used solely for agriculture. Thus the value of a tract of farmland depends on the products grown or raised on it, on the skill of the farmer, and on fluctuations in national and international prices of various farm products. Farmland can also be valuable because it is cleared and has access to water: When situated near a populated area, it may be desirable for eventual residential development.

3. Totally improved land: This type of land is converted for use, and qualifies for zoning for commercial or residential use. Such classification means that the land has undergone extensive development, including installation of sewers, utilities, streets and other basics. The value of totally improved land is far greater than that of other types. For example, a 300-unit condo complex on a 2-acre site could be worth as much as $6 million! Such multi-family sites are sold not by "size" but by the number of buildable units that can be erected on them. The $6 million value is based on a per unit cost of $20,000—not unusual in many areas.

WHAT MAKES A HOMESITE A HOMESITE?

This discussion points out the essence of what makes land valuable—*use*. The magic of land's *use* is the springboard to real estate worth. If a piece of land has no utility, it has no economic value. With utility, there is value.

A residential property is more than just a piece of land. It needs access to many services to become usable, habitable, and valuable. Such services and facilities—expensive to install and provide—elevate land to homesite status. Since a homesite enjoys higher status and improved utility, it will also be more valuable because people want and need such property.

Real estate that is sold by either a large developer or an individual for residential construction must be serviced with several basic utilities that are not merely desirable but *essential* if the homesite is to have real utility and subsequent worth. These services include:

1. Central Water System: This is probably the single most important element in a future homesite. Except in certain remote areas, wells are vanishing as a source of limitless, acceptable-quality water. Health department codes have found well water to

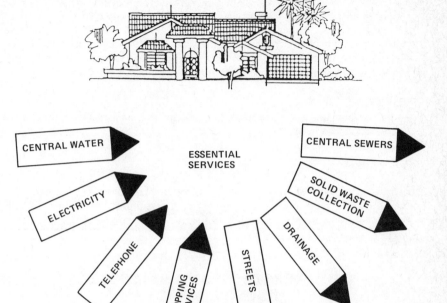

Figure 8-1: A Homesite is Land which has been or will be Fully Improved

be increasingly unsatisfactory. This shrinking supply may deny people residential use of land. These problems are particularly acute in such states as New Mexico, Nevada, and California, where water rights are as valuable as the land itself.

2. Central Sewer System: Unbridled dumping of waste through septic systems has created health problems by contaminating many of our aquifers, which are underground water-bearing rock formations. After investigating such abuses, health departments may be required to forbid development, thus rendering local real estate useless and worthless.

For example, in Florida, the health department will allow only one septic tank per acre. Therefore, in a cluster of ¼-acre homesites, the installation of one system serving only one home will *prevent* development of three adjacent sites. The only guarantee against such a setback is a central sewer system.

3. Drainage System: The value of flood-prone areas is questionable at best and properties in such regions should not be considered for any long-term investment. Guideline: The area should not have been flooded in the preceding century. The U.S. Corps of Engineers will provide and verify these data.

4. Solid Waste Collection: The facilities to handle this service must be available.

5. Paved Roads: Access roads must be available or installed. Conformity to city, town or county specifications is critical if the local authorities are going to assume responsibility for maintenance and repair.

6. Telephone and Electricity: Most purchasers consider these utilities as vital as the air we breathe, but the *cost* of installing them can be prohibitive in remote and unpopulated areas. Their absence can play havoc with property values.

In addition to the above basics, another body of services should also be available within reasonable distance of the homesite. These are facilities that enhance the residents' standard of living and lifestyle. They include:

- Shopping centers
- Recreational and cultural facilities (theaters, sports centers, galleries, museums, libraries, and so on)
- Hospitals
- Houses of worship

Only when the proposed property fulfills all of these requirements should you consider a homesite purchase. Unless you scrutinize the above list of prerequisites for a viable homesite, you may find yourself a victim of the "Mercedes Mirage."

THE INTERSTATE LAND SALES FULL DISCLOSURE ACT

Fortunately, the federal government wants to help you avoid the horrors of the "Mercedes Mirage." By the late 1960s, growing complaints about abuses in the real estate field alarmed Congress, leading it to pass the Interstate Land Sales Full Disclosure Act of 1968. Previously, almost no protections had existed for the real estate buyer; those on-record regulations that did exist had no effect.

The new law mandated that sellers of more than 100 lots file a detailed property report with the Housing and Urban Development Agency (HUD) in Washington, D.C. (see Figure 8-2). However, the act deals only with real estate sales across state lines. We must thus distinguish between two types of real estate sales:

1. Intrastate: real estate located in one state and sold to someone residing in that *same* state. These sales are regulated by that state's real estate commission.
2. Interstate: real estate located in one state and sold to someone living in *another* state.

The federal government is empowered to be concerned only with interstate sales.

The 1968 land-sale reforms compel developers to conform to mandated procedures. Developers must secure the approval of two sources and file documents with HUD. (see Figure 8-2):

- The real estate commission of the state where the property is located.
- The real estate commission of the state(s) where the prospective buyers live.

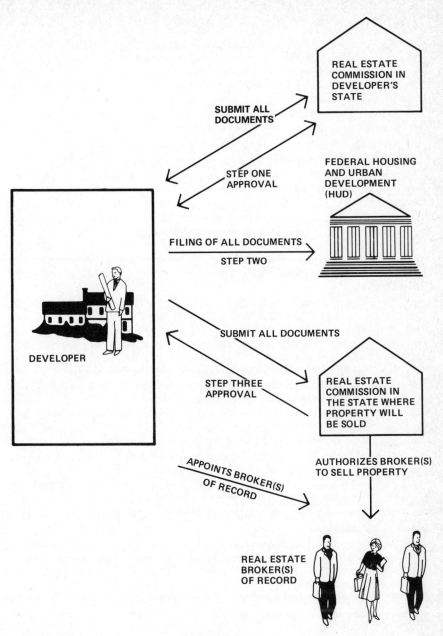

REAL ESTATE
COMMISSION IN
DEVELOPER'S
STATE

SUBMIT ALL
DOCUMENTS

STEP ONE
APPROVAL

FEDERAL HOUSING
AND URBAN
DEVELOPMENT
(HUD)

FILING OF ALL DOCUMENTS

STEP TWO

SUBMIT ALL DOCUMENTS

DEVELOPER

STEP THREE
APPROVAL

REAL ESTATE
COMMISSION IN
THE STATE WHERE
PROPERTY WILL
BE SOLD

APPOINTS BROKER(S)
OF RECORD

AUTHORIZES BROKER(S)
TO SELL PROPERTY

REAL ESTATE
BROKER(S)
OF RECORD

Figure 8-2

We'll examine each of these agencies in turn.

1. Real Estate Commission of State Where Property is Located: The developer intending to market property must prepare a thorough *offering*, or property report, for the real estate commission of the state where the property is located. This report is a massive document that answers literally every "who," "what," and "where" question pertinent to the location.

When the state real estate commission is satisfied with the offering, it approves the use of this document in the developer's sales promotion and transactions.

A typical property report must reveal information, *positive or negative*, on:

Property: The report outlines the location, size and types of buildings.

Risk: A variety of warnings about buying the land is described. These are "red flags" to the prospect. The real estate salesperson should address these issues before the sale.

Encumbrances: Existing mortgage amounts and holders are itemized. The rights of the buyer must be defined. Release clauses and rights in case the developer defaults must be defined, too.

Access: The report must tell how to get to the location via all modes of transportation. The directions must include roads, primary and secondary highways, and so on.

Land Use: The exact way in which the property will be used and fitted into the surrounding developed area must be detailed. One of the most important considerations is flooding. If the area is in a flood zone, the report must say so. If there is no flooding, this must be stated and substantiated by referring to the U.S. Corps of Engineers study.

Area Facilities: Availability of services such as police and fire protection, schools, hospitals, houses of worship, and recreational facilities must be disclosed, along with the number of all such services and their distance from the site.

Improvements: Proposed completion dates for the developer's various tasks must be stated. This section gives the "when" and "how" of such basics as roads, sewage disposal, water supply, drainage, surveys, and street maintenance.

Public Utilities: Rates and information on the local companies are explained. Hook-up or deposit costs for electric, phone, water, and natural gas are itemized.

Public Transportation: The nearest buses, trains, and airlines are listed, no matter how far away. If none are anywhere nearby, that's mentioned, too.

Government Control: Tax rates on the property are given, as is any other pertinent tax information.

Method of Sale: This advises you of deed rights and who owns them. Interest rates, prepayment rights, and refund privileges are also noted. For example, you can cancel a contract within two years of signing if no one showed you a property report before you signed. Or you can cancel for any reason within one week of signing.

Another prerequisite must be adhered to if a property in a given state is to be deemed suitable for sale in that state: The state insists on preapproving all documents—including films, maps, and advertising brochures—that describe the property. For example, if a photograph is featured in a flyer, the developer must state whether the depicted scene is on the property or, if it is not, how far away it is from the site. If the developer fails to identify photos accurately, fraud is perpetrated.

2. HUD: Once the developers have complied with the requirements of their own state, they must then file with a federal agency, HUD, if they wish to sell property interstate. Appropriate documents and material are sent to HUD's interstate land sales

division. Again, the offering must provide the information just outlined. In anticipation of selling land in other states, the prospectus must also cover information on:

1. The developer's *corporate charter* with relevant financial facts per the law.
2. *Title* of one property and facts pertinent to it.
3. *Mortgages*, with details of obligations.
4. *Local regulations* that affect your undisturbed use of the property. (Zoning laws are common, but a *deed of restriction* is much better—it's a legal document and can only be changed by court action.)
5. *Local facilities* such as schools, hospitals, houses of worship, and police departments.
6. *Costs* and availability of improvements.
7. *Recreational facilities*—availability and use.

These data are generally encompassed in the original property report. HUD does not approve or inspect the property. It will file the documents as evidence of the property offering. It will not investigate or verify any information in it. The document is a legal description of the property and the improvements and services that the developers have promised. If they do not keep their word, their noncompliance may be referred to the Justice Department for criminal action.

3. Real Estate Commission in the Buyer's State: The second source from which developers must obtain approval is the real estate commission of the state(s) in which they wish to sell their property. All the same documents, contracts, property reports, and so on, are submitted for each outside state's approval, and the other state's specific rules or regulations must be complied with. State commission representatives travel to the project to verify the accuracy of the information submitted. The expense of this trip is borne by the developers.

Only after all of these procedures have been followed to the state's satisfaction will it permit real estate brokers within its borders to be officially named "brokers-of-record." When so designated, these brokers can sell the out-of-state property to residents of the state in which they are licensed.

Why Does The "Mercedes Mirage" Persist?

With all of these legal protections in place, it would appear that consumers were safe from the "Mercedes Mirage." Surely these regulations assure purchasers that the land they buy in interstate transactions will live up to all the promises that the developers make. But, unfortunately, we live in an imperfect world, and countless unsatisfactory and questionable real estate sales are still being made.

Why? Essentially, the system of controls and safeguards was legislated with the purpose of protecting buyers against the sellers, but *not against themselves.*

This situation results from the sound principle that the government does *not* and should *not* dictate or interfere with the actions of a buyer. Therefore, even if an offering is laden with inadequacies and could be considered terrible by any normal standard, the government cannot and should not prevent someone from buying it.

In addition, the government has stated that anyone who offers a *homesite* for sale is committing fraud if that *homesite* does not provide the improvements or services that define a *homesite*. But the government cannot prevent someone from simply offering *real estate* for sale. Real estate that is less developed than a homesite *can* be sold, and therein lies the rub.

For example, a nationally known organization is presently offering *real estate* for sale. The property report on this land makes a number of statements. For example:

- Water:
  "A central water system is not available. You will need to install your own. . . .by drilling a well."
  "The estimated cost for drilling a well. . . .should range from $3,200. . . .to $2,500." "There is no assurance a productive well can be installed and, if it cannot, no refund of the purchase price of the lot will be made."
- Sewer:
  "Sewers are not available. . . .Septic tanks will. . . .cost. . . .$1,325 to $4,800."
- Utilities:
  "Power extension costs will vary depending on the distance(s). . . .estimated costs for a primary user will be $100 per pole [spaced] about 300 feet or. . . .$1,800 per mile plus clearing charges, if required, at. . . .$1,250 per mile."
  "Telephone facilities have not been extended to the individual lots, and there is no estimated schedule for their installation."
  "The cost to extend telephone facilities to lots. . . .will be. . . .$50 for each one-tenth of a mile above the first (free) mile."
  "The estimated cost to extend (telephone) service for the most distant lot. . . .is $400."

Local Services

- Fire:
  "The Volunteer Emergency Squad (is) located. . . .19 miles (away)."
- Police:
  "Police protection is available 19 miles (away)."
- Hospital:
  ". . . .The nearest hospital (is) located. . . .45 miles (away)."
- Doctors:
  "Physicians are . . . . 15 miles (away). . . .dentists 19 miles (away)."
- Public Transportation:
  "Public transportation is not available . . . . to nearby communities."
- Soil Erosion:
  "We do not have a comprehensive plan to control [soil erosin that] could result in property damage and create a possible safety and health hazard."

Most of the above statements can hardly be described as "selling points." In fact, the ethical salesperson would be upset or at least displeased if charged with the responsibility of selling such land.

Such negative statements certainly can't help the developers sell the property. But the developers are *compelled* to reveal all such facts; interstate regulations make such disclosures mandatory. Any misinformation in the offering is an indictable offense, punishable by severe fines and/or imprisonment.

The offering quoted above was for *land*. Had such conditions as stated existed in an advertised *homesite* offering, fraud would have been perpetrated and charges brought. But the developer has avoided promoting the property as a *homesite* and is marketing it as *land* instead. This procedure is fully legal. Remember, the regulations make the *seller* declare accurately what he or she is offering. The regulations do not *judge* either the quality of lack thereof of the properties. Nor does the legislation place any restraints or guidelines on the buyer. The buyer must study the property report to judge whether the offering is a good or bad investment. If he or she makes a bad choice, no one else is to blame.

Therefore, you will have to ask both obvious and not-so-obvious questions about any property you are considering. Only your probing inquiries will give you the information you need to make a sound decision as to whether or not to buy.

Everything is in position for you. Legal mechanisms are available to enforce protective legislation, and HUD and the state real estate commissions are behind you. Since these sources don't appraise the offering, though, the final decision to buy will be up to *you*.

The Buy Procedure: We have detailed the information that state and federal authorities demand of *sellers*. Government regulations also require that you be given the chance to read and study the property report thoroughly. Only after you've examined the property report should you sign the receipt for it. The salesperson also witnesses that you have received the report, stating that *only* information in the report has been used to sell the property. The salesperson's signature is important and strengthens his or her credibility with the client. Any misrepresentation subjects the salesperson to civil and/or criminal action.

As an added protection, be sure to ask and expect to receive signed verification of any information *not* in the original report or in subsequent sales presentations. Insist that such data be written down, signed, and given to you.

Your objective now is to review the property report to learn all you can. You are doing this for your own benefit and protection. It is your duty to yourself to gather as much information as you can and to ascertain that you understand it.

By now, you may want to throw up your hands in despair, wondering how you can absorb and remember all this. With your need to ferret out pertinent information, how can you wade through oceans of documents to make a sound decision?

We believe the best way for you to inform and protect yourself is to be inquisitive. Therefore, we recommend you ask the following questions of the salesperson from whom you are contemplating buying real estate. If the answers are already in the property report, have the salesperson indicate the appropriate page and section. If they are not, ask him or her to put the answers to the following questions *in writing*. If the salesperson doesn't know an answer, insist that he or she find out. If he or she refuses to do so, or to write down and personally sign any needed information, take your business elsewhere! You'll be much safer. An unwillingness to confirm the information in writing indicates that the salesperson is less than expert and/or candid. The list of questions follows:

KNOW THE CRITICAL FACTS ABOUT THE SELLER OR DEVELOPER

- Is the organization a private or public corporation?
- Are reports available on the organization's financial strength?
- Do the sellers develop the land and build their own homes?
- How many homes has the developer built in this project?
- Has the developer built any recreational facilities? If so, what are they?
- Will the seller provide clear, insured title to the property?
- How many years has the developer been engaged in this type of activity?
- Is the property in a flood zone?
- What are the required building requirements to meet the above?

The Land or Homesite

- Does the developer have assets that can be attached in a legal action and judgment?
- Will the services listed below be *unconditionally* guaranteed by the developer?
- Are any additional costs required or assessed?

	Yes	No	Costs
Central sewer system			
Central water system			
Streets			
Storm drains			
Street lighting			
Electrical power			
Telephone service			
Trash collection			
Water hydrants			

- Are there any maintenance fees or special assessments required of property owners?
- Are all promised facilities in the contract?
- How are promised improvements guaranteed—bonds, cash, or other vehicles?
- Who will maintain roads during and after the project is complete?
- Who will manage the project after the developer moves out?
- Is there a homeowner's association? If so, what is required of members?

About Area Facilities

The distance in miles to the nearest:

Large shopping center _____

Police department _____

Fire station _____

Hospitals (number of beds) _____

Major airline service _____

Medical & dental offices _____

Houses of worship _____

Banks, law offices, etc. _____

About Other Matters

The distance to the closest:

Golf Course _____

Marina _____

Park _____

Is the property protected by a
deed of restrictions? _____

These questions and the answers you receive should serve as your "blueprint" for accepting or rejecting a real estate proposal. Even though protective procedures now promote the consumer's interests, the best way to protect yourself in a real estate transaction is knowledge. Follow the guidelines set forth in this chapter, and you will never purchase a useless or valueless property.

INTRASTATE SALES

All the protections we have described so far refer to *interstate* sales. No such extensive requirements are mandated for people who buy property in their own state (*intrastate*).

The only regulations for an intrastate purchase require the seller to furnish the buyer with:

- Clear title
- Property description (not a full *report*)

The absence of extensive rules and regulations regarding intrastate sales must make us take serious note when considering a purchase within our own state. This is especially true in light of the critical role of thorough disclosures and definitions in making a sound decision.

Therefore, I urge *intrastate* buyers to rise up and act like *interstate* buyers. You have to initiate all requests for information because of the

minimal obligations placed on the seller. You should use the checklist we've just outlined by asking any seller to provide answers to *all* the requested data.
    Specifically, take these two steps:

1. Use all guidelines that I've used to define a homesite.

2. Have your sales agent *commit to writing* all pertinent facts and information about the property. Be sure that the agent and/or salesperson executes and signs the documents. This step is imperative, since only a written and signed declaration has any value in a civil or criminal case involving real estate. Hearsay or word of mouth is inadmissable—even with witnesses! If the agent won't comply fully, you are best advised to forget the anticipated purchase and consider yourself saved from possible disaster.

Having armed yourself with knowledge and your vital checklist of questions, you are now in a stronger position to consider the real estate IRA. Furthermore, you now can be more confident about going out to buy a homesite. You are now in a better position to spot the "Mercedes Mirage," that may conjure up illusions of attractive homesites but will actually bring you only troubles and regrets.

NINE

How to Set Up and Maintain a Self-Directed IRA

- "Where's the beef?"
- "It takes a tough man to make a tender chicken."
- "Good to the last drop!"

These memorable slogans are among thousands that barrage us daily via radio, television, newspapers, and magazines. They sell tons of hamburgers, carloads of chicken, and cauldrons of coffee.

What does this have to do with a self-directed IRA? Nothing directly. But, you see, the above products are highly recognizable because of expensive advertising. And guess who pays for these ad campaigns? Everybody who buys the beef or chicken and washes it down with coffee. When you see the next ad, remember, you helped pay for it!

You may also be familiar with print and broadcast messages for bank, insurance company, and brokerage house IRAs. This advertising is also costly. In fact, the better you remember the ad, the more costly the campaign. Can you imagine the enormous cost of all the bank IRA ads in the country? And guess who paid for them all? The same person who paid for the burger and coffee ads—little old *you*.

But the trustees of self-directed IRAs, on the other hand, do not make any money on your assets. Such organizations only earn fees for their administrative work, as we noted in Chapter Six. These trustees cannot afford widespread promotion or advertising. Consequently, they have such low visibility that most people are completely unaware of them. But rest assured, trustees for totally self-directed IRAs do exist. And they can work very much to your advantage.

THE ROLE OF THE TRUSTEE IN YOUR
SELF-DIRECTED PLAN

The first order of business in your overall strategy is to locate a trustee for your self-directed IRA. If you're a financial planner or if you subscribe to a professional financial publication, this search is comparatively simple. However, for the lay person, the task is not so easy. To assist the uninitiated, I have compiled a small but growing list of these independent self-directed trust organizations. If you cannot find such a trust in your area, please send your request, along with a stamped, self-addressed business envelope, to the following address. You will be sent the most current list.

HOUSEPOWER
P.O. Box 1679
West Caldwell, New Jersey 07007

These trust companies have been organized to administer all types of accounts. With IRS approval, they have designed IRAs for the general public. The details or covenants of the independent trust must conform to the same regulations that govern all IRAs. As we have noted, these trustees do *not* advise or exercise any investment control over your funds. All such decisions are vested in you, the individual IRA participant, alone. When you hold an IRA with one of these trust companies, it is truly a self-directed plan. The only controls or limitations on investments are those imposed by law under ERISA, TEFRA, or whatever other acronyms the government can dream up.

Totally self-directed trust companies offer you more than just the opportunity to invest in real estate. As shown in Figure 9-1, and as we saw in Chapter Six, once you are inside the fortress, you can invest in any vehicle approved by legislation covering IRA investments. You can design a personal portfolio to your own specifications—it's your right! A typical trust company's document explains:

> You can select from a wide range of investments. These include stocks, bonds, mutual funds, money market funds, savings certificates, U.S. Treasury investments, real property, promissory notes secured by mortgages or deeds of trust, limited partnerships, and covered call options. The list of acceptable investments is updated to conform with changes in regulations, and includes all investments that are considered permissible under ERISA, and administratively feasible for the trustee.

In order to comply with IRS regulations, you must make contributions directly to the trustee. The trust company then forwards the funds to the institutions that offer the investment or savings vehicles that you have chosen.

For example, if you want to deposit your IRA money in a CD, you simply instruct your self-directed IRA trustee to purchase that specific bank's CD. Your self-directed trustee is the official owner of the CD on your behalf. Therefore, the bank will treat your trustee like any regular customer making this purchase.

Flexibility is a key feature of a self-directed IRA. You won't be violating IRS regulations as long as: The transaction is made without violating any

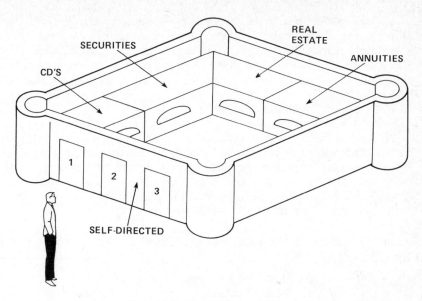

Figure 9-1: The Self-Directed IRA

covenants of the preapproved trust instrument. Because of potentially turbulent economic and financial cycles, it may well be to your advantage to be able to shift funds from one investment vehicle to another. Nevertheless, some warnings are in order! Switching investments may carry penalties and restrictions imposed *not* by the trustee but by the product sponsor. If you own a CD and you direct your trust to liquidate that CD prior to its maturity date, you will incur a bank penalty, thereby reducing your expected yield.

Before you can take advantage of the flexibility of selecting your own investments, there are certain actions you must take in order to set up your self-directed real estate IRA. You must:

1. Adopt, or sign up, for the plan.
2. Fund the IRA.
3. Select the property.
4. Negotiate the real estate purchase.
5. Instruct your trustee to purchase.
6. Maintain the IRA.

Adopting the Plan

To adopt a self-directed plan, all you have to do is execute an adoption agreement. There is no uniform document to use; each marketer designs its own. (A typical adoption agreement is shown in Figure 9-2.) The document must contain the details of operation, restrictions, fee schedules, and investment penalties. It should also itemize all investment vehicles designed into the trustee's plan.

The trust document is legally binding. You should know your rights and restrictions under its provisions, or you may be in trouble. For example, some little-known restrictions concern IRA deposits in jumbo CDs. While these accounts are attractive because of their higher yields, you may not be able to retrieve your money for many years; multimillion-dollar CDs are not very liquid. For such reasons, it's important that you understand the document and any specific investment restrictions in it.

In addition to personal data, you must indicate on the trust document which type of IRA you are adopting. The distinction among the five types listed in the Adoption Agreement in Figure 9-2 lies in the source of the funds. The first two are technically new IRAs, either individual or spousal. In the other three, the money will come from other IRAs or qualified plans. Your trustee will be able to accept more than the yearly limits if money is being transferred from these previously established sources.

Funding the Plan

There are only two sources with which you can fund your IRA—your present year's contributions and the previous years' accumulations. It is your right to move any or all assets from other previous IRAs into your new one. You can do this through either of two authorized procedures: *Transfer* and *Rollover*.

TRANSFER

Transfer involves only the two trustees. A simple letter from you to your present IRA trustee will do the trick. A typical, convenient form letter, supplied by your new trust, is shown in Figure 9-3. In this transfer letter, you state, through the new trust, that you have engaged a new trust and request the existing trust to transfer all assets to it. The old trust must comply. Remember, you are the boss.

In transferring assets, you can ask that the assets be moved to the new trustee. You do not have to liquidate the investment; you simply put someone else in charge. Moving the asset intact is prudent, as in the case of a CD that has not come due. By allowing the CD to mature, you will avoid the bank's penalty.

For example, if you have a CD coming due three months after you adopt the new trust, you should change its trustee, but should not change the CD itself until its maturity date. By so doing, you avoid a penalty for disruption. You instruct the new trust to cash in the CD only when it matures. After that, you are free to invest the funds in the new vehicle of your choice.

Transfers can be made from one or all of the IRAs that you may have previously established. Remember, your IRA does not have to be one monolithic instrument. You can use contributions to set up separate IRAs with as many trustees as you have accounts. The only limitation is on the dollar *amount* that you can contribute in a given year. However, it is advisable that you place all IRAs under the total control of one trustee. You benefit by doing this because you will receive a *single* annual report to review *all* your holdings—a much easier task.

IRA
ADOPTION AGREEMENT

The undersigned hereby establishes an Individual Retirement Account ("IRA") under
Retirement Plan and Trust Agreement which is incorporated within this Adoption Agreement by this reference. The undersigned
designates   as Trustee under the Individual Retirement Account established and
makes the following declarations.

Participant's Name: _____   Date of Birth: _____ / _____ / _____
                          (Please print)   (Mo.)   (Day)   (Yr.)

Street Address: _____

City and State: _____   Zip Code: _____

Daytime Telephone Number: _____ / _____   Social Security Number: _____
                              (Area Code)

Indicate below which type of IRA you wish to establish at this time: (more than one box may apply)

☐ Regular tax-deductible deposit
☐ Spousal IRA deposit
☐ Transfer from another IRA
☐ Rollover from another IRA
☐ Rollover-Qualified Plan or TSA

Rollover Statement. If this is a Rollover IRA, I certify that the cash or other property I now deposit as a rollover contribution meets the requirements for a Qualifying Rollover Contribution as provided in the Internal Revenue Code and as defined
in the Plan and Trust Agreement, including the requirement that deposit of such cash or property is being made within 60
days after receipt by me of the qualifying distribution.

In addition to the initial rollover contribution, I may make annual contributions of earned income to my Rollover account
(these should be itemized as such). If I choose this option, I will not be allowed to roll the account into a qualified plan in the
future. For this reason, I may also open a separate IRA with   to accumulate these additional
contributions of earned income. This will require a separate Adoption Agreement.

Beneficiary Designation. I hereby designate the following persons as first and contingent beneficiaries to receive my
interest in this IRA according to the terms of the Plan and Trust Agreement, hereby revoking any such prior designations made
by me.

Participant's Primary Beneficiary(ies)   Participant's Contingent Beneficiary(ies)
(list full name(s), relationship(s) and social security #(s))   (list full name(s), relationship(s) and social security #(s))

_____   _____

_____   _____

Figure 9-2: IRA Adoption Agreement

TRANSFER LETTER

TO (Your *Current* Trustee):   FROM (Yourself):

_____   _____
(Name)

_____
(To the Attention of)

_____   _____
(Street)

_____   _____
(City, State and Zip Code)

_____/_____   _____/_____
(Area Code)   (Telephone)   (Area Code)   (Telephone)

Account Number with Current Trustee: _____

I wish to terminate your administration of my _____ account. I have adopted a new plan and have designated _____ as my successor trustee. Please transfer my assets to _____ as indicated below.

TO THE CLIENT: All assets in your plan MUST BE LISTED INDIVIDUALLY BELOW. For each asset, you must indicate how it is to be transferred. If no selection is made, the asset will be liquidated and the cash forwarded to

- Check the box marked SELL if you want current trustee to sell an asset and send the proceeds to
- Check the box marked RE-REGISTER if you want to keep an asset in its present form in your new retirement plan. In this event, your current trustee will transfer the registration of the asset to _____ If certificates of deposit or insurance products are to be re-registered, you must check with your current trustee to be sure that re-registration is possible. Also, check to see if it is required that your signature be guaranteed. Upon transfer, the actual certificate or policy must be sent to
- If accounts held by different trustees are to be transferred, each transfer requires a separate transfer form.
- _____ reserves the right to reject the transfer of assets deemed unacceptable. If this should occur, a new transfer letter must be executed authorizing liquidation of the asset prior to the transfer.

CASH _____ $_____

NON-CASH ASSETS (Explain fully, including Face Amount or Number of Shares as applicable.)	Face Amount or Number of Shares	Sell	Re-Register*
_____	_____	☐	☐
_____	_____	☐	☐
_____	_____	☐	☐
_____	_____	☐	☐
_____	_____	☐	☐

*Registration should be changed to include _____ name, address, and tax

All checks should be made payable to:

       TRUSTEE FOR _____IRA
(Participant's Name)

CLIENT SIGNATURE. I have initiated and approved this transfer. I certify that all assets in my plan are listed and that I am fully aware of any and all penalties incurred by my request (if any) for premature liquidation of any certificate of deposit or insurance product involved in this transfer.

_____   _____
(Client Signature)   (Date)

To *Current* Trustee: Please complete this section.

_____   _____   _____
(Name)   (Date)   (Phone #)

_____
(Signature)

Figure 9-3: Transfer Letter

106

ROLLOVER

In the rollover process, you will take *personal* delivery of the funds and then contribute them to the new trustee. You are allowed to hold the funds for a period of 60 days from the date when you take constructive receipt before you can be taxed. Before that deadline, you must redeposit the funds into the new trust. Rollover may be a more efficient method than transfer, since many trustees are very slow to transfer funds. Their inordinate delays shouldn't surprise you, because they are losing out on the use of your money when they relinquish your funds.

Selecting a Property

Having adopted a self-directed IRA and moved funds into it, you are now ready to make your first investment in real estate. You will base your selection on a number of factors, but none will be more important than your available funds.

You can now indulge in some adult fantasy and start to think about where you want to live when you retire. This will involve some practical considerations and careful deliberations. You may want to stay close to home or move across the country. Migration around the nation has been facilitated by today's rapid, lower-cost air transportation.

In the last ten or fifteen years, increasing numbers of people have moved from the industrialized Northeast and Midwest to the Sunbelt. Many factors have contributed to this trend, which is projected to continue steadily. Chief among these reasons is the lower cost of living, due to lower energy costs, in warm areas. Real estate taxes and state taxes are more lenient in many Sunbelt states, too.

If you're fortunate enough to know where you want to live when you retire, you are free to concentrate right away on selecting a specific site. If you're less certain, abundant literature is available to help you make a wise choice. One source that will furnish you with information is the American Association of Retired Persons; write to your state's chapter of this organization. The Chamber of Commerce of the state where you plan to retire will also be glad to send you information.

The sooner you make this decision the better. If you purchase a property, save, or invest early, your money accumulates longer from a smaller dollar sum and will appreciate to a satisfactory level by retirement.

After choosing an area, you should visit it to ascertain that it is practical and suitable for you. Then you should contact local real estate brokers to help you locate specific sites for purchase. Professionals know the area, they can save you much time and energy. You and your broker must thoroughly discuss the specific type of location you seek and your purchase objectives.

The dramatic growth of our aging population has triggered a new awareness of retirement goals in the real estate profession. Knowledgeable brokers can help you select those communities that offer high-quality recreational facilities and essential support services. It's the broker's business to accommodate you and fulfill your requirements.

While brokers have always marketed individual properties, many major developers all over the country have begun to develop small and large projects to cater to the retiree market. Their aggressive campaigns have influenced tens of thousands of people, with mixed results. The positive experiences are the ones you hope to match. You can do this by being aware of and avoiding all the pitfalls. Be sure to adhere to the standards and guidelines outlined in Chapter Eight.

When talking to your broker, you should exercise extreme care in examining all zoning regulations, master plans, and other documents that will influence the long-term character of your target community. Surely, the future desirability of the area must be your prime consideration. Although it's impossible to be totally clairvoyant, there is a real-estate instrument that does provide a level of predictability—*a deed of restriction*. This is a legal document that imposes limitations on the use of the property through deed covenants such as types of improvements, architectural designs, construction materials, building size or height limits, setback standards, and so on. Buyers *must* observe its conditions.

A deed of restriction is far more reliable than the more common zoning regulations. It is very difficult to alter, while local zoning regulations can be modified at the whims of a small and changing community board.

Remember: *never* purchase unless the points discussed in Chapter Eight are committed to writing. Additionally, the seller should have "deep pockets." In other words, the person or organization who sells you the property must have sufficient financial strength (or "pockets" into which you can reach) to redress any loss you might suffer. We reemphasize that any verbal guarantees or statements by a broker or his or her representatives *must* be put in *writing* and witnessed by the involved sellers and personnel to be valid. You should disregard any promises or projections made *only* verbally. You must remember that *any promises or statements are worthless unless they are put in writing*. If the seller or agent refuses to do this and asks you to "trust me," do yourself a favor and walk away.

Negotiating the Purchase

After you have selected a suitable site, you are now ready to conduct the discussions that precede the purchase of a homesite with your IRA money. Your negotiation of the financial terms of the purchase will depend on three conditions: The funds available in your IRA; the debt service that you can handle with your IRA; and your ingenuity. The details of the initial down payment and the debt service are so extensive that we will treat them separately in the next chapter. The terms of the purchase are established between you and the seller. These negotiations are generally made with a real estate broker acting as the agent for the seller. Just remember that these terms must be compatible with the financial limitations discussed in the next chapter.

You may decide to purchase property offered by a large developer. One advantage of working with such a seller is that the terms are prearranged. This means little sparring will be involved. Otherwise, the legal paperwork in this type of sale is similar to and follows the same course as that of any other real estate transaction.

The proceedings begin with a *contract for sale,* which is an agreement between the parties for the buyer to purchase the property from the seller. This document is contingent on conditions that both buyer and seller must satisfactorily meet. The contract for sale is finalized by a deed and mortgage. The contract will be drawn according to the laws and regulations of the state(s) in which the property is located and sold. Since space does not permit detailed discussion of this matter, we advise that you, your broker, and your attorney ensure that all pertinent paperwork and contracts are legally executed.

Instructing Your Trustee to Purchase

After negotiating price and terms with the seller—based on the funds available in your IRA—you must make the seller aware that you are buying the property through your IRA. Remember, regulations mandate that all IRA assets must remain in a trustee's custody. Your financial arrangements with the trust must be made completely clear to the seller of the property.

All parties involved in this transaction should understand the uniqueness of this comparatively uncommon procedure. The real estate broker, and especially the attorneys, should become acquainted with the mechanics of IRA sales transactions. If necessary, you can refer any person who has a question on this matter to your trustee. But if everyone follows the directions set forth herein, no problem should arise, since this is *not* an untried procedure. It has been followed for almost 10 years.

To place the IRA purchase in proper perspective, let's examine the more familiar procedure of a non-IRA real estate transaction. Figure 9-4 shows the flow of paperwork, instructions, and responsibilities in a real estate purchase that is initiated by the buyer but executed through an attorney. As the diagram indicates, you can give your lawyer a limited "power of attorney" to effect the sale for you. In addition to giving your attorney the power to buy, you must furnish him or her with the purchase details. Your attorney must also be given sufficient money with which to bind the contract. Now the attorney has both the legal authority and necessary funds to execute the purchase.

Your attorney is empowered to sign all papers and hold any sale contract, deed, or other legal papers "in trust" for you. Furthermore, you can make all payments through the attorney, whom you must supply with both the funds and the authority to make all payments. This type of transaction has been common for years.

Now let's replace your attorney with your self-directed IRA trustee. The flow is exactly the same (see Figure 9-5). You are now authorized by the trust agreement to direct your trustee to purchase the property you have picked. Of course, along with such instructions to purchase, you must also provide the funds to do so.

If you're buying a property with IRA funds, one covenant ought to be added to the contract. Let us explain. The legal purchaser of the property

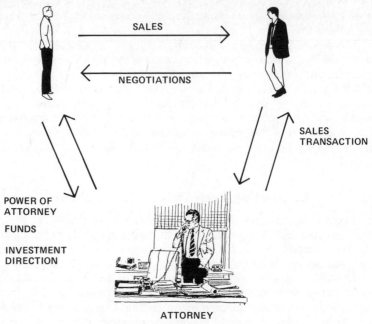

SALES

NEGOTIATIONS

SALES
TRANSACTION

POWER OF
ATTORNEY

FUNDS

INVESTMENT
DIRECTION

ATTORNEY

Figure 9-4:   Power of Attorney

(your trust) is dependent on your having sufficient monies in your IRA to buy the property and/or to maintain the continuing flow of annual payments to satisfy the debt service. If this were a direct, non-IRA leveraged purchase and the financial obligations were not met, conventional retrieval methods would be used. The mortgagee (loaner) could offer the property for sale and obtain his or her unpaid balance. If there were a lack of available funds, the mortgagee could look to the debtor for full satisfaction. Thus the mortgagee could look both to the property and to the purchaser's personal liability for payment of the unsatisfied claims.

This procedure is not possible in an IRA transaction. In such a purchase, the trustee and the participants *cannot* be targeted for deficiency action. Therefore, a clause must be added to the contract restricting the mortgagee to look *only* to the property for liquidating damages in the event of the worst. In effect, this means that *personal* liability cannot be charged against you or your IRA trustee to satisfy any terms of the contract. The buyer must be clearly apprised of this restrictive clause. Your lawyer should be likewise advised of it and should add the appropriate covenant to the agreement.

Since large developers have sold properties to IRA holders, their contracts do contain such a clause, as presented here in guideline form:

> *Default of this Purchase Agreement by the purchasers or their heirs, personal representatives, or their assigns shall incur no personal liability of purchaser or heirs, representatives, or assigns but the Company shall retain the land and payments made under this Purchase agreement subject to the limitations contained herein.*

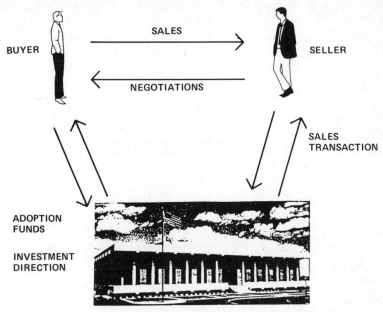

Figure 9-5: IRA Trustee

Once you have negotiated the terms, the sale contracts with the seller must be executed. When the terms and all financial considerations have been defined, the paperwork is sent to the IRA trustee, along with your authorization to purchase the property.

A form known as an IRA investment authorization is shown in Figure 9-6. Since the official buyer is the trust, these papers must be signed by your trustee as "participant." In addition, you must have sufficient funds in your IRA to execute the purchase. Only when your authorization has been received and there are sufficient funds in your IRA can the trustee act on your behalf. The trustee will then countersign all the papers and execute the purchase.

MAINTAINING THE IRA

When all documents are executed by both your trustee and the seller, your trust now "owns" the property. If it is a leveraged purchase, your trustee will use your contributions to satisfy any unpaid balance. You are *never* to make any payments directly to the seller. Your contributions must *always* be sent directly to the trust in order to be considered tax-deductible contributions to your IRA. This is true for your other purchase obligations as well. When the real estate taxes are due, the tax bill will be sent to the trust. The trust will then make payment from existing monies.

At the end of the payment cycle, the real estate becomes your property, but it *must* be held in trust by your trustee. The deed will be recorded in your trust's name on your behalf. It is not to be commingled with anyone else's IRA assets.

IRA INVESTMENT
AUTHORIZATION

Plan Name: _____ IRA
(Type or print Participant's name)

Account Number (if available): _____

I hereby authorize _____ to invest the funds of my IRA as follows:

(Explain fully, including face amount or number of shares as applicable. If IRA funds are not adequate to complete all transactions below, _____ will invest the available funds in the order in which the transactions are listed. Any remaining funds will be deposited into a daily money account for your benefit.)	Face Amount or Number of Shares	Buy	Sell
_____	_____	☐	☐
_____	_____	☐	☐
_____	_____	☐	☐
_____	_____	☐	☐
_____	_____	☐	☐
_____	_____	☐	☐
_____	_____	☐	☐
_____	_____	☐	☐
_____	_____	☐	☐
_____	_____	☐	☐
_____	_____	☐	☐
_____	_____	☐	☐

I hereby verify that I meet the suitability requirements (if any) of the offering(s) indicated above. And I understand that all of the above must be deemed acceptable investments by _____ before they will be executed.

_____   _____
(Participant's Signature)   (Date)

Complete back of this page as applicable.

Figure 9-6: IRA Investment Authorization

112

Congratulations!

You have just purchased one homesite to secure one-quarter of a debt-free replacement home, an equation we discussed in Chapter Four. As we noted there, you should consider this homesite not as a source of income but rather as one-fourth of a retirement house. It is a long-term real estate investment that you should *not* liken to a bank account or to shares of stock. Those investments can only create dollars, that must be converted to the goods and services you need in retirement. But your commitment to real estate can give you a debt-free place to live.

Regardless of the real estate you select, your initial choice is not rigid or ironclad. If conditions change and your retirement plans are redirected to another location, you can sell your first property and purchase another homesite elsewhere. You should be aware that the sale of real estate is influenced by certain relatively simple factors. Sales really depend almost exclusively on two basic elements—supply and demand. The supply of real estate will never increase. Actually, it is shrinking drastically, as we explained in Chapter Eight. And population shifts alter the demand side of the equation. In general, supply is decreasing while the demand is increasing—an ideal set of conditions for any investment.

Again, discouraging events can temporarily act adversely on a specific market. But such downside trends are short-term. Since you're looking for long-term rewards with real estate, it is inappropriate to worry about the influence of transitory "bearish" factors.

You should now have a sufficient grasp of the procedures. With the help of your trustee, you can work your way through the seemingly complicated but actually simple paperwork. All you need now is to get a handle on one final and important factor—the limits on your purchase. It might appear that the IRA imposes severe limitations here, but we have a surprise in store for you. The maximum purchase can be substantial, and it will at least be adequate enough to meet your basic objective—securing all or part of your retirement house!

TEN

How Much Real Estate Can You Purchase With an IRA?

You are now aware that it is your own responsibility to negotiate the purchase of the real estate you buy with your IRA. Your self-directed trust does the administrative work, but you must determine precisely what and how much property to purchase. To help you make these decisions correctly, this chapter will discuss how much real estate you can buy with your IRA.

In a conventional real estate purchase, the amount of property you can buy depends on two factors—the sum you have available for a down payment and the size of the mortgage you can secure from a lender. The down payment reflects the amount of cash that you have saved or accumulated. The mortgage is determined by your financial ability to service the debt you incur. A simple formula is:

$$\text{Purchase price} = \text{Down payment} + \text{Mortgage}$$

Similar principles apply to real estate purchases in an IRA. However, the basic formula must be restated as:

$$\begin{array}{ccccc} \text{Maximum} & = & \text{Accumulated} & + & \text{Debt-service} \\ \text{purchase price} & & \text{IRA assets} & & \text{limit} \end{array}$$

The amount you have accumulated in your IRA depends on your previous contributions and the interest they have earned. These totals will vary widely among IRA holders, causing a dramatic range in the amount of real estate different IRA participants can afford, since the down payment *must* come from these accumulations.

114

Table 1.5 Cumulative IRA Contributions
(Without Interest)

	Single IRA		Spousal IRA	
1975	1,500		1,750	
1976	3,000		3,500	
1977	4,500		5,250	
1978	6,000		7,000	
1979	7,500		8,750	
1980	9,000		10,500	
1981	10,500		12,250	
1982	12,500	2,000	14,500	2,250
1983	14,500	4,000	16,650	4,500
1984	16,500	6,000	19,900	6,750
1985	18,500	8,000	22,150	9,000
1986	20,500	10,000	24,400	11,250

From 1975 through 1981, the contribution limits were $1,500 for an individual IRA and $1,750 for a spousal IRA. The limits were raised to the present levels—$2,000 and $2,250 respectively—in 1982. Table 1.5 lists the maximum possible contributions and their cumulative sums since the inception of the program.

These data provide the cumulative totals of the maximum allowable contributions *without taking investment yield into account.* When we do add in an estimated average yield of 8%, the accumulations reach levels at which respectable real estate transactions are possible. Such total amounts range from $12,611 to a high of $39,634, as shown in Table 1.6.

The second factor involved in the maximum purchase price, the debt service, concerns the ongoing obligation of your mortgage. The debt-service limit of the IRA is the same for all participants, since it is controlled by how much we can invest annually in the account—$2,000 for an individual IRA,

TABLE 1.6 IRA Accumulations Maximum Contribution
Accumulation Yield = 8%

	Single IRA		Spousal IRA	
1975	$ 1,620		1,890	
1976	3,370		3,931	
1977	5,259		6,136	
1978	7,300		8,517	
1979	9,504		11,088	
1980	11,884		13,865	
1981	14,455		16,865	
1982	17,771	2,160	20,643	2,430
1983	21,353	4,474	24,725	5,054
1984	25,221	6,975	29,133	7,889
1985	29,399	9,677	33,893	10,950
1986	33,911	12,611	39,634	14,256

TABLE 1.7 How Much Principal $2,000 Per Year Pays Off
(Simple Interest Included)

	5 Years	10 Years	15 Years
10%	$7,800	$12,500	$15,440
11%	7,630	12,000	14,600
12%	7,460	11,560	13,833
13%	7,452	11,118	13,122
14%	7,134	10,689	12,462
15%	6,977	10,290	11,857
16%	6,825	9,910	11,300

$2,250 for a spousal. The amount of debt obligation that IRA contributions of $2,000 and $2,250 can satisfy is shown in Table 1.7 and Table 1.8 respectively; the debt ceiling is located in the appropriate term column and interest row. For example, Table 1.7 shows that a $2,000 annual contribution can satisfy a debt of $11,560 at an interest rate of 12% for a term of 10 years. If the term is extended to 15 years, the debt can be increased to $13,833. Table 1.8 gives similar information for the annual spousal limit of $2,250. The specific details of amortization that produce these data are discussed later in this chapter.

By adding the appropriate limits above to the total of your accumulated IRA funds, you will be able to compute how much real estate you can buy with your IRA. This simple procedure will become familiar as we examine a number of varied cases.

As we progress through these examples, you may find your own situation among them. So follow along.

INDIVIDUAL IRA PURCHASE WITH AN ACCOUNT OPENED IN 1975

Between 1975 and 1981, as we have seen, qualified employees could contribute up to $1,500 per year to their individual IRAs. In 1982 the maximum was raised to $2,000 per year. As shown in Table 1.5, the

TABLE 1.8 How Much Principal $2,250 Per Year Pays Off
(Simple Interest Included)

	5 Years	10 Years	15 Years
10%	$ 8,823	$14,183	$17,441
11%	8,624	13,606	16,490
12%	8,426	13,066	15,625
13%	8,241	12,558	14,822
14%	8,057	12,073	14,076
15%	7,881	11,624	13,392
16%	7,709	11,194	12,763

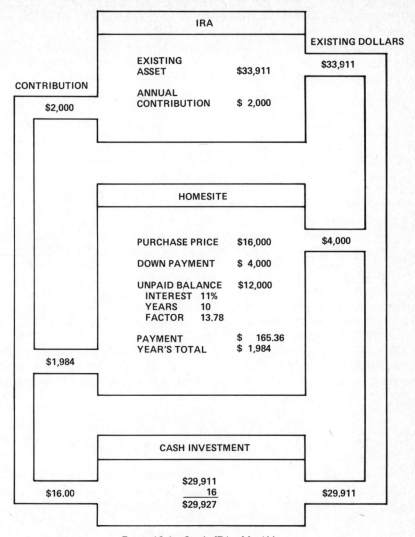

Figure 10-1: Single IRA—Mr. Abbott

maximum total of contributions (not counting return on earnings) is $20,500 for the 1975 group and $10,000 for the 1982 group.

Let's introduce an employee, Mr. Abbott, to illustrate the potential purchasing capacity of the 1975 group. Mr. Abbott became eligible for an IRA in 1975 and diligently contributed the maximum sum every year. By 1986, he had deposited $20,500. Through the power of compounding on an 8% return, his IRA funds had grown to $33,911, as shown in Figure 10-1.

Mr. Abbott elects to buy a homesite in a developed retirement community for $16,000. His down payment will be $4,000, and the seller has agreed to finance the $12,000 balance at 11% for 10 years. The monthly payment is found by using the amortization table in Table 1.9, which lists the factor for the number of dollars required to satisfy $1,000 of debt at various interest rates and lengths of time. To find the total monthly payment, we multiply the monthly factor by the number of thousands of mortgage dollars. In this case, the monthly payment is:

Factor	Number of thousands	Monthly payment
$13.78 ×	12 =	$165.36

-or-
$1,984 per year

Let's track this transaction and cash flow in Figure 10-5. Mr. Abbott's existing asset balance of $33,911 will be supplemented annually by a $2,000 contribution. He will take $4,000 from existing assets to make his down payment, and he will invest the remaining $29,911 in a cash instrument. He will use his subsequent annual contributions to make the yearly total mortgage payment of $1,984. He will add the remaining $16.00 ($2,000 − $1,984) to the cash account, raising the sum in that account to $29,927.

Note that an 8% yield on the balance of $29,927 in Mr. Abbott's IRA cash account will be $2,394, a sufficient return to satisfy the loan's debt service. This means that his IRA's purchasing capacity has not been fully exploited. Mr. Abbott could actually purchase a second homesite of equal value and still have *excess* funds in his IRA.

Now let's suppose Mr. Abbott purchases a luxurious $40,000 homesite (Figure 10-2). He uses $30,000 of his total $33,911 IRA funds as a down payment. That leaves him with a $10,000 mortgage. At terms of 10% for nine years, his monthly payments will be:

Factor × Balance in thousands
(from Fig. 10-2)
14.08 × 10 = $140.80, or $1,690 per year

He will add the balance of his annual contribution, $310 ($2,000 − $1,690), to his cash balance of $3,911. His cash fund will now total $4,221 and grow at prevailing interest rates. This flow is shown in Figure 10-2.

Mr. Abbott has several other alternatives. For instance, he could buy *two lots* outright for $13,000 each and finance a *third* one of similar price with future contributions. His options enable him to vary the number of lots and their prices, the down payment, the interest rate and the term of the balance.

Individual Purchase With a 1982 IRA

Participants who opened an IRA in 1982 or later have less to invest than Mr. Abbott. As we noted earlier, an individual IRA begun in 1982 has amassed $12,611 at 8% (Table 1.6).

That brings us to our second buyer, Ms. Banks. She can use up to the $12,611 total in her IRA as a down payment. But how much of a mortgage can she finance?

Ms. Banks' maximum allowable IRA contribution is $2,000. To find out

Table 1.9 Factor for Monthly Amortization of $1000

Interest Rates (%)

Years	9.0	9.5	10.0	10.5	11.0	11.5	12.0	12.5	13.0
5	20.76	21.00	21.25	21.49	21.74	21.99	22.25	22.50	22.75
6	18.03	18.28	18.53	18.78	19.04	19.29	19.55	19.81	20.07
7	16.09	16.34	16.60	16.86	17.12	17.39	17.65	17.92	18.19
8	14.65	14.91	15.17	15.44	15.71	15.98	16.25	16.53	16.81
9	13.54	13.81	14.08	14.35	14.63	14.90	15.18	15.47	15.75
10	12.67	12.94	13.22	13.49	13.78	14.06	14.35	14.64	14.93
11	11.96	12.24	12.52	12.80	13.09	13.38	13.68	13.98	14.28
12	11.38	11.66	11.95	12.24	12.54	12.83	13.13	13.44	13.75
13	10.90	11.19	11.48	11.78	12.08	12.38	12.69	13.00	13.31
14	10.49	10.78	11.08	11.38	11.69	12.00	12.31	12.63	12.95
15	10.14	10.44	10.75	11.05	11.37	11.68	12.00	12.33	12.65

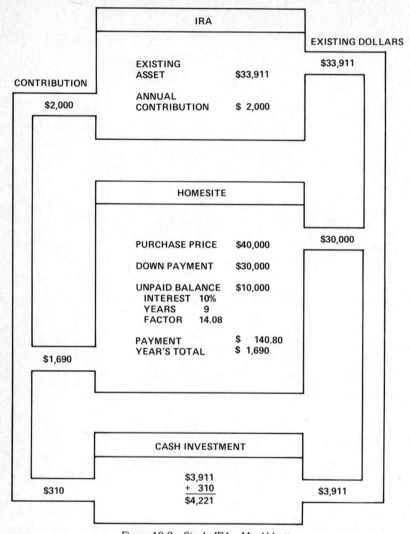

Figure 10-2: Single IRA—Mr. Abbott

how much debt this amount can service, we simply divide the *yearly amount* required to satisfy $1,000 into $2,000. The yearly amount is determined using the monthly factors in Table 1.9. For an obligation at 10% interest for 10 years, the factor is 13.22. The yearly total for each $1,000 is therefore:

$$13.22 \times 12 = \$158.64$$

Dividing $2,000 by this yearly total gives the maximum allowable serviceable debt in thousands:

$$\frac{\$2,000}{158.64} = 12.607, \text{ or } \$12,607$$

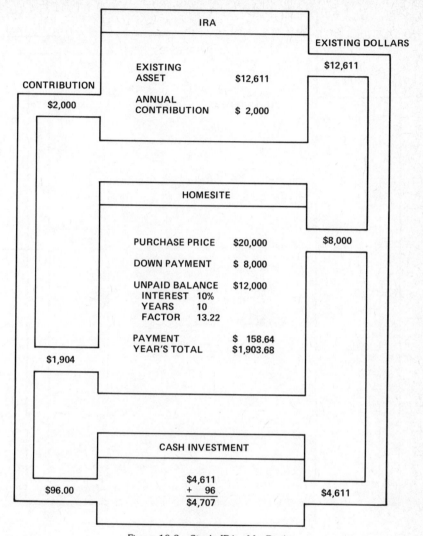

Figure 10-3: Single IRA—Ms. Banks

If Ms. Banks adds her existing assets to this maximum allowable figure, she finds that she can buy as much as $25,218 ($12,607 + $12,611). Armed with this information, Ms. Banks decides to buy a $20,000 homesite. Knowing that her $2,000 contribution will support a $12,607 mortgage at 10% over 10 years, she will use $8,000 of her existing IRA funds for a down payment, making the unpaid balance $12,000. She purchases the property, as shown in Figure 10-3.

A second option for Ms. Banks is to buy a lower priced homesite. Let's say she selects a $14,500 offering and commits future contributions to service the debt, using the same terms as the first purchase (10%, 10 years). On a

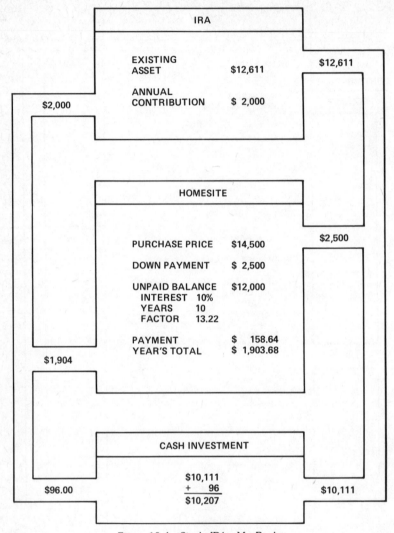

Figure 10-4: Single IRA—Ms. Banks

purchase price of $14,500, she makes a down payment of $2,500. She finances $12,000, as shown in Figure 10-4.

In each example, note that a cash investment fund is present. Any difference between the annual mortgage payments and the maximum contribution is deposited and is available for your *IRA trustee* to handle real estate taxes and property costs. These are minor expenses, but they must be satisfied, and this small fund can meet these obligations neatly.

Individual Purchase With a First-Time IRA

The first-time IRA holder can afford the least amount of real estate, since he or she has not accumulated any contributions with which to make a down payment. Nevertheless, effective price negotiation and good timing can still make homesite sales available to the IRA newcomer. For example, he or she can purchase a $12,000 lot with the same terms that Mr. Abbott and Ms. Banks received (10%, 10 years).

Figure 10-5 plots three time frames—the last quarter of the *previous* year, the entire present year, and the first four months of the *next* year. The contribution period for a designated year runs from January 1 of that year to April 15 of the following year. But from January 1 to April 15 of the designated year, there is an overlap period during which the *previous* year's contribution (if not already made) can be combined with the current year's. The two years' contributions total $4,000, a sum that makes possible many purchases not feasible with only one year's contribution.

For example, our third buyer, Mr. Carpenter, wants to buy a $14,000 homesite at the same terms as his coworker, Ms. Banks. The purchase details are:

Purchase price	=	$14,000
Down payment	=	2,000
Balance	=	12,000
Monthly payment	=	158.64
Yearly payment	=	1,903

If he were to put down $2,000 and pay the present year's monthly sums ($1,903 yearly), he would be contributing:

$$\$2,000 + \$1,903 = \$3,903$$

Since $3,903 far exceeds the annual IRA limit, Mr. Carpenter has a problem. But here's how he can solve it: He can make the down payment with the previous year's contribution. He can then make monthly payments against the current year's limits. Of course, this tactic can only be used in the overlap period, January 1-April 15.

Here's a variation of this timing situation. Let's say the sale was made between April 15 and December 1. If payment terms can be arranged on an annual basis, Mr. Carpenter can make the $2,000 down payment with his

Figure 10-5: IRA Funds

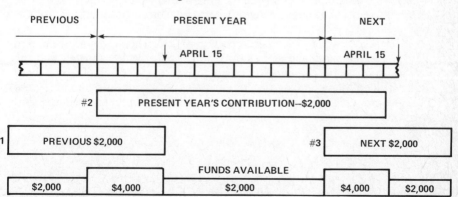

present year's funds and the annual payment with the following year's contribution. His yearly payment will be higher than monthly terms would be ($1,953 versus $1,903), but within allowable IRA limits.

SPOUSAL IRA PURCHASE

If you're married, you should become familiar with the spousal IRA. The general public perceives the spousal IRA as one IRA because it is based on the earnings of one person in a married couple. However, it is *not* one account held jointly by two persons, but *two* separate IRAs. One is yours, and the other is your spouse's. The total spousal contribution can be divided between husband and wife in any desired proportion, as long as neither person's contribution is more than $2,000 in a given year. In this case, the remaining $250 belongs to the spouse. The contribution can just as legitimately be split equally, $1,125 to each, even though one member of the couple doesn't work for wages.

A real estate purchase in a spousal IRA is permissible—it's a type of partnership—but the purchase procedure will differ slightly from that in an individual account. However, to avoid confusion about technicalities, we will here treat the spousal IRAs *not* as separate accounts but as *one*, even though the trust that handles them must treat them as two.

Table 1.6 showed that the spousal IRA enjoys an extra $250 contribution yearly. This means that a married couple with a spousal IRA can buy higher-priced real estate, or more real estate, than someone with an individual account can.

To demonstrate, let's say that the Davises have contributed maximum totals to their spousal IRA since 1975. Together they have garnered $39,634 based on an 8% compounded yield. The Davises—who have divided their IRA assets equally between them—have located a desirable lakefront homesite and are ready to proceed with the acquisition. (We remind you that a waterfront purchase is even better than money in the bank! While it's admittedly a judgment call, investment in scarce waterfront—lake, ocean, or river—property has always been a winner. Such property has become even more valuable than ever, since the government placed a moratorium on waterfront development as a result of environmental and ecological factors. This intervention has sent prices of coveted waterfront property skyrocketing.)

The Davises' target homesite costs $40,000. The sellers are willing to grant a 10-year mortgage of $12,000, at 11%. Table 1.8 showed that the Davises' spousal IRA can handle a maximum mortgage of $13,606 with these terms. Taking their combined accumulated assets into consideration (Figure 10-6), the couple can make a maximum affordable purchase of $53,240 based on the formula:

Accumulated IRA asset	+	Debt-service limit	=	Maximum purchase price
		or		
$39,634	+	$13,606	=	$53,240

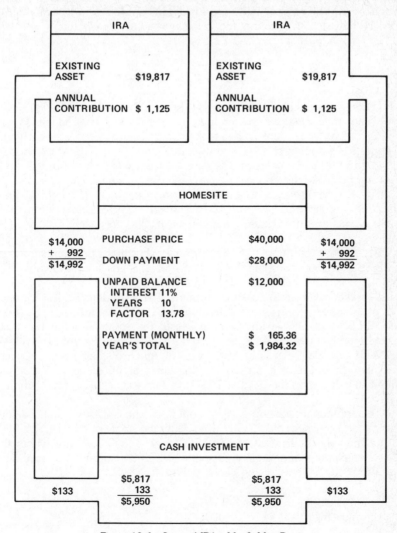

Figure 10-6: Spousal IRA—Mr. & Mrs. Davis

Since the Davises' IRA funds can support more than the $40,000 purchase price, they can use one of several financing options. They can make a large down payment and assume a small debt service, or they can make a small down payment and carry a larger mortgage.

The first alternative is shown in Figure 10-6. Each Davis owns half the existing assets—$19,817 each. The total spousal contribution of $2,250 is divided equally, at $1,125 each. Their individual total assets are thus $20,943 apiece.

The $40,000 homesite purchase is made with a total down payment of $28,000—$14,000 from each spouse. The monthly debt service is found by taking the balance, $12,000 ($40,000 − $28,000), dividing it by 1,000 and multiplying 12 (the balance in thousands) by the amortization factor of 13.78 (11%, 10 years). This provides the following payment schedule:

$$12 \times 13.78 \ = \ \$165 \ monthly$$

or

$$\$165 \times 12 \quad = \ \$1,984 \ yearly$$

Each Davis is responsible for 50% of the annual debt service of $1,984 ($992 each). When they have paid this amount, they will each have $133 left ($1,125 − $992) for cash investment. Added to their original asset balance, the cash fund will equal $5,950 for each (see *asset* box in Figure 10-6). This account could grow to $15,000 in 10 years at 8%. A cash investment of that size will easily satisfy any purchase-related expenses and still leave a sizable excess.

The Davises' second option—a low down payment ($10,000) with a bigger debt—is pictured in Figure 10-7. The assets and annual contributions are the same and the down payment is $5,000 for each spouse. The remaining $14,817 ($19,817 − $5,000) in each Davis's IRA will be deposited in a cash account returning 10%. The annual debt service payments for each are $2,380 ($4,760 combined). This sum far exceeds their allowable IRA contributions of $1,125 each. The additional sum of $1,255 ($2,380 − $1,125) will come from the cash instrument, that is yielding $1,482 for each Davis at 10% for a year-end asset value of $16,299 ($14,817 − $1,482). After $1,255 has been withdrawn to satisfy the mortgage, the net asset growth in the first year is $227, bringing the total in the account to $15,044.

While the Davises will have to draw off much of their assets' earnings yearly, they do not have to tap any of their principal. In fact, since the annual withdrawal is less than the yield at 10%. this sum will actually grow, although slowly.

Yet another interesting option would see the Davises purchase four lower-priced homesites at $12,500 each. Both the single purchase ($12,500) and the multiple total purchase ($12,500 × 4 = $50,000) are within the couple's maximum affordability capacity of $53,240. Each homesite purchase will require the following yearly payment:

Purchase price	=	$12,500
Down payment	=	2,500
Balance	=	10,000
Interest	=	10%
Monthly payment	=	132.50
Yearly total	=	1,590

Figure 10-8 shows the calculations for the purchase of four homesites. If the Davises use existing funds, the yields from these dollars, and their annual contributions, they will have sufficient funds to make $2,500 down payments and to sevice the debt.

The down payment and the monthly and yearly payments are shown for one and for all four $12,500 homesites. After the down payment of $10,000 and the year's IRA contribution of $2,250 have been made, the

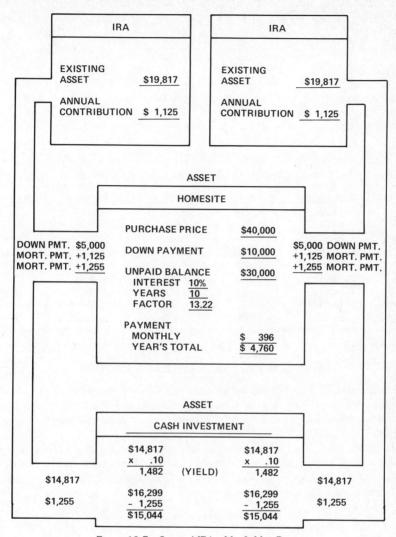

Figure 10-7: Spousal IRA—Mr. & Mrs. Davis

account balance at the beginning of the next year is $31,884. This money is deposited in a cash instrument yielding 8%.

At the end of that year, the yield will be $2,550, thereby increasing the account to $34,434. After the Davises make the annual payment of $6,300, the balance will be $28,075. The opening amount at the start of the following year will be increased by the new contribution, giving a new total of $30,325.

Figure 10-8 traces this procedure over ten years. At that time, the Davises will have acquired their home equivalency of four lots and a cash balance of $7,046. They are having their cake and eating it, too.

Annual Contribution	$ 2,250	
Fund Available	29,634	
Homesite Price	12,500	

Number of Homesites	1	4
Down Payment	2,500	$10,000
Unpaid Balance	10,000	40,000
Monthly Payment	133	530
Yearly Payment	1,590	6,360

Year	Balance (+2250)	Yield (8%)	Total	(Payment)	Balance
1	$31,884	$ 2,550	$34,434	($6,360)	$28,075
2	30,325	2,426	32,751	(6,360)	26,391
3	28,641	2,291	30,932	(6,360)	24,572
4	26,822	2,146	28,968	(6,360)	22,608
5	24,858	1,989	26,847	(6,360)	20,487
6	22,737	1,819	24,556	(6,360)	18,195
7	20,446	1,636	22,081	(6,360)	15,721
8	17,971	1,438	19,409	(6,360)	13,049
9	15,299	1,224	16,523	(6,360)	10,163
10	12,413	993	13,406	(6,360)	7,046

Figure: 10-8

Spousal Purchase With a 1982 IRA

Most spousal IRAs have probably been established since 1982. Our next couple—Mr. and Mrs. Evans—have contributed the maximum since they began participation in 1982. Their combined assets, appreciating at 8%, have grown to $14,256.

Table 1.8 tells us the maximum real estate purchase that this couple can make. Again, we use purchase terms of 10% for 10 years, for which the debt serviceable by the spousal IRA is $14,183. Consequently, the maximum real estate purchase for the Evanses is:

Accumulated IRA assets	+	Debt service limit	=	Maximum purchase price
		or		
$14,256	+	$14,183	=	$28,439

After selecting a desirable homesite, the Evanses agree to a purchase price of $25,000 (Figure 10-9). Their down payment is 10%, or $2,500. The terms of the purchase-money mortgage in which the seller holds the mortgage are 10% for 10 years. Since the Evanses have chosen to divide their IRAs 50-50, they own the property and share the responsibility equally.

Notice that the Evanses' individual IRA asset balance after making the down payment decreases to $5,878 ($7,128 − $1,250). This total will yield $700, providing a year-end balance of $7,703. Adding the next annual contribution of $1,125 to the account will swell each balance to $7,703. After

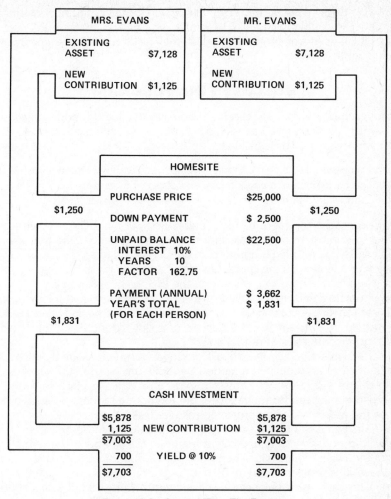

Figure 10-9: Spousal IRA—The Evanses

paying their share of the annual debt service of $1,831, the asset balance will be $5,872. Since the debt service of $1,831 is greater than the annual contribution, existing assets must be used to fund it. The deficiency of $706 ($1,831 − $1,125) will come from the cash investment. The Evanses have purchased a $25,000 homesite, and they still maintain a reasonable cash investment fund for other expenses.

Single Purchase With a Double IRA

Under the spousal IRA, we saw that the purchase of one homesite was treated as if it had come from one source. But a husband and wife who are both wage earners can each adopt an individual IRA and can each contribute $2,000 annually. Known as a *double IRA,* this strategy presents a number of options, whether the couple have had IRAs since 1982 or are first-time IRA holders. Essentially, whatever choice they select, they just *double* the payments of an individual IRA holder.

ROLLOVER IRA PURCHASE

Rollover IRAs are used to preserve tax-shelter qualities of money distributed to participants of qualified pension plans. Rollover distributions can take place for many reasons. These include:

1. Lump-sum distribution of a retiring employee's vested pension monies.
2. Discontinuation of a pension plan and dispersal of funds.
3. Lump-sum distribution of a resigning employee's pension fund.

If you ever take receipt of pension funds, they will normally be taxed after a 60-day moratorium. You have that much time to deposit the funds into a rollover IRA. A warning is appropriate here. You can keep the funds *only* 60 days from the date on the check. On the 61st day, you will be taxed and may incur penalties. There's no relief from the IRS, so act promptly.

Prior to 1986, funds rolled over into this IRA qualified for the special 10-year forward averaging tax treatment. This privilege having been revoked, all money in IRAs—new contributions or rollover funds—will be taxed at ordinary income rates at distribution.

Let's examine two individuals employed for many years by their firms. Mr. Ferris has accumulated a modest pension sum of $35,000; Ms. Gage, a large one of $125,000. Mr. Ferris' company terminated its plan; Ms. Gage has changed employers. Both employees are too young to retire, so each opts to place the assets into a tax-protected rollover IRA.

Mr. Ferris can make a maximum real estate purchase of $35,000. But he will act conservatively and buy a homesite for $14,500. The terms are a $2,000 down payment with a mortgage of $12,500 for 15 years at 10%. This transaction is profiled in Figure 10-10.

The cash asset balance, which increased from $33,000 ($35,000 − $2,000 down payment) to $34,688 after the first year, will have compounded to $87,771 by the end of the mortgage, when the homesite is paid off.

Ms. Gage moves to purchase four homesites at $15,000 each (Figure 10-11). She eventually intends to use them to build her retirement home. The terms of sale are 20% down and a mortgage at 10% for 10 years. The details are shown in Figure 10-11.

The cash account portion of Ms. Gage's portfolio is increasing each year and will total more than $170,000 when the four homesites are paid off. Ms. Gage has achieved her retirement security goal through fulfillment of the four-lot concept.

Should You Buy Inside or Outside The IRA?

A valid, widely raised issue is how best to purchase homesites. Should they be acquired within the IRA or outside its confines? This question is triggered

Existing Assets	$35,000
Purchase Price	14,500
Down Payment (D.P.)	2,000
Mortgage Balance	12,500
Monthly	134
Yearly	1,612
Cash Asset Balance after D.P.	33,000

Year	Beginning Balance	Yield (10%)	Sub-total	Mortgage	Cash Asset Balance
1	$33,000	$3,300	$36,300	$1,612	$34,688
2	34,988	3,499	38,487	1,612	36,875
3	36,875	3,687	40,562	1,612	38,950
4	38,950	3,895	42,845	1,612	41,233
5	41,233	4,123	45,357	1,612	43,744
6	43,744	4,374	48,119	1,612	46,507
7	46,507	4,650	51,158	1,612	49,546
8	49,546	4,955	54,500	1,612	52,888
9	52,888	5,289	58,177	1,612	56,565
10	56,565	5,656	62,221	1,612	60,610
11	60,610	6,060	66,671	1,612	65,058
12	65,058	6,505	71,564	1,612	69,952
13	69,952	6,995	76,948	1,612	75,336
14	75,336	7,533	82,862	1,612	81,257
15	81,257	8,126	89,383	1,612	87,771

Figure: 10-10

Figure 10-11: Original Assets: $125,000

Original Assets: $125,000

	(1)	(2)	(3)	(4)	Total
Purchase Price	$15,000	$15,000	$15,000	$15,000	$60,000
Down Payment	3,000	3,000	3,000	3,000	12,000
Balance	12,000	12,000	12,000	12,000	48,000
Mortgage Monthly	159	159	159	159	636
Yearly	1,903	1,903	1,903	1,903	7,612
Asset Balance:				$113,000	

Year	Balance	Yield (10%)	Sub-total	(Payment)	Total
1	$113,000	$11,300	$124,300	$7,612	$116,688
2	116,688	11,669	128,357	7,612	120,745
3	120,745	12,075	132,820	7,612	125,208
4	125,208	12,521	137,728	7,612	130,116
5	130,116	13,011	143,127	7,612	135,516
6	135,516	13,552	149,067	7,612	141,455
7	141,455	14,146	155,601	7,612	147,989
8	147,989	14,799	162,788	7,612	155,176
9	155,176	15,518	170,694	7,612	163,082
10	163,082	16,308	179,390	7,612	171,778

by the entrenched concept that successful real estate investment is dependent upon tax deductions and the now obsolete capital gains treatment of profits. As we saw in Chapter Six, the tax-neutral environment of the IRA fortress makes any tax treatment impossible, and the IRS will treat all distributions from the IRA the same—as ordinary income.

To resolve the question, we will compare the net after-tax returns on the same real estate purchased in an IRA and in a conventional manner. To keep everything fair and equal in these comparisons, we must begin at the same starting point—with the same number of earned dollars. Because of the IRA limitations, we will use $2,000.

The conventional investor must pay taxes. At the 28% bracket, he or she owes $560 to Uncle, leaving him $1,440 for the real estate investment. But our IRA investor has the entire $2,000 ($2,250 for spousal) to invest. Now, to simplify the analysis, you recall that the contribution consists of tax-deferred dollars *and* personal dollars (refer to Chapter Five). Before 1986, everyone's contributions were tax-deductible and the individual tax brackets determined how many deferred dollars and how many personal ones were used. We now have three types of IRA contributors, as shown below:

1	2	3
Contributions Fully deductible	*Contributions Partly deductible*	*Contributions Non-deductible*
No pension plan or earnings less than: $25,000 (single) $40,000 (married)	With pension plan and earnings between: $25,000 to $35,000 (single); $40,000 to $50,000 (married)	With pension plan and earnings more than: $35,000 (single) $50,000 (married)

Wage earners who qualify to enter the IRA fortress through gate 1 are treated the same. Nothing has changed for them, and their IRA dollars are treated as discussed (see Chapter Five). Conversely, contributors who use gate 3 cannot take any deduction. Their entire contribution is personal after-tax dollars. Although all three contributor groups invest $2,000, whose money it is and where it goes or belongs varies. The table below identifies the status of the dollars for the different types of IRA participants and the conventional non-IRA investor.

Tax Bracket: 28%

Earned Income $2,000	Conventional Non-IRA	Gate 1	Gate 2	Gate 3
Taxes	$ 560	$0	$0-560	$ 560
Deferred taxes	0	$560	$0-560	$ 0
Personal dollars	$1440	$1440	$1,440	$1,440

Note that in each case the amount of personal dollars is the same: $1,440. The remaining $560 is either in the IRA as IRS' deferred dollars or paid as taxes immediately.

To simplify this evaluation, we will assume that the real estate appreciates 7½ times the original personal investment, as demonstrated in Figure 3-4, Chapter Three.

The segment that is the personal investment dollars will grow in value to: $1,440 × 7.5 = $10,800.

The first factor that could influence investment performance is the treatment of expenses normally associated with real estate interest, taxes, and so on. In the tax-free environment of the IRA, no treatment occurs since the IRS has no presence.

For the conventional non-IRA real estate investment, there is access by the IRS. But as of 1987, favorable deductions have been eliminated. Any advantage of tax deductibility over the IRA real estate investment no longer exists.

The next important issue is the tax treatment of the profit or appreciation. As we have stated often, IRA distributions are taxed at ordinary income tax rates. On the other hand, non-IRA investors have become accustomed to having the tax on the profits reduced by the capital gains tax treatment. Unfortunately for them, Congress has eliminated capital gains from the tax code. Profits will now be treated as ordinary income. Again, the conventional and IRA investors have been legislated into equality.

At sale or distribution time, each investor will receive the same amount—$10,800. However, the IRS will tax both the profits and previously untaxed distributions. The following table shows the after-tax yields for all three contributor groups, and the non-IRA investor.

Real Estate Results: IRA vs. Conventional

	Conventional	#1	#2	#3
Personal dollars	$ 1,440	$ 1,440	$ 1,440	$ 1,440
Asset Value	10,800	10,800	10,800	10,800
Profit	9,360	9,360	9,360	9,360
Tax @ 28%	2,621	0	0-3,024	2,621
Net	8,179	10,800	10,800 to 8,179	8,179

The conventional investor will net $8,179 after paying ordinary taxes of $2,621 on the $9,360 profit. Since the participant entering through gate 3 paid taxes up front (like the conventional investor) and his profit was taxed at ordinary rates, the net result is also $8,179.

There is no comparative advantage or disadvantage for either of these individuals. However, if the real estate is *sold within* the IRA, there is no immediate tax action—as in a *conventional,* or non-IRA sale. The IRA participants will receive their original personal dollars and the profit on this portion of their contribution TAX FREE. While that seems incredible, it's true. It's just a restatement of the tax-free delivery of any investment return by the totally deductible IRA discussed in Chapter Five.

The IRA investor who can take a *full* deduction (gate 1) is the clear winner in the investment comparison. The investor who takes a partial deduction (gate 2) will also win—but his or her advantage diminishes as the deductibility approaches zero. If any property is sold, tax treatment is delayed until distribution. All of this once again leaves the IRA as the best course to follow.

These results should not let you lose sight of the basic reason for real estate purchases within the IRA. It is not financial. As stressed in Chapter Four, the purpose of this part of your overall retirement strategy is functional. Homesites will provide you with part, and perhaps all, of the price of your debt-free replacement home. Thus, your objective here is not to amass more dollars but to provide yourself with a debt-free home where you can live after you've retired and sold your principal residence.

To review the procedure, we repeat the simple two-component formula for affordability:

$$
\begin{array}{ccc}
\text{Maximum} & = & \text{Debt service} & + & \text{Accumulated} \\
\text{purchase} & & \text{limit} & & \text{IRA assets} \\
\text{price} & & & &
\end{array}
$$

After deciding which IRA you will use in your purchase—a single IRA, spousal IRA, double IRA, or rollover IRA—the remaining steps fall in line in logical sequence:

1. Determine the current value of your IRA(s).
2. Establish a self-directed IRA.
3. Transfer or roll over assets into that account.
4. Using Tables 1.7 and 1.8, determine the amount of debt your IRA contributions can service.
5. Fix the maximum purchase price by adding your IRA assets to the debt you can service.
6. Using this figure, pick out a homesite and negotiate the terms.
7. Execute all documents and request your new trustee to purchase the property on your behalf.

Your first purchase with your tax-sheltered IRA dollars puts you on track toward the fulfillment of your total retirement objective.

ELEVEN

The Ultimate Payoff: Converting Your Homesites Into a Debt-Free Home

As we have progressed through this book, we have challenged many traditional concepts about financial planning for retirement. We have done this to introduce you to an innovative—but simple and workable—plan for achieving a financially secure retirement.

As we have seen, a key objective of this plan is your acquisition of a debt-free replacement home. The sale of your principal residence enables you to reap the substantial equity tied up in it, completing the income transfer process that will satisfy your financial needs in retirement. But to replace your home, you must purchase another one—or its equivalent, four homesites, that you can eventually convert into your debt-free retirement home. In this chapter, we will demonstrate precisely how this ultimate conversion is accomplished. But first, as we've done before, let's back track a bit.

We assume you will acquire your homesite with your real estate IRA. This may be difficult, but it's possible, as we saw in Chapter Ten, particularly if both you and your spouse have IRAs or if you have a substantial rollover IRA.

Whatever the status of your IRA, as you approach retirement, you must face one of your old nemeses—taxation. Until now the IRS has been kind to your IRA, permitting it to grow tax-deferred. But at distribution, the IRS will be ready to claim its deferred taxes. At that point, your IRA withdrawals will be added to your other taxable income, increasing your tax obligation. You must carefully plan the size and timing of your IRA distributions to minimize your tax obligation and you will have to carefully integrate these distributions with your other sources of income. You can do this only when your retirement income becomes available to you.

So let's fast-forward to that time and examine the situation more closely. Regardless of your precise age, tax planning should be very important to you *now*.

THE AVAILABILITY AND TAX TREATMENT
OF RETIREMENT FUNDS

The timing of your retirement will depend on the readiness of your three income-transfer sources: Social Security, pension plans and savings and investments. You must orchestrate the three so as to assure yourself maximum retirement income.

Your first source of retirement income is Social Security. Except for unexpected disability, the eligibility age is 65 for full benefits and 62 for reduced payments. Your monthly check will increase if you do not start drawing benefits until after age 65. Your Social Security benefits will normally not be taxable.

The second transfer source is your pension plan, if you have one. Except for a minority of plans—such as "20 years and out" for police officers, fire fighters, military personnel, and so on—pension plans tend to favor retirement at age 62. Many of them grant retirement benefits as early as age 55 if the employee has completed the prescribed number of years of service. Payment of pension benefits is controlled by the contractual obligation built into your employer's pension plan. For your planning purposes, though, we'll assume that you can begin to draw your benefits at 55.

Pension benefits will be taxed as ordinary income. But you may escape taxes on these for a while if you have contributed to your pension plan. Your own dollars will be the first funds that you will be paid. Since you made these contributions with taxed dollars, the IRS allows you to receive them tax-free now. This means that you may draw up to 1½ years of pension checks before they are taxed.

Therefore, in your first year or more of retirement, two components of your retirement income may *not* be subject to taxation. This gives you a *window of opportunity* to distribute funds from your third source of retirement income, savings and investments, that are treated as ordinary income. The pattern of the taxes on income sources is shown in Figure 11-1.

The window of opportunity allows you to devise safe, legal financial strategies for reducing your taxes and increasing your discretionary dollars. We have all been encouraged to do exactly this by no less a personage than famed jurist Learned Hand. Recall that we quoted Hand, who stated categorically that citizens should arrange their affairs so that they pay only the *minimum* taxes that are due. Hand insisted that the public legally maneuver around the taxes that Congress lays down.

With Hand's admonition in mind, let's now turn to the third source of retirement income, your savings and investments. This source of income is the one that you must create yourself. And because you can control it—

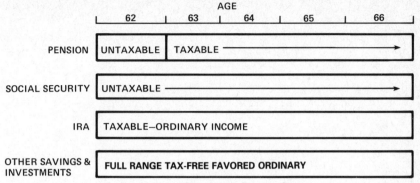

Figure 11-1: Contributory Pension Case

whereas you have little control over your Social Security and pension benefits—this is the one you should focus on primarily. Note that even your S&I vehicles have conditions that, if violated, can trigger financial penalties and adverse tax consequences. You should be aware of some common traps:

- Penalties on early distribution of IRAs: If you take an IRA withdrawal before age 59½, you will be penalized 10% of the distribution.
- House profit at age 55: The one-time tax-free profit of up to $125,000 on the sale of your principal residence is available only after you reach age 55.
- Savings penalties: Bank CDs, annuities and bonds have maturity dates that must be honored.
- Profits from investments in limited partnerships: These investments have very little resale potential, and any profits on them may be available only at the conclusion of the program, when the general partner is to sell the property or asset.

Although we have been discussing different sources of retirement income in the last page or two, the two principal agents in your planning will be your *principal residence* and your *real estate IRA*. To maximize the value of these assets, you must pay particular attention to the size and timing of their distribution, because these factors will make a big difference in the taxes you'll pay.

The investment over which you will be able to exercise the greatest degree of control is your principal residence, although, as we've just noted, the accrued profit of up to $125,000 from its sale can be obtained tax-free *only* after you reach age 55. Your home equity and its investment yield can provide 25% of your pre-retirement income, as we explained in Chapter Two. So these funds are of paramount importance.

Monitoring the final payoff from your IRA will be more complicated. Many key options, regulations, restrictions, and administrative conditions apply to this program. They include the following:

1. All distributions from IRAs, minus any after-tax contributions, will be taxed as ordinary income.

2. You will be permitted to spread distributions over a period of time.

3. You will be permitted to start withdrawing funds without penalty at 59½, or you may wait until as late as 70½.

4. At age 70½, you must start withdrawals based on your life expectancy, and these withdrawals will have to be completed by a determined age—likely somewhere in your eighties. Failure to start withdrawals at 70½, and to maintain a distribution schedule, will incur a staggering 50% penalty on the nondistributed amounts. The only relief from this punitive condition is that you are permitted to use the life-expectancy average of yourself and the beneficiary of your IRA funds. Even so, 50% of the accumulated assets in your IRA must be withdrawn by the time you reach your life expectancy.

5. You can elect to have a portion of your IRA money distributed as a *lump sum* and can then spread out payments on the balance.

Arranging for the distribution of your IRA funds and integrating them with your other income are your responsibilities. Integrating them carefully can save you thousands in taxes.

Obviously, you can't seriously consider retiring until you have a sufficient flow of funds (65% of pre-retirement income) from your transfer sources. Figure 11-2 plots the availability of these various sources. It shows that if you need *all three* sources to retire, your earliest retirement age will be 62 with reduced Social Security benefits or 65 with full Social Security benefits. If you are fortunate enough to be able to meet your retirement

Figure 11-2: Age

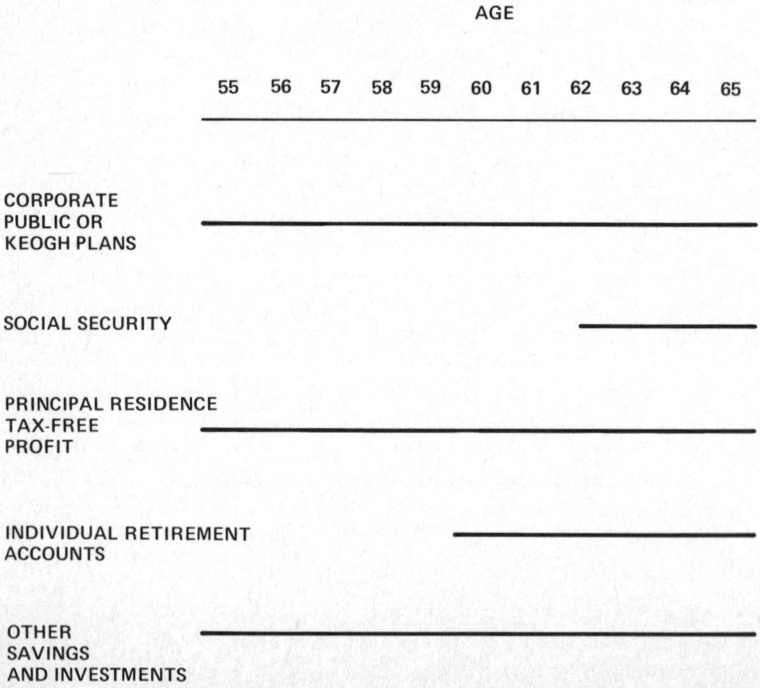

income objectives *without* Social Security, earlier retirement becomes a viable option.

OK. Let's zero back in on your real estate IRA and your homesites. But don't forget your other income sources. Remember, they're all interrelated parts of a complex system.

To help you attain your retirement objective with the real estate IRA, we will discuss how distributions from the IRA are made and how people who are able to purchase four homesites are taxed. To keep our discussion simple, we will use as an example a single IRA holder who buys four homesites, but the details will be exactly the same for a married couple filing jointly. Next, we will look at some cases of people who have bought only *one* homesite. This should help you interpret the modifications in these cases and apply them to your own situation.

THE DISTRIBUTION PROCEDURE

The distribution of CDs and similar cash instruments from an IRA at retirement is a simple procedure: On request, your trustee will send you all or some of your accumulated funds. But the distribution of either stock or real estate from an IRA may require an additional step. These assets are normally liquidated before distribution. The stock or real estate transaction is made by your IRA trustee within the trust, and the proceeds are then remitted to your account. Since you yourself have not yet received any distribution, you will not be taxed at the time of sale. After the sale, you can withdraw or distribute the cash now in your IRA on request. You do have the option of taking a stock instrument directly as a distribution. If you do, its market value will be deemed to be the amount of the withdrawal.

With real estate, it is also possible to distribute the homesite to the IRA participant without first converting it to cash. But since you can't divide the property, it must be treated as a whole entity. When the lot is delivered, the market value of the entire lot is taken to represent the dollar distribution, and this large sum is added to your other taxable income for that year. To avoid this unpleasant situation, your trustee can sell the homesite and place the cash into your account.

You or a broker of your choice can execute the sale of your homesite. He or she will send the proceeds to your trustee. (Otherwise, the entire amount will be considered a distribution and you will be taxed accordingly.) The money can be housed in a cash instrument, such as a CD, and distributed to you as you need it.

BUYING A DEBT-FREE HOUSE WITH FOUR HOMESITES

Alert to how the distribution process works, let's now focus on an individual who has obtained four homesites with IRA funds (Figure 11-3). As we've seen, four homesites are the financial equivalent of a home. In Figure 11-3, the individual homesites have been valued at $25,000 each, making four lots

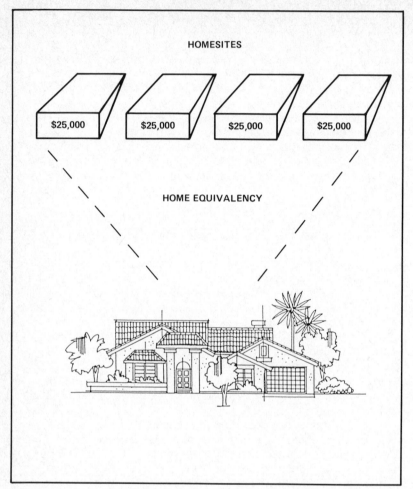

Figure 11-3: Individual Retirement Account

equal to a $100,000 home. No matter what price we assign to the home—
whether $150,000, $200,000, or $300,000—the equivalency principle re-
mains the same, and the price of each homesite is still 25% of that of a house.

But the cash value of your homesites will be diminished because you
must pay deferred taxes as the assets are distributed to you. One strategy—
one that will deliver the *least* value—is to distribute the entire $100,000 from
your IRA in a lump sum. This will incur a maximum tax obligation, leaving
you the least amount of money possible to purchase your retirement home.
Because none of your IRA contributions were taxed, and if you are in the
28% bracket, your taxes will be $28,000, leaving you only $72,000 with
which to pay for your retirement home (Figure 11-4). While you will acquire
a debt-free home, you will have maximized your tax burden and minimized
your available cash. Justice Hand would urge you to seek a better solution.

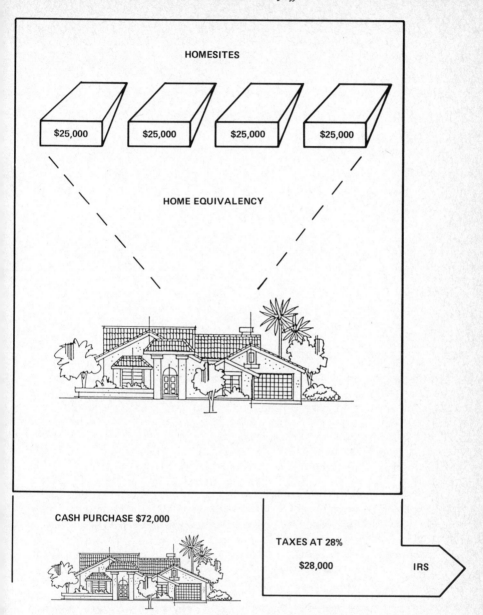

HOMESITES

$25,000 $25,000 $25,000 $25,000

HOME EQUIVALENCY

CASH PURCHASE $72,000

TAXES AT 28%

$28,000

IRS

Figure 11-4: Individual Retirement Account

A more effective strategy is to buy your house with a down payment and satisfy the mortgage payments with *periodic* distributions from your IRA. Since your IRA will be supplying the funds to cover the debt service, you need not use your other income to meet this obligation. Thus this strategy too will give you a debt-free home. To see the advantage of this strategy over the

```
PRICE          $ 70,000

DOWN
PAYMENT        $ 14,000

MORTGAGE       $ 56,000

(10.5% – 30 YEARS)

PAYMENT:
    MONTHLY   = $  512
    YEARLY    = $6,147
    INTEREST  = $5,867

TAX SAVINGS ON INTEREST PAYMENT:
    SAVINGS   = INTEREST x TAX BRACKET
              = $5,867 x .28
              = $1,643

NET IRA FUNDS REQUIRED:
              = (6,147 – 1,643)
              = $4,504

PRE-TAX DISTRIBUTION FROM IRA:
              = $4,504/(1-TAX BRACKET)
              = $4,504/(1-.28)
              = $4,504/.72
              = $6,256
```

Figure 11-5: Retirement Home

one discussed in Figure 11-4, look at Figure 11-5. In this case, you will buy the same $70,000 home, but instead of making a cash purchase, you will put 20% down and assume a mortgage of $56,000 for 30 years at a 10.5% fixed rate.

The first requirement is to obtain the down payment from your IRA. This will involve the distribution of an amount that will yield a net of $14,000 *after* the IRS tax bite. In a 28% tax bracket, this distribution will have to be $19,444. You might not initially like the idea of taking this large lump-sum distribution, because the tax obligation seems high. But the tax burden in this case will not be onerous. In fact, your total tax will probably only be about 15%, thanks to the window of opportunity discussed earlier in this chapter. Let's look into this more fully.

As we've noted, your pension checks are not taxable in your first year of retirement, and your Social Security benefits are not taxable at any point. Because of this, the tax on any IRA distribution you take during this period will be low. Since we are unable to forecast future swings in the tax bracket, let us—for the sake of argument—assume that your first $9,000 of income will not be taxed and that the remainder will be taxed at 15%. To net $14,000 under these conditions, you will need a distribution of $14,880, which we'll round off to $15,000 for simplicity:

Total funds needed	=	$14,000
Distributed untaxed funds	=	9,000
Balance needed	=	5,000

Pretax dollars, to net
 $5,000 at 15% tax:
 $5,000/(1-.15)   = $ 5,880
 $5,000/.85

Total funds to be distributed = $14,880 -or-
                                $15,000

You direct your trustee to sell two homesites (for simplicity, we ignore brokerage commissions) for $50,000 and to *send you a check for $15,000*. The $35,000 balance from the sale remains in your IRA, along with your other two homesites. Your IRA trustee deposits the $35,000 in a cash instrument yielding 8%, while the two unsold homesites continue to appreciate. This procedure is outlined in Figure 11-6.

Satisfying the mortgage (Figure 11-5) will require a monthly payment of $512 or $6,147 yearly. Since the interest paid will be deductible, your tax savings in the 28% bracket will be $1,643. This reduces your actual yearly out-of-pocket cost to $4,504 ($6,147 − $1,643). Despite this lower net after-tax cost, you will have to withdraw $6,256 from your IRA annually to net $4,504 after taxes. The cash remaining from the sale of the two homesites—$35,000 appreciating at 8%—will provide mortgage payments for seven years. Then you will have to find another cash source within your IRA to complete the 10-year term of payments.

Enter the two homesites still in your IRA. They have been appreciating quietly over the seven year period. Although we have no crystal ball to predict the exact increase in their value, experience demonstrates that *homes* have appreciated 8% and better over long periods. And this is a conservative figure, considering that spurts of 20% and 30% are common in many parts of the country. In fact, *hold on a minute!* As we noted in Chapter Four, the homesite may well have risen in value 2½ times faster than the total home package. But we will be cautious and settle for a 12% annual homesite appreciation in our calculations.

So how much are our two remaining lots now worth? Well, Figure 11-6 shows that the two $25,000 homesites will be valued jointly at $110,539 after seven years. Amortization tables will show that the original $56,000 mortgage has been reduced to $53,257. You are in a position to settle everything here and now. If you take full distribution of the two lots valued at $110,539, your 28% tax bite will be $30,950. That will leave you $79,584. After paying off the mortgage balance of $53,257, you'll have $26,327 left. That's a bonus from your real estate IRA, which has already delivered on its big promise— your debt-free retirement home.

These encouraging calculations are not mathematical magic. The only sleight of hand is the appreciation on your third and fourth homesites. By keeping them until the seventh year, you've enabled them to grow in value to the point where you are able to pay off the remaining obligation on your retirement home. This appreciation is the basic reason you receive your replacement house debt-free.

You will fare even better if you allow *three* homesites, instead of two, to

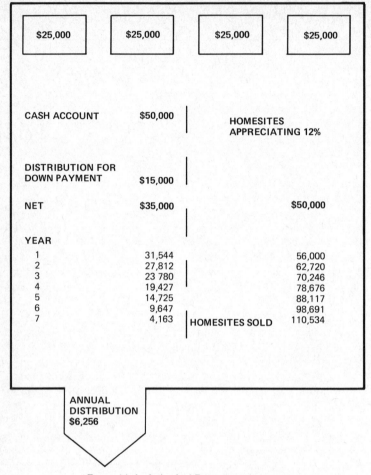

Figure 11-6: Individual Retirement Account

appreciate and sell them as needed. Delaying their sale as long as possible gives you a chance to realize more dollars.

In the above example, we used a lower-priced home to reflect the general trend among retirees. You may need a large home to raise your family, but your retirement home probably won't be as big. While you're willing to accept a smaller house, though, you may wonder whether you can still live in a highly desirable area. What if you want a home on the water or next to a golf course? The smaller *size* of the house may reduce its cost, but its excellent location may jack that cost right back up. And so you're back to square one.

Can you afford to purchase a $100,000 home, for example, with the $100,000 worth of homesites in your real estate IRA? (Remember: The $100,000 is only a figure we're using for argument's sake; we could replace it with *any* sum.)

Let's look at a hypothetical purchase of a $100,000 home, using a

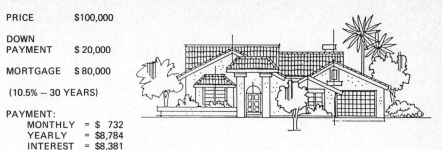

PRICE $100,000

DOWN
PAYMENT $ 20,000

MORTGAGE $ 80,000

(10.5% – 30 YEARS)

PAYMENT:
    MONTHLY = $ 732
    YEARLY   = $8,784
    INTEREST = $8,381

TAX SAVINGS ON INTEREST PAYMENT:
    SAVINGS   = INTEREST x TAX BRACKET
             = $8,381 x .28
             = $2,347

NET FUNDS REQUIRED:
             = $8,784 – $2,347
             = $6,437

PRE-TAX DISTRIBUTION FROM IRA:
             = $6,437/(1-TAX BRACKET)
             = $6,437/(1-.28)
             = $6,437/.72
             = $8,940

Figure 11-7: Basic Replacement Home

down payment of 20% and assuming a 30-year mortgage of $80,000 at a fixed rate of 10.5%. The funds required to satisfy this are shown in Figure 11-7.

To keep it simple, we'll say you use funds from the sale of your principal residence to make the $20,000 down payment.

As shown in Figure 11-7, you will have to withdraw $8,940 from your IRA each year to pay income taxes of $2,503 ($8,940 × .28) on the distribution and have enough ($6,437) for the net mortgage payments ($8,784 – $2,503). Remember, as our example in Figure 11-5 shows, this is possible because of the tax savings on the interest payment. The total year's mortgage payment equals $8,784; interest of $8,381 plus the principal of $403. At the 28% rate, this tax savings is $2,347 ($8,381 × .28), that when added to your after-tax IRA net funds of $6,437 covers your annual mortgage commitment of $8,784. Again, you will sell homesites as needed to continue your payments. The cash and asset flow schedule is shown in Figure 11-8, assuming a 12% appreciation on the assigned homesite value of $25,000.

After selling the fourth homesite in the 18th year, your IRA will have a cash balance of $215,319. Setting aside the mandatory distribution requirements at age 70½ for the time being, the 8% yield on this sum will be $17,225. After paying the 28% tax on this distribution, you will be able to net $12,402 each year.

This sum exceeds your annual total mortgage payments of $8,784. You can continue paying the mortgage in installments, or you can distribute enough to pay off the mortgage balance, which after 18 years of payments will have been reduced to $62,148. This will require a distribution of $86,317

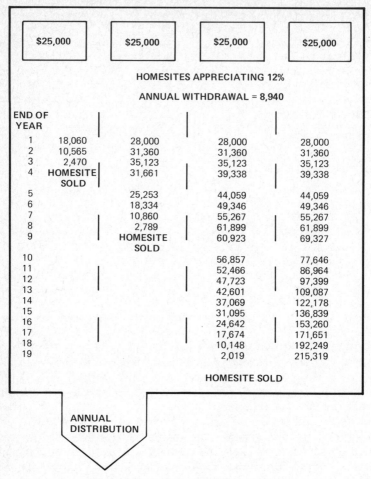

| | $25,000 | $25,000 | $25,000 | $25,000 |

HOMESITES APPRECIATING 12%

ANNUAL WITHDRAWAL = 8,940

END OF YEAR				
1	18,060	28,000	28,000	28,000
2	10,565	31,360	31,360	31,360
3	2,470	35,123	35,123	35,123
4	HOMESITE SOLD	31,661	39,338	39,338
5		25,253	44,059	44,059
6		18,334	49,346	49,346
7		10,860	55,267	55,267
8		2,789	61,899	61,899
9		HOMESITE SOLD	60,923	69,327
10			56,857	77,646
11			52,466	86,964
12			47,723	97,399
13			42,601	109,087
14			37,069	122,178
15			31,095	136,839
16			24,642	153,260
17			17,674	171,651
18			10,148	192,249
19			2,019	215,319

HOMESITE SOLD

ANNUAL DISTRIBUTION

Figure 11-8: Individual Retirement Account

($62,148/(1-.28.) You'll still have an IRA asset balance of over $100,000. How's that for an investment?

One thing you *must not* forget: The IRS mandates that you must start IRA distributions no later than age 70½. This fact can influence how much you withdraw, but your assets will still be enough to more than cover the debt service and deliver your debt-free retirement home.

If you begin distribution at 70½, you must take out funds at a rate based on your estimated life expectancy. The IRS allows this calculation to be an average of your own age *and* your beneficiary's—normally, your spouse's. Recent regulations disallow a beneficiary's receipt of any benefits in the principal's lifetime. They also require that the account be reduced to at least 50% of its predistribution value during the life expectancy of the principal.

Because these rules may require increased distributions, you can apply these sums to mortgage *prepayments* if these are in keeping with your overall financial plan. Doing this need not compromise the basic objective of your real estate IRA.

Detailing all the eventualities involved in acquiring four homesites is beyond the scope of this book. The salient point is that if you do acquire four homesites, *you will need no other retirement income* to pay for the debt service on your retirement home. This fact will work in your favor in your battle with inflation, as measured by the CPI. By owning a debt-free replacement home, you will eliminate a major expense once you've retired, increasing the likelihood of achieving all your retirement objectives. Because the real estate IRA will help you to tame inflation by giving you full financial means to acquire a debt-free replacement home, it will have performed an invaluable service.

Clearly, the key to our argument is the fact that the real estate IRA delivers most or all of your debt-free retirement home. This is the central, pivotal benefit of the example cited here. A closely allied *second* advantage is that you'll be able to invest all or most of the profits from the sale of your main residence. Instead of using these funds to buy a retirement home, you can use them to obtain a sizable extra pension.

Values of homes some 20 years from now may grow to what might currently appear to be incomprehensible totals. But these inflated sums, however large, will be no impediment to you. You need not be concerned about the absolute dollar value of the replacement home you choose. Only its *relative* worth should concern you. For instance, if four $10,000 lots today sell for a total of $320,000 in 20 years, this increase will not adversely affect your goal. When the time comes, you will be able to convert the lots to a residence, *regardless* of how housing costs have inflated. You own the ingredients. For that, you can thank appreciation and leverage—real estate's shining performers.

Earlier chapters made clear what a favorable strategy it is to secure retirement shelter by the wise use of IRA funds. This single action removes the biggest retirement cost of all from your shoulders. With debt-free housing, you will have a much lower overall shelter cost—a condition that will relieve you of worry and bolster your security. Furthermore, we cannot emphasize too strongly the link between this strategy—using a real estate IRA to obtain a replacement home—and the other strategy we have mentioned, using profits from the sale of your principal residence to obtain a handsome pension. The interdependence between these two strategies is the key to your comfortable future.

BUYING A DEBT-FREE HOUSE WITH ONE HOMESITE

So far, our examples have demonstrated that, using the real estate IRA, the four-lot equivalency concept can deliver your debt-free retirement home. The best tactic seems to be to keep the homesites intact so that they can appreciate as much as possible *inside* the IRA until it is advantageous to sell them. The longer the delay, the better. Against this background, we will examine the options if you have acquired fewer than the optimum four lots.

Bear in mind that your ability to obtain your retirement home will be directly proportional to the number of homesites you own. Let's say you have been able to buy only one homesite within your IRA (or even via a conventional purchase). Since one homesite equals only 25% of the total purchase price of a house, you will have to look to the profit from your principal residence for the funds to make up the difference. But you will still be ahead of the game.

Let's say the retirement home you want to buy is the same $70,000 unit we encountered in Figure 11-5. With the $25,000 you have in the form of one homesite, you could take the following three steps:

1. Sell the homesite for $25,000 cash; then,

2. Withdraw the cash. In the first year of retirement, the tax distribution will be zero on the first $9,000 and 15% on the remaining $16,000. The tax is $2,400, leaving you $22,600 net; then,

3. Pay the difference of $47,400 ($70,000 − $22,600) with funds from another source—possibly from the tax-free profit from the sale of your principal residence.

This three-step strategy has merit, but there is another, much more productive strategy you could follow instead. It suggests that you purchase the home with *part* of the $47,400 and use the balance to pay the mortgage for as long as the money lasts. Then you can sell the well-appreciated homesite in the IRA and continue making mortgage payments.

Refer back to Figure 11-5 for the details of the $70,000 purchase. After making a $14,000 down payment, you have $33,400 ($47,000 − $14,000) available in cash to pay the mortgage. The annual funds required are:

Yearly payment	-	$6,147
Tax Savings	-	$1,760
Net dollars required	-	$4,387

If you invest $33,400 in a cash instrument yielding 8% and make the $4,387 payments, the funds will last approximately 12 years. As shown in Figure 11-9, you will have a cash balance of $854 at that time.

During that same period, the value of your homesite will have appreciated to $97,399 and the balance you owe on your mortgage will be $49,627. Paying off this obligation will require a pretax lump-sum distribution of $68,926. Here's how we arrive at this figure:

$$\frac{\$49,627}{(1 - \text{tax bracket})}$$

$$\frac{\$49,627}{(1 - .28)}$$

$$\frac{\$49,627}{.72} = \$68,926$$

When you sell, the IRA cash balance will be $98,253 (cash balance of $854 + homesite value of $97,399.) To satisfy the $49,627 mortgage, you

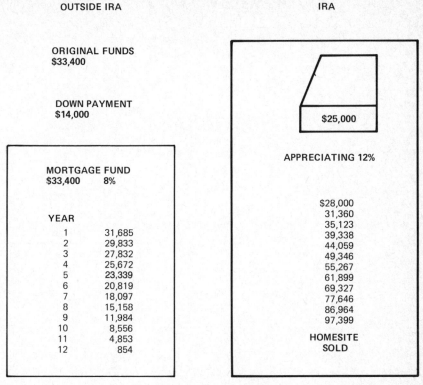

OUTSIDE IRA   IRA

ORIGINAL FUNDS
$33,400

DOWN PAYMENT
$14,000

$25,000

APPRECIATING 12%

MORTGAGE FUND
$33,400   8%

YEAR		
1	31,685	$28,000
2	29,833	31,360
3	27,832	35,123
4	25,672	39,338
5	23,339	44,059
6	20,819	49,346
7	18,097	55,267
8	15,158	61,899
9	11,984	69,327
10	8,556	77,646
11	4,853	86,964
12	854	97,399

HOMESITE
SOLD

Figure 11-9: Outside IRA

must withdraw $68,926 from your IRA. You will still have $29,327 in your
IRA ($98,253 − $68,926). Just look at what has happened: As a homesite
owner, you allocated $47,400 from the $100,000 you received for sale of
your principal residence to purchase your retirement home. When this fund
was depleted by payments, you were then able to take $68,926 from the sale
of your IRA homesite, pay the remaining mortgage balance, and still have
$29,327 in the IRA. It's almost like getting your original cash back!

Thus even a single homesite can be a valuable ally in the quest for the
financial security of a debt-free retirement home. And owners of two or three
homesites will receive proportionally greater benefits. While the dollars
amassed are vastly different, all homesite owners reach their basic goal and
reap the expected benefits, whether they own one lot or four.

All of the above cases seem to deal with homeowners only. However,
a debt-free replacement home can be even more valuable for non-home-
owners. A replacement house will safeguard renters from the special economic crunch that menaces them. It will help them to avoid escalating rents
that can cramp their style—and possibly do worse—in retirement, when their
income is relatively fixed.

Fortunately, the real estate IRA does provide a partial—possibly a full—
solution to the renter's need for a retirement home. We will explore this
situation next.

TWELVE

The Embattled Renter

It appears that the only people who benefit from the real estate IRA strategy we've been discussing are those who own their homes or condos. And, with two-thirds of all American wage earners in the homeowner category, we naturally directed our program to them first.

But fully one-third of American workers are not home owners. They are the nation's renters. Can these people also take advantage of our real estate IRA logic? The answer—absolutely. Renters have the same goal of fiscal security as homeowners do, and they require our special attention.

SHELTER COST AND CPI

Figure 12-1 demonstrates that the needs of renters and homeowners are the same. Both are obliged to provide for shelter and the other goods and services listed in the Consumer Price Index. Both are also subjected to the same inflationary spiral and must pay increasing dollars for goods and services. But the cost of the major CPI component—shelter—will exert different degrees of pressure on the two groups. The homeowner finds some welcome relief, the renter none. Let's see why.

The homeowner's monthly mortgage payments can be likened to the non-homeowner's cost for shelter, which is rent. The major difference is that the homeowner's "rent" will decrease as a percentage of total income, since, as income increases the mortgage payment remains constant and eventually becomes zero when the mortgage is satisfied (Figure 12-2). At retirement, the

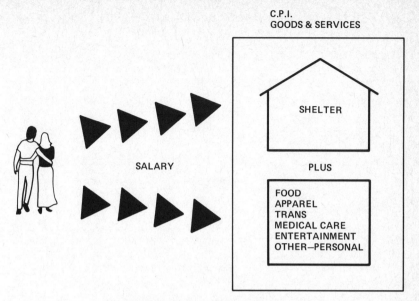

Figure 12-1: CPI Goods & Services

homeowner's principal residence can either: Serve as a debt-free retirement residence or be sold to assure his or her financial security.

A simplified example will make this dramatically clear. Figure 12-3 visualizes it for you. In 1974 Mr. Wood bought a home for $90,000 with a 20% down payment of $18,000. He was granted a fixed 9%, 30-year mortgage of $72,000. His monthly mortgage payment was $579; his yearly payments totaled $6,952. (We used a fixed mortgage here for simplicity's sake.)

Figure 12-2: Years

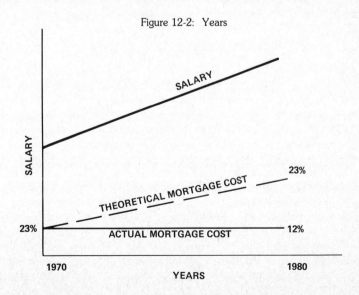

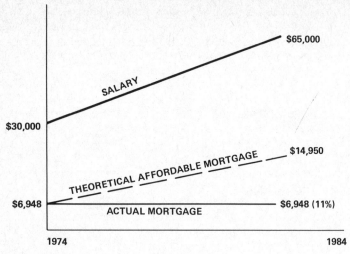

Figure 12-3

Mr. Wood's annual salary when he purchased his house was $30,000, or $577 per week. With guidelines allowing up to 25% of income to be spent on shelter, he was barely able to qualify for his mortgage, because the obligation of $6,948 ($597 × 12) represented 23% of his gross earnings. The first year's tax-deductible interest is $6,460. The tax saving at in 28% tax bracket is $1,809 ($6,460 × .28). This will reduce the mortgage cost to $5,139 ($6,948 − $1,809), that is only 17% of Mr. Wood's gross income.

Now let's fast-forward to 1984. We know that Mr. Wood's mortgage payment is still $579. But his annual salary had kept pace with inflation and increased to $65,000 ($1,250 a week). Note that by comparison, his mortgage had declined to only 7.9% of his salary:

$$\frac{\text{Year's mortgage payments}}{\text{Year's Salary}} = \frac{\$5,139}{\$65,000} = 7.9\% \text{ of salary}$$

Since Mr. Wood's 1984 salary could have supported a mortgage payment of 23%, or $14,950 per year, he enjoyed a surplus of $9,811 ($14,950 − $5,139) in that year. This is vivid testimony that Mr. Wood significantly outdistanced inflation, even though his salary only kept pace with it. The 11% differential he no longer needs for his mortgage payment becomes discretionary income. He has extra money to spend or invest as he pleases, and he has defied inflation almost effortlessly.

Interestingly, the mortgage amount that Mr. Wood had paid during the period is *less* than the surplus available to him in 1984! This suggests that he could actually assume and carry *another* mortgage essentially comparable to the one he now holds on his primary residence.

No matter how big the mortgage, this scenario unveils two pleasant advantages. First, Mr. Wood has defeated inflation—no mean task. Second, he has accrued extra monies to invest. All without expending any energy or using any complex strategy!

Like Mr. Wood, all home buyers have probably viewed the purchase of their house as a sound, comfortable and sensible way to raise a family. Shelter has been their main reason for buying and they have hardly realized that they will reap these extra financial rewards. No such good fortune awaits renters, however.

As shown in Figure 12-1, renters are committed to paying rent to secure their shelter. No tenant needs to be reminded that this cost is neither fixed nor insignificant. Except for people in rent-controlled apartments, rents have risen steadily and will continue to climb. In general, the shelter cost is not only affected by inflation; it may well *cause* much of the inflation.

Unlike the homeowner, renters' shelter cost increases never abate. The growing burden of rising rents never seems to lessen throughout these people's working lives. Although renters do not benefit from the reduced costs of the track shown in Figure 12-2, this situation may present no serious problem for them, as long as their pay raises keep pace with or outrun inflation. However, serious problems will surely surface when a renter prepares to retire.

On retirement, changes in lifestyle affect both homeowners and renters. We'll focus on the financial impact of this transition. As discussed in Appendix C, retirement will alter the pattern of use of all components in the total CPI. The average changes in these spending patterns are shown for both homeowners and renters in Figure 12-4.

For a variety of reasons, certain needs may increase (possibly medical care, for example), while others will diminish or disappear completely. The most significant distinction between the homeowner's and the renter's needs is the shelter cost. The homeowner's mortgage cost will, in most cases, have been satisfied, and that cost will no longer have to be paid. This welcome development is the main reason why shelter costs drop so much in retirement—to only 4%. In fact, this factor accounts for more than *half* of the total reduction of the CPI from 100% to 65% on retirement.

Our retirement needs analysis shows that the lifelong renter does not share the same relief. Instead, the renter faces an uphill battle to stay on an even keel in retirement.

RENT—THE PERSISTENT PROBLEM

Like the homeowner, the renter will likely be living on a relatively fixed income when retired. This income may be subject to very small inflation-sensitive raises at best. However, the renter's housing cost will continue to increase at a pace minimally equal to and probably *more* than inflation.

A renter's plight is shown in Figure 12-5. This graphic tracks Ms. Steele's steadily increasing income during her working career. At retirement, her income is abruptly reduced to a level *below* her final year's salary. In the very first year of retirement, Ms. Steele will be in for a rude awakening. Until recently, her income and rent have been both rising, causing no problem since both have increased proportionately. Now her income suddenly drops by a third. At that moment, her rent cost immediately becomes a much larger percentage of her income.

This unpleasant condition will not improve, either. Ms. Steele's rent will

Retirement/Renters CPI

CPI Components	National Percent	Retirement Percent	Renter in Retirement
Food & Beverages	20.069	15%	15%
• Food at home	12.866		
• Away from home	6.097		
• Alcoholic beverages	1.106		
Housing	37.721	16%	36%
• Shelter (Including rent & owners' equivalent rent)	21.339		
• Fuel & utilities	8.377		
• Household furn. & operation	8.005		
Apparel and Upkeep	5.205	2%	2%
Transportation	21.791	13%	13%
• Private (gas, insurance, fees, maintenance)	20.250		
• Public transportation	1.541		
Medical Care	5.954	8%	8%
• Commodities (prescriptions, etc.)	.976		
• Services (doctors, dentists)	5.018		
Entertainment	4.206	8%	8%
• Commodities (newspapers, magazine hobbies, sporting goods)	2.485		
• Services (admission fees, sporting events)	1.721		
Other Goods & Services	5.014	3%	3%
• Tobacco	1.387		
• Personal Care	1.857		
• Educational, Misc.	1.770		
TOTAL	100.000	65%	85%

Figure 12-4: Retirement Renters' CPI

keep rising steadily, causing the percentage of her shelter costs in relation to her diminished income to escalate. And that's just the beginning of her troubles. As the years pass, her income remains constant, while her rent goes up continuously. Each year, she is forced to spend more of her limited retirement income for rent. In other words, as shown in Figure 12-5, her housing expenses will account for an ever-greater percentage of her CPI, reducing the funds she has available for her other needs. Theoretically, if she lives long enough, the two lines in Figure 12-5 will eventually intersect. If they do, it means all of Ms. Steele's income will ultimately be assigned to rent. She will have no money for all her other basic necessities!

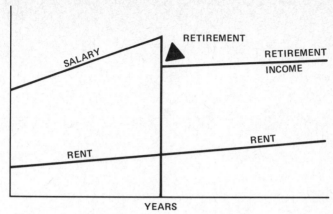

YEARS

Figure 12-5: The Renter's Dilemma

Although this frightening situation will, in reality, likely never materialize, it does prove that the relentless shrinkage of income for non-housing costs is a distinct possibility that menaces the renter. And as rental costs rise, his or her lifestyle will necessarily become more pinched.

THE RENTER'S RELIEF

Renters are not doomed to follow this dire path, though. There is a solution for them. Because the shelter cost is the largest CPI component by far, it is imperative they adopt the objective of obtaining a debt-free retirement home without delay. If they fail to do so, they will be big losers in the retirement game.

The means by which renters can acquire a retirement home have been described in this book. They are the same methods that homeowners must use. Careful attention to the material in the preceding chapters provides the key to the renters' financial security. This course of action is essential to their economic survival.

In fact, renters have even *more* to gain, in a sense, by possessing a debt-free retirement house than existing homeowners do. Renters gain liberation from an economic morass that could ultimately swallow up a disproportionate share of their resources. While the homeowner who acquires a paid-up replacement home will derive an additional and substantial pension, which will be most welcome, the renter has literally saved his or her very economic life—a more precious accomplishment.

We have now seen that the real estate IRA is truly beneficial to the renter as well as the homeowner. For the renter, the program has the added value of proving that "it's never too late!"

The message is clear. No matter how many lots you possess in or out of an IRA, and no matter whether you now own or rent your house or apartment, real estate ownership puts you on the path to a better retirement.

THIRTEEN

Your Map to The Treasure

Now that you know all about our plan for ensuring your financially secure retirement, you are adequately informed. In fact, you may have assimilated everything we've talked about so well that you may have no need to read this short chapter. If so, you can go right out and do what you must do to set up your real estate IRA. We know you'll have good luck. You'll get the reward of your life.

On the other hand, you may feel you need a little help to nudge you along the path toward fulfilling your retirement dreams. If so, this chapter is for you. We will fall back, regroup, and summarize just what you must do to realize the objectives of your plan.

Having read this book, you know, and most probably accept, the reasoning and concepts behind our program. You've learned *how* they work and *why* they're the best ones to pursue. Every chapter has justified them logically. At this point, we will recap just *what* you must do. We'll give you a road map, as it were, to get you where you want to go.

ESTABLISH YOUR FINANCIAL OBJECTIVES

First and foremost, this book has addressed the importance of retirement planning. In Chapter One, you learned that having a successful plan requires you to establish clear objectives.

Then, in Chapter Two, we evaluated these objectives in a somewhat unusual way. Instead of estimating how many *dollars* you will need in retirement, we used a *percentage* method based on your final working year's salary. This percentage proved much easier and more accurate than projected dollar sums as a way to forecast your needed retirement income. You learned that 65% of your final working year's income will be a sound estimate of your financial needs in your golden years.

THE TRANSFER PROCESS

Chapter Two also explained that your retirement income will come from three sources—Social Security, pensions, and savings and investments. It traced how these three sources of income evolve during your working years. We described this phenomenon as the income transfer process; we show it again in Figure 13-1 because it is so significant.

Figure 13-1: The Income Transfer Process.

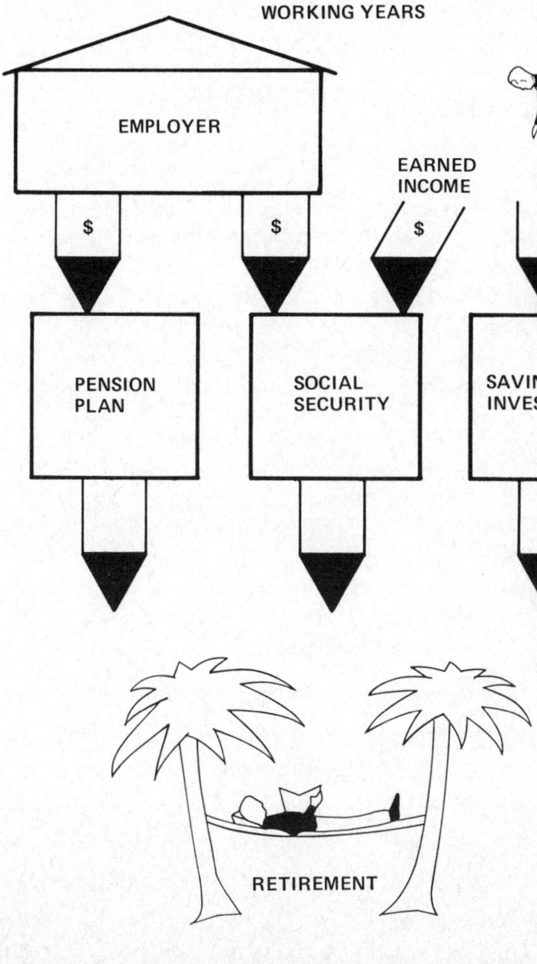

The first transfer source we covered was Social Security. We showed you how to get a close approximation of the benefits you can expect, even though the Social Security Administration will give you, on request, a more exact figure within five years of your retirement. We found that you can expect 10% to 40% of your last working year's income from Social Security.

In Chapter Two we also examined your second source of retirement income—pensions. We showed that, if you are covered by a pension plan, you can expect your pension to deliver up to 30% of your last salary. If necessary, you should review your pension with your company's pension officer to determine your specific benefits. Be sure to note and record the percentage of pre-retirement income you expect to receive from this transfer source.

The third income source will be your home—the *only* savings and investment choice you will need to complete your plan. Chapter Three discussed this point. We saw how your home will provide a big 25% of your last working year's salary, bringing the total from all three sources to the required 65%. Thus, Chapters Two and Three demonstrated how the three transfer components—Social Security, pensions, and your principal residence—will fully furnish all of your financial needs in retirement.

THE FUNCTIONAL PLAN

Having fulfilled the *fiscal* side of your plan, you must now act on the only *major undertaking* needed to complete your plan. You will have to address the *functional* side of your plan—acquiring your housing for retirement. Much of this book has been devoted to this overall objective, especially Chapter Four. Your first step in achieving this goal will be to look closely at the assets in your IRA, because you will use them to buy your four lots—the essence of our unique real estate IRA plan. You'll be shifting your IRA assets into a self-directed IRA because, as Chapter Nine showed, this device best serves your plan and suits your purposes. You will need to know where you can open a bona fide self-directed IRA. If you send an enclosed, self-addressed envelope to us, we will forward you the current list of self-directed IRA trustees in the United States. Write to the address listed on p 102.

After you receive this information, you should select and contact a self-directed trust. Then you must deposit some money with your trust to prepare for your down payment on your first homesite. This is done via transfer or rollover. The formulas in Chapter Ten show you how your existing IRA funds, plus the debt service your IRA can handle, will determine how much you can buy. Next, you must tackle a question that, alas, this book *cannot* answer for you:

WHERE SHOULD YOU BUY YOUR HOMESITES?

Only you can resolve this matter. We can only help by pointing out the many factors that affect this important decision—for example, population density, desirability, climate, and services. These factors were discussed in Chapter Eight.

BE SURE YOU'RE ACTUALLY BUYING A HOMESITE

Once you settle on a general location, you have to select a specific homesite. Be careful here. Never buy land. Be sure you're buying a homesite. This distinction was explained in Chapter Eight. Make sure you are well acquainted with the important differences between the two so that you make a sound decision at this most critical stage. For your protection, you must be aware of all the caveats presented in Chapter Eight. Review the questionnaire presented there thoroughly when considering any potential purchase of property, and be sure that all the offering conforms to the definition of a true homesite. Once again, you must be sure to get the seller to verify this data in *writing!*

NEGOTIATING AND FINANCING YOUR PURCHASE

When you have settled on a homesite you like, you can begin discussions with the seller. After you are satisfied that the promised services and improvements have been or will be delivered, you should enter into serious negotiation about price and terms. These must be commensurate with your IRA's capacity to meet the debt.

With these matters settled and the purchase agreed on—through a broker, developer, or financial planner—you must now complete the appropriate paperwork. How to do this was spelled out in Chapter Nine.

You send the executed documents and any additional monies to your trust, directing it to purchase the property on a form similar to the one shown in Chapter Nine. Your trust then executes the documents and forwards them to the seller of the property. The seller, in turn, executes the agreement and returns the papers to the trust. The sale is then official.

Once you have completed one homesite purchase, you will repeat the process when buying a second, third, or fourth lot. The payoffs of our various acquisitions are explored in Chapter Eleven, which showed the advantages you reap, whether you own four homesites or only one. Fulfillment of these objectives may be premature for many of you at this point, but don't fail to act. You will assuredly benefit a few years hence.

That's our road map to successful retirement. Any legislative modifications that affect any of these steps will be discussed in later editions of this book to enable you to adjust your plan accordingly and to make sure that your retirement objectives remain up to date, realistic, and within your grasp.

Appendix A: Money and Tax Principles

In this appendix, we will identify and discuss some key money and tax principles. Doing this will help us to understand fiscal fundamentals as they relate to the IRA.

Taxes are a recurring theme in IRA literature. To grasp their true relationship to the IRA, we should learn exactly how they work and how they really affect the intricate interplay between our income and investments.

SOME BASIC TAX TERMS

Taxes eat away at our dollars in countless ways from the outset of our careers. Complex and extensive federal tax laws and regulations besiege us at every turn, and we will be doing ourselves a big favor if we try to understand how taxation works and how we can cope with it. Some of the following terms are therefore essential for us to know.

1. Tax-Deferred Income: This term refers to income that is free from taxation for a specified period. As interest compounds on a body of money that is undiminished by any tax bite, the total will grow more rapidly. Tax-deferred income includes money that goes into deferred compensation programs, such as the 401(k), the 403(b), and in most IRAs. The advantage of such programs is that taxes are deferred on all or part of the original dollar and on all of the earnings. Taxes must be paid on the deferred compensation at withdrawal, however. The term *tax-deferred* also applies to the profits or appreciation on investments that include annuities, stocks, and real

160

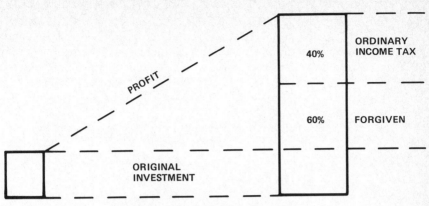

Figure A-1: Capital Gain Treatment

estate. In these, the invested dollars have been taxed. However, their yields or profits are tax-deferred until distribution to the individual.

2. Tax-Favored Income: This term refers to income that benefits from preferential tax treatment in some way. Capital gains was an example. Until 1987, this tax-favored treatment reduced the taxes you paid on the profit from the sale of an asset that you had held for at least six months before selling it. If you held it less than six months, all your profit was treated as ordinary income. Taxes were due on only 40% of the profit at ordinary income tax rates. Figure A-1 shows how capital gains were treated.

You should be aware that the 1986 tax reform legislation has eliminated capital gains tax advantages. Profits from the sale of an asset after 1986 will now be taxed as ordinary income regardless of how long the asset has been held. The repeal of capital gains imposes a maximum income tax rate of 28% on these profits, compared to a maximum of 20% before repeal (40% of your profit, times a maximum marginal tax bracket of 50%.)

3. Tax-Free Income: This is income that is excluded from *any* tax obligation at any time. Sources of tax-free income include:

- Interest on state or city municipal bonds.

- Profit, up to $125,000, from the sale of one's principal residence after age 55. This is a once-only exclusion.

- Proceeds of a life-insurance policy.

- Social Security benefits.

4. Tax Shifting: Tax shifting allows you to give anyone—usually your children—a sum of money. New limitations have been placed on this technique. Parents can transfer an income-producing asset to their children, but income in excess of $1,000 will be taxed at the parent's higher rate if the child is under fourteen years old. If the child is over fourteen, the income will be taxed at the child's lower rate.

5. Tax Shelters: This term is applied to certain tax-favored investments such as real estate, oil, and gas. They have also included esoteric investments in horses, records, and certain creative ventures. These investments usually involved accelerated depreciation, major interest deductions, and many statutory deductions that offset current income. For all practical purposes, the 1986 legislation virtually eliminated these tax-sheltering techniques.

Deductions from passive activities (losses) generally may not be deducted against other income. Passive activities include businesses (including rental activities) in which the investor does not materially participate. Active participation in real estate investments does provide tax sheltering of up to $25,000 of losses each year against nonpassive income of the taxpayer.

We've been kicking around some pretty complicated terms. Perhaps you're at a stage in your life where tax-free income and once-only exclusions are still as alien to you as Godzilla. So let's get back to basics and discuss how we amass the money to play these convoluted financial games.

HOW DO WE GET MONEY?

This has always been a big question. You may have first asked it when you were a teenager. You may have gotten your first answer when you took a job delivering newspapers or working as a supermarket checkout clerk. This was a simple beginning. Nevertheless, what you received for your work was:

1. Earned Income: This term refers to how you are rewarded for "active" effort. Any money you receive in compensation for services you've performed is considered earned income.

Now, suppose that you liked your work experience and its rewards very much, so much so that you wanted to save some money for a "rainy day." You put a little aside to build for the future. When you did this, your account accumulated interest. You began to learn about:

2. Unearned Income: Unlike earned income, unearned income is "passive" in nature: Your money "works" and grows for you, instead of you working for it. Examples are bank interest, dividends, and rental income.

All this money of yours interests the IRS. This agency has a stake in your income because it anticipates taxes from your labors or investments. This makes us wonder:

How Does The IRS View My Earnings?

Well, it initially takes a plain view of your earnings. Quite simply, it calls them:

1. Ordinary Income: This consists of the two types of income just described— earned and unearned. Although both are taxable, only your *earned* income can be used to determine how much income you are qualified to put in your IRA. Contributions to an IRA must be determined *solely* on the basis of earned income. If unearned income is your only source of earnings, you cannot have an IRA.

Once the IRS has defined your earnings, it demands a share of them. This blow to your psyche and your wallet was first struck in 1914 when the federal personal income tax went into effect, and it has become increasingly harsh ever since. The part of our earnings that the IRS feels it has a right to is called:

2. Taxable Income: This is your ordinary income minus the exclusions, deductions, exemptions, and credits (such as IRAs and alimony) that the tax code allows. Income tax obligations are based on this net figure.

The basic types of income we've been discussing should be familiar to most of you. After all, you go to work and receive a regular paycheck, you pay taxes, and maybe you have some money accumulating interest in the bank. But you may still be thinking about those rarefied tax terms we introduced earlier in this appendix. You may be wondering how you will ever reach a position where those terms will have any practical meaning for you. Well, if you invest wisely, they will! And to help you make sound investment choices, we should address a question that will lead us into the intriguing realm of mathematics:

HOW DOES OUR INVESTED MONEY GROW?

The most intriguing feature of our investments is how they "make" or amass money for us. One of these methods is a phenomenon as old as investing and the very use of money itself. This is the marvel of:

COMPOUNDING

Compounding is the process by which interest is accumulated not only on the original principal (the amount originally invested), but also on interest that the principal earns. Figure A-2 tracks the steady growth of a $1,000 principal. At 8%, the interest earned ($80) is added to the original $1,000 at the end of the first year. This becomes the next year's starting balance. At the end of ten years, the total in the account will be $2,159.

The power of compounding can be extremely beneficial, especially if a

Figure A-2: Compounding Yearly @ 8%

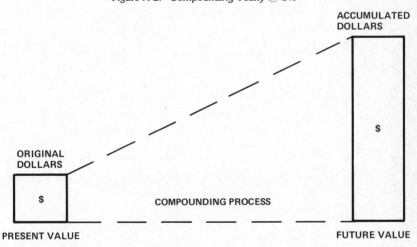

YEAR	BEGINNING AMOUNT	INTEREST	BALANCE
1	$1,000	$ 80	$1,080
2	1,080	86	1,166
3	1,166	93	1,260
4	1,260	101	1,360
5	1,360	109	1,469
6	1,469	118	1,587
7	1,587	127	1,714
8	1,714	137	1,851
9	1,851	148	1,999
10	1,999	160	2,159

TABLE 1.10 Future Value Of One Dollar Invested At Beginning Of Year

Year	Annual Rate Of Return										
	5	6	7	8	9	10	11	12	13	14	15
1	1.05	1.06	1.07	1.08	1.09	1.1	1.11	1.12	1.13	1.14	1.15
2	1.103	1.124	1.145	1.166	1.188	1.21	1.232	1.254	1.277	1.300	1.323
3	1.158	1.191	1.225	1.260	1.295	1.331	1.368	1.405	1.443	1.482	1.521
4	1.216	1.262	1.311	1.360	1.412	1.464	1.518	1.574	1.630	1.689	1.749
5	1.276	1.338	1.403	1.469	1.539	1.611	1.685	1.762	1.842	1.925	2.011
6	1.340	1.419	1.501	1.587	1.677	1.772	1.870	1.974	2.082	2.195	2.313
7	1.407	1.504	1.606	1.714	1.828	1.949	2.076	2.211	2.353	2.502	2.660
8	1.477	1.594	1.718	1.851	1.993	2.144	2.305	2.476	2.658	2.853	3.059
9	1.551	1.689	1.838	1.999	2.172	2.358	2.558	2.773	3.004	3.252	3.518
10	1.629	1.791	1.967	2.159	2.367	2.594	2.839	3.106	3.395	3.707	4.046
11	1.710	1.898	2.105	2.332	2.580	2.853	3.152	3.479	3.836	4.226	4.652
12	1.796	2.012	2.252	2.518	2.813	3.138	3.498	3.896	4.335	4.818	5.350
13	1.886	2.133	2.140	2.720	3.066	3.452	3.883	4.363	4.898	5.492	6.153
14	1.980	2.261	2.579	2.937	3.342	3.797	4.310	4.887	5.535	6.261	7.076
15	2.079	2.397	2.759	3.172	3.642	4.177	4.785	5.474	6.254	7.138	8.137
16	2.183	2.540	2.952	3.426	3.970	4.595	5.311	6.130	7.067	8.137	9.358
17	2.292	2.693	3.159	3.700	4.328	5.054	5.895	6.866	7.986	9.276	10.76
18	2.407	2.854	3.380	3.996	4.717	5.560	6.544	7.690	9.024	10.58	12.38
19	2.527	3.026	3.617	4.316	5.142	6.116	7.263	8.613	10.20	12.06	14.23
20	2.653	3.207	3.870	4.661	5.604	6.727	8.062	9.646	11.52	13.74	16.37

21	2.786	3.400	4.141	5.034	6.109	7.400	8.949	10.80	13.02	15.67	18.82
22	2.925	3.604	4.430	5.437	6.659	8.140	9.934	12.10	14.71	17.86	21.64
23	3.072	3.820	4.741	5.871	7.258	8.954	11.03	13.55	16.63	20.36	24.89
24	3.225	4.049	5.072	6.341	7.911	9.850	12.24	15.18	18.79	23.20	28.63
25	3.386	4.292	5.427	6.848	8.623	10.83	13.59	17.00	21.23	26.46	32.92
26	3.556	4.549	5.807	7.396	9.399	11.92	15.08	19.04	23.99	30.17	37.86
27	3.733	4.822	6.214	7.988	10.25	13.11	16.74	21.32	27.11	34.39	43.54
28	3.920	5.112	6.649	8.627	11.17	14.42	18.58	23.88	30.63	39.21	50.07
29	4.116	5.418	7.114	9.317	12.17	15.86	20.62	26.75	34.62	44.69	57.58
30	4.322	5.743	7.612	10.06	13.27	17.45	22.89	29.96	39.12	50.95	66.21
31	4.538	6.088	8.145	10.87	14.45	19.19	25.41	33.56	44.20	58.08	76.14
32	4.765	6.453	8.715	11.74	15.76	21.11	28.21	37.58	49.95	66.21	87.57
33	5.003	6.841	9.325	12.68	17.18	23.23	31.31	42.09	56.44	75.48	100.7
34	5.253	7.251	9.978	13.69	18.73	25.55	34.75	47.14	63.78	86.05	115.8
35	5.516	7.686	10.68	14.79	20.41	28.10	38.57	52.80	72.07	98.10	133.2
36	5.792	8.147	11.42	15.97	22.25	30.91	42.82	59.14	81.44	111.8	153.2
37	6.081	8.636	12.22	17.25	24.25	34.00	47.53	66.23	92.02	127.5	176.1
38	6.385	9.154	13.08	18.63	26.44	37.40	52.76	74.18	104.0	145.3	202.5
39	6.705	9.704	13.99	20.12	28.82	41.14	58.56	83.08	117.5	165.7	232.9
40	7.040	10.29	14.97	21.72	31.41	45.26	65.00	93.05	132.8	188.9	267.9

high interest rate or percentage of return is at work for you. Small fortunes have grown through compounding. Over 30 to 40 years, undisturbed sums can grow into handsome totals, as heirs to estates that were sprinkled with ancient passbooks will attest. Understanding this phenomenon leads us to consider what is known as:

Future Value (FV): Simply expressed, if we put a certain sum in the bank, we know its earnings will accrue to a specific level based on the length of time and rate of return. When we plug in these variables, we can determine the *future value* of our money.

Suppose we deposit $1,000 in a bank for 10 years at 8% interest, that is the payment rate the bank agrees to give you for the use of your money. Let's assume the bank policy is to compute the interest once per year. You may then want to know the factor by which you can multiply the $1,000 to determine its value 10 years from now.

For the record, the formula for determining future value is:

$$FV = PV (1 + i)^n$$

In ordinary English, this equation says that if you want to know the future value (*FV*) of a sum of money, you multiply the present value (*PV*) by the sum of one plus the interest rate paid on it (*i*), raised to the power of the number of compounding periods (*n*). The formula may be simple for math majors, but it is probably a turnoff for the average reader. You can relax, take heart, and forget the formula. Mathematicians have developed future-value factor charts for various combinations of interest rates and numbers of years, to save you from having to make these calculations. Such a chart is shown in Table 1.10.

Let's go back to the $1,000 deposited in Figure A-2. To find the future value (FV) of this deposit, you refer to Table 1.10. At the intersection of the 8% yield column and the 10th-year row is the factor 2.159. The $1,000 is multiplied by this number to provide the value of the account in 10 years.

$$\$1,000 \times 2.159 = \$2,159$$

This is the same value we calculated in Figure A-2. Using a similar formula, mathematicians have developed factors for the regular yearly investment of $1.00 for a variety of lengths of time and yields. In this case, one dollar is deposited yearly or added to the compounding sum. These factors are presented in Table 1.11. For example, if you deposited $1,000 each year for twelve years in an investment yielding 9%, the factor is 21.95 and the future value (FV) is:

$$\$1,000 \times 21.95 = \$21,950$$

The converse of future value is known as:

Present Value (PV): Present value can best be understood by contrasting it to future value. FV tells us how much a known sum invested today will be worth at a specific future date, as was shown in Figure A-2. On the other hand, PV tells us how much we must deposit today to have a known amount at a specific future date.

A good example of how PV functions in a financial product is government EE bonds. These bonds generally are issued in face amounts of multiples of $1,000 and are purchased at a discount, usually at $750. The face amount is the future value (FV) and the amount you pay for it is the present value (PV). The bond earns interest that is added to the present value price you paid.

To determine a given PV, we use the same basic formula we used to find FV. We know *how much* we want and *when* in the future we want it. What we have to find out is *how much to invest now* to deliver what we want. The present value principle is also shown in Figure A-2.

As with FV, we do not need to use a formula to calculate PV; we need only refer to Tables 1.12 and 1.13. Figure 1.12 gives the factor to be used on a *once only* deposit of $1.00 for various combinations of time and yield.

If $12,000 is the desired goal in 12 years in a vehicle paying 8%, we use the factor from Table 1.12 (.397) to determine the *one-time* deposit required:

$$\$12,000 \times .397 = \$4,765$$

You merely multiply the PV factor .397 (for 12 years and an 8% interest rate) by the known future sum, $12,000, to find how much you must invest now. To emphasize the interplay between PV and FV, let's reverse the process. We'll take a present value of $4,765 and calculate its *future* value in the same 12 years at 8%.

$$\$4,765 \times 2.518 = \$12,000 \text{ (From Table 1.10)}$$

These compounding charts and equations provide us with exact data. But sometimes we wish to have more general information at our fingertips, without having to refer to complex tables. A popular shortcut is the:

• Rule of 72: This handy device helps you to track the magical way in which interest compounds. It's a formula that tells you how long it takes money to double at any given interest rate. You simply divide the interest rate into the number 72 to find the number of years in which your money will double. For example:

72 divided by	6%	=	12	years
72 divided by	9%	=	8	years
72 divided by	10%	=	7.2	years
72 divided by	14%	=	5.1	years

While it is useful to know how much compounding will mean to us in income of future or present value, another important consideration involves the real or actual value of any gain we realize.

Our FV factor charts (Tables 1.10 and 1.11) told us how much a given sum invested now will yield in the future. But they don't take taxes into account! When we consider taxes, a different set of numbers emerges.

Table 1.14 shows the future-value factors of $1.00 compounded annually for a person in the 28% marginal tax bracket. Clearly, the factors are lower because taxes must be subtracted from the total accumulation. Again, just multiply the invested sum by the factor for the corresponding year and

TABLE 1.11 Future Value Of One Dollar Invested At Beginning Of Each Year

Year	5	6	7	8	9	10	11	12	13	14	15
						Annual Rate Of Return					
1	1.05	1.06	1.07	1.08	1.09	1.1	1.11	1.12	1.13	1.14	1.15
2	2.153	2.184	1.215	2.246	2.278	2.31	2.342	2.374	2.407	2.440	2.473
3	3.310	3.375	3.440	3.506	3.573	3.641	3.710	3.779	3.850	3.921	3.993
4	4.526	4.637	4.751	4.867	4.985	5.105	5.228	5.353	5.480	5.610	5.742
5	5.802	5.975	6.153	6.336	6.523	6.716	6.913	7.115	7.323	7.536	7.754
6	7.142	7.394	7.654	7.923	8.200	8.487	8.783	9.089	9.405	9.730	10.07
7	8.549	8.897	9.260	9.637	10.03	10.44	10.86	11.30	11.76	12.23	12.73
8	10.03	10.49	10.98	11.49	12.02	12.58	13.16	13.78	14.42	15.09	15.79
9	11.58	12.18	12.82	13.49	14.19	14.94	15.72	16.55	17.42	18.34	19.30
10	13.21	13.97	14.78	15.65	16.56	17.53	18.56	19.65	20.81	22.04	23.35
11	14.92	15.87	16.89	17.98	19.14	20.38	21.71	23.13	24.65	26.27	28.00
12	16.71	17.88	19.14	20.50	21.95	23.52	25.21	27.03	28.98	31.09	33.35
13	18.60	20.02	21.55	23.21	25.02	26.97	29.09	31.39	33.88	36.58	39.50
14	20.58	22.28	24.13	26.15	28.36	30.77	33.41	36.28	39.42	42.84	46.58
15	22.66	24.67	26.89	29.32	32.00	34.95	38.19	41.75	45.67	49.98	54.72
16	24.84	27.21	29.84	32.75	35.97	39.54	43.50	47.88	52.74	58.12	64.08
17	27.13	29.91	33.00	36.45	40.30	44.60	49.40	54.75	60.73	67.39	74.84
18	29.54	32.76	36.38	40.45	45.02	50.16	55.94	62.44	69.75	77.97	87.21
19	32.07	35.79	40.00	44.76	50.16	56.27	63.20	71.05	79.95	90.02	101.4

20	34.72	38.99	43.87	49.42	55.76	63.00	71.27	80.70	91.47	103.8	117.8
21	37.51	42.39	48.01	54.46	61.87	70.40	80.21	91.50	104.5	119.4	136.6
22	40.43	46.00	52.44	59.89	68.53	78.54	90.15	103.6	119.2	137.3	158.3
23	43.50	49.82	57.18	65.76	75.79	87.50	101.2	117.2	135.8	157.7	183.2
24	46.73	53.86	62.25	72.11	83.70	97.35	113.4	132.5	154.6	180.3	211.8
25	50.11	58.16	67.68	78.95	92.32	108.2	127.0	149.3	175.9	207.3	244.7
26	53.67	62.71	73.48	86.35	101.7	120.1	142.1	168.4	199.8	237.5	282.6
27	57.40	67.53	79.70	94.34	112.0	133.2	158.8	189.7	226.9	271.9	326.1
28	61.32	72.64	86.35	103.0	123.1	147.6	177.4	213.6	257.6	311.1	376.2
29	65.44	78.05	93.46	112.3	135.3	163.5	198.0	240.3	292.2	355.8	433.7
30	69.76	83.80	101.1	122.3	148.6	180.9	220.9	270.3	331.3	406.7	500.0
31	74.30	89.89	109.2	133.2	163.0	200.1	246.3	303.8	375.5	464.8	576.1
32	79.06	96.34	117.9	145.0	178.8	221.3	274.5	341.4	425.5	531.0	663.7
33	84.07	103.2	127.3	157.6	196.0	244.5	305.8	383.5	481.9	606.5	764.4
34	89.32	110.4	137.2	171.3	214.7	270.0	340.6	430.7	545.7	692.6	880.2
35	94.84	118.1	147.9	186.1	235.1	298.1	379.2	483.5	617.7	790.7	1013.
36	100.6	126.3	159.3	202.1	257.4	329.0	422.0	542.6	699.2	902.5	1166.
37	106.7	134.9	171.6	219.3	281.6	363.0	469.5	608.8	791.2	1030.	1343.
38	113.1	144.1	184.6	237.9	308.1	400.4	522.3	683.0	895.2	1175.	1545.
39	119.8	153.8	198.6	258.1	336.9	441.6	580.8	766.1	1013.	1341.	1778.
40	126.8	164.0	213.6	279.8	368.3	486.9	645.8	859.1	1145.	1530.	2046.
41	134.2	175.0	229.6	303.2	402.5	536.6	718.0	963.4	1296.	1745.	2354.
42	135.6	176.8	232.1	306.5	406.9	542.5	725.9	974.1	1310.	1765.	2381.
43	137.1	178.7	234.6	309.8	411.4	548.5	734.0	985.1	1325.	1785.	2408.

TABLE 1.12 Present Value Of One Dollar

Annual Rate Of Return

Year	5	6	7	8	9	10	11	12	13	14	15
1	.9524	.9434	.9346	.9259	.9174	.9091	.9009	.8929	.8850	.8772	.8696
2	.9070	.8900	.8734	.8573	.8417	.8264	.8116	.7972	.7831	.7695	.7561
3	.8638	.8396	.8163	.7938	.7722	.7513	.7312	.7118	.6931	.6750	.6575
4	.8227	.7921	.7629	.7350	.7084	.6830	.6587	.6355	.6133	.5921	.5718
5	.7835	.7473	.7130	.6806	.6499	.6209	.5935	.5674	.5428	.5194	.4972
6	.7462	.7050	.6663	.6302	.5963	.5645	.5346	.5066	.4803	.4556	.4323
7	.7107	.6651	.6227	.5835	.5470	.5132	.4817	.4523	.4251	.3996	.3759
8	.6768	.6274	.5820	.5403	.5019	.4665	.4339	.4039	.3762	.3506	.3269
9	.6446	.5919	.5439	.5002	.4604	.4241	.3909	.3606	.3329	.3075	.2843
10	.6139	.5584	.5083	.4632	.4224	.3855	.3522	.3220	.2946	.2697	.2472
11	.5847	.5268	.4751	.4289	.3875	.3505	.3173	.2875	.2607	.2366	.2149
12	.5568	.4970	.4440	.3971	.3555	.3186	.2858	.2567	.2307	.2076	.1869
13	.5303	.4688	.4150	.3677	.3262	.2897	.2575	.2292	.2042	.1821	.1625
14	.5051	.4423	.3878	.3405	.2992	.2633	.2320	.2046	.1807	.1597	.1413
15	.4810	.4173	.3624	.3152	.2745	.2394	.2090	.1827	.1599	.1401	.1229
16	.4581	.3936	.3387	.2919	.2519	.2176	.1883	.1631	.1415	.1229	.1069
17	.4363	.3714	.3166	.2703	.2311	.1978	.1696	.1456	.1252	.1078	.0929
18	.4155	.3503	.2959	.2502	.2120	.1799	.1528	.1300	.1108	.0946	.0808

19	.3957	.3305	.2765	.2317	.1945	.1635	.1377	.1161	.0981	.0829	.0703
20	.3769	.3118	.2584	.2145	.1784	.1486	.1240	.1037	.0868	.0728	.0611
21	.3589	.2942	.2415	.1987	.1637	.1351	.1117	.0926	.0768	.0638	.0531
22	.3418	.2775	.2257	.1839	.1502	.1228	.1007	.0826	.0680	.0560	.0462
23	.3256	.2618	.2109	.1703	.1378	.1117	.0907	.0738	.0601	.0491	.0402
24	.3101	.2470	.1971	.1577	.1264	.1015	.0817	.0659	.0532	.0431	.0349
25	.2953	.2330	.1842	.1460	.1160	.0923	.0736	.0588	.0471	.0378	.0304
26	.2812	.2198	.1722	.1352	.1064	.0839	.0663	.0525	.0417	.0331	.0264
27	.2678	.2074	.1609	.1252	.0976	.0763	.0597	.0469	.0369	.0891	.0230
28	.2551	.1956	.1504	.1159	.0895	.0693	.0538	.0419	.0326	.0255	.0200
29	.2429	.1846	.1406	.1073	.0822	.0630	.0485	.0374	.0289	.0224	.0174
30	.2314	.1741	.1314	.0994	.0754	.0573	.0437	.0334	.0256	.0196	.0151
31	.2204	.1643	.1228	.0920	.0691	.0521	.0394	.0298	.0226	.0172	.0131
32	.2099	.1550	.1147	.0852	.0634	.0474	.0355	.0266	.0200	.0151	.0114
33	.1999	.1462	.1072	.0789	.0582	.0431	.0319	.0238	.0177	.0132	.0099
34	.1904	.1379	.1002	.0730	.0534	.0391	.0288	.0212	.0157	.0116	.0086
35	.1813	.1301	.0937	.0676	.0490	.0356	.0259	.0189	.0139	.0102	.0075
36	.1727	.1227	.0875	.0626	.0449	.0323	.0234	.0169	.0123	.0089	.0065
37	.1644	.1158	.0818	.0580	.0412	.0294	.0210	.0151	.0109	.0078	.0057
38	.1566	.1092	.0765	.0537	.0378	.0267	.0190	.0135	.0096	.0069	.0049
39	.1491	.1031	.0715	.0497	.0347	.0243	.0171	.0120	.0085	.0060	.0043
40	.1420	.0972	.0668	.0460	.0318	.0221	.0154	.0107	.0075	.0053	.0037

Table 1.13 Present Value of One Dollar Per Year

Annual Rate Of Return

Year	5	6	7	8	9	10	11	12	13	14	15
1	.9524	.9434	.9346	.9259	.9174	.9091	.9009	.8929	.8850	.8772	.8696
2	1.859	1.833	1.808	1.783	1.759	1.736	1.713	1.690	1.668	1.647	1.626
3	2.723	2.673	2.624	2.577	2.531	2.487	2.444	2.402	2.361	2.322	2.283
4	3.546	3.465	3.387	3.312	3.240	3.170	3.102	3.037	2.974	2.914	2.855
5	4.329	4.212	4.100	3.993	3.890	3.791	3.696	3.605	3.517	3.433	3.352
6	5.076	4.917	4.767	4.623	4.486	4.355	4.231	4.111	3.998	3.889	3.784
7	5.786	5.582	5.389	5.206	5.033	4.868	4.712	4.564	4.423	4.288	4.160
8	6.463	6.210	5.971	5.747	5.535	5.335	5.146	4.968	4.799	4.639	4.487
9	7.108	6.802	6.515	6.247	5.995	5.759	5.537	5.328	5.132	4.946	4.772
10	7.722	7.360	7.024	6.710	6.418	6.145	5.889	5.650	5.426	5.216	5.019
11	8.306	7.887	7.499	7.139	6.805	6.495	6.207	5.938	5.687	5.453	5.234
12	8.863	8.384	7.943	7.536	7.161	6.814	6.492	6.194	5.918	5.660	5.421
13	9.394	8.853	8.358	7.904	7.487	7.103	6.750	6.424	6.122	5.842	5.583
14	9.899	9.295	8.745	8.244	7.786	7.367	6.982	6.628	6.302	6.002	5.724
15	10.38	9.712	9.108	8.559	8.061	7.606	7.191	6.811	6.462	6.142	5.847
16	10.84	10.11	9.447	8.851	8.313	7.824	7.379	6.974	6.604	6.265	5.954
17	11.27	10.48	9.763	9.122	8.544	8.022	7.549	7.120	6.729	6.373	6.047
18	11.69	10.83	10.06	9.372	8.756	8.201	7.702	7.250	6.840	6.467	6.128

19	12.09	11.16	10.34	9.604	8.950	8.365	7.839	7.366	6.938	6.550	6.198
20	12.46	11.47	10.59	9.818	9.129	8.514	7.963	7.469	7.025	6.623	6.259
21	12.82	11.76	10.84	10.02	9.292	8.649	8.075	7.562	7.102	6.687	6.312
22	13.16	12.04	11.06	10.20	9.442	8.772	8.176	7.645	7.170	6.743	6.359
23	13.49	12.30	11.27	10.37	9.580	8.883	8.266	7.718	7.230	6.792	6.399
24	13.80	12.55	11.47	10.53	9.707	8.985	8.348	7.784	7.283	6.835	6.434
25	14.09	12.78	11.65	10.67	9.823	9.077	8.422	7.843	7.330	6.873	6.464
26	14.38	13.00	11.83	10.81	9.929	9.161	8.488	7.896	7.372	6.906	6.491
27	14.64	13.21	11.99	10.94	10.03	9.237	8.548	7.943	7.409	6.935	6.514
28	14.90	13.41	12.14	11.05	10.12	9.307	8.602	7.984	7.441	6.961	6.534
29	15.14	13.59	12.28	11.16	10.20	9.370	8.650	8.022	7.470	6.983	6.551
30	15.37	13.76	12.41	11.26	10.27	9.427	8.694	8.055	7.496	7.003	6.566
31	15.59	13.93	12.53	11.35	10.34	9.479	8.733	8.085	7.518	7.020	6.579
32	15.80	14.08	12.65	11.43	10.41	9.526	8.769	8.112	7.538	7.035	6.591
33	16.00	14.23	12.75	11.51	10.46	9.569	8.801	8.135	7.556	7.048	6.600
34	16.19	14.37	12.85	11.59	10.52	9.609	8.829	8.157	7.572	7.060	6.609
35	16.37	14.50	12.95	11.65	10.57	9.644	8.855	8.176	7.586	7.070	6.617
36	16.55	14.62	13.04	11.72	10.61	9.677	8.879	8.192	7.598	7.079	6.623
37	16.17	14.74	13.12	11.78	10.65	9.706	8.900	8.208	7.609	7.087	6.629
38	16.87	14.85	13.19	11.83	10.69	9.733	8.919	8.221	7.618	7.094	6.634
39	17.02	14.95	13.26	11.88	10.73	9.757	8.936	8.233	7.627	7.100	6.638
40	17.16	15.05	13.33	11.92	10.76	9.779	8.951	8.244	7.634	7.105	6.642

Table 1.14 Future Value Of One Dollar Invested At Beginning Of Year
28% Tax Bracket

	Annual Rate Of Return										
Year	5	6	7	8	9	10	11	12	13	14	15
Year	3.6	4.32	5.04	5.76	6.48	After Tax Rate Of Return 7.2	7.92	8.64	9.36	10.08	10.8
1	1.036	1.043	1.050	1.058	1.065	1.072	1.079	1.086	1.094	1.101	1.108
2	1.073	1.088	1.103	1.119	1.134	1.149	1.165	1.180	1.196	1.212	1.228
3	1.112	1.135	1.159	1.183	1.207	1.232	1.257	1.282	1.308	1.334	1.360
4	1.152	1.184	1.217	1.251	1.286	1.321	1.356	1.393	1.430	1.468	1.507
5	1.193	1.235	1.279	1.323	1.369	1.416	1.464	1.513	1.564	1.616	1.670
6	1.236	1.289	1.343	1.399	1.457	1.518	1.580	1.644	1.711	1.779	1.850
7	1.281	1.345	1.411	1.480	1.552	1.627	1.705	1.786	1.871	1.959	2.050
8	1.327	1.403	1.482	1.565	1.653	1.744	1.840	1.941	2.046	2.156	2.272
9	1.375	1.463	1.557	1.655	1.760	1.870	1.986	2.108	2.237	2.373	2.517
10	1.424	1.526	1.635	1.751	1.874	2.004	2.143	2.290	2.447	2.613	2.789
11	1.476	1.592	1.718	1.852	1.995	2.149	2.313	2.488	2.676	2.876	3.090
12	1.529	1.661	1.804	1.958	2.124	2.303	2.496	2.703	2.926	3.166	3.424
13	1.584	1.733	1.895	2.071	2.262	2.469	2.694	2.937	3.200	3.485	3.793
14	1.641	1.808	1.991	2.190	2.409	2.647	2.907	3.190	3.500	3.836	4.203
15	1.700	1.886	2.091	2.316	2.565	2.837	3.137	3.466	3.827	4.223	4.657
16	1.761	1.967	2.196	2.450	2.731	3.042	3.386	3.766	4.185	4.649	5.160

17	1.824	2.052	2.307	2.591	2.908	3.261	3.654	4.091	4.577	5.117	5.717
18	1.890	2.141	2.423	2.740	3.096	3.495	3.943	4.444	5.006	5.633	6.335
19	1.958	2.233	2.545	2.898	3.297	3.747	4.255	4.828	5.474	6.201	7.019
20	2.029	2.330	2.674	3.065	3.510	4.017	4.592	5.246	5.986	6.826	7.777
21	2.102	2.431	2.808	3.242	3.738	4.306	4.956	5.699	6.547	7.514	8.617
22	2.177	2.536	2.950	3.428	3.980	4.616	5.349	6.191	7.160	8.272	9.547
23	2.256	2.645	3.099	3.626	4.238	4.949	5.772	6.726	7.830	9.105	10.58
24	2.337	2.759	3.255	3.835	4.513	5.305	6.229	7.307	8.563	10.02	11.72
25	2.421	2.879	3.419	4.055	4.805	5.687	6.723	7.939	9.364	11.03	12.99
26	2.508	3.003	3.591	4.289	5.116	6.096	7.255	8.624	10.24	12.15	14.39
27	2.598	3.133	3.772	4.536	5.448	6.535	7.830	9.370	11.20	13.37	15.94
28	2.692	3.268	3.962	4.797	5.801	7.006	8.450	10.18	12.25	14.72	17.66
29	2.789	3.409	4.162	5.074	6.177	7.510	9.119	11.06	13.39	16.20	19.57
30	2.889	3.557	4.372	5.366	6.577	8.051	9.841	12.01	14.65	17.83	81.69
31	2.993	3.710	4.592	5.675	7.003	8.631	10.62	13.05	16.02	19.03	24.03
32	3.101	3.870	4.823	6.002	7.457	9.252	11.46	14.18	17.52	21.61	26.62
33	3.213	4.038	5.066	6.348	7.940	9.918	12.37	15.41	19.16	23.79	29.50
34	3.328	4.212	5.322	6.713	8.455	10.63	13.35	16.74	20.95	26.19	32.69
35	3.448	4.394	5.590	7.100	9.003	11.40	14.41	18.18	22.91	28.83	36.22
36	3.572	4.584	5.872	7.500	9.586	12.22	15.55	19.75	25.06	31.73	40.13
37	3.701	4.782	6.168	7.941	10.21	13.10	16.78	21.46	27.40	34.93	44.46
38	3.834	4.988	6.479	8.399	10.87	14.04	18.11	23.31	29.97	38.45	49.26
39	3.972	5.204	6.805	8.883	11.57	15.05	19.54	25.33	32.77	42.33	54.58
40	4.115	5.429	7.148	9.394	12.32	16.14	21.09	27.52	35.84	46.59	60.48

interest rate to find the total. For example, the after-tax total for $12,000 invested at 8% for 10 years would be:

$$\$12,000 \times 1.75 = \$21,000$$

It is, therefore, imperative that when we consider how to invest our money, we distinguish between *pretax* and *after-tax returns*. These phrases have confused many harried consumer investors.

• Pretax: Marketers use this adjective to describe the return you may expect from an investment, but it refers to any gain *before* it is subjected to taxation. When a fund sends out literature boasting a return of 10%, its claim is correct in theory but not in practice. A return of 10% on $1,000 will be $100 *pretax*. The unspoken implication is that you will enjoy the full $100, which, of course, is not true. You will receive the $100, but you must pay taxes on it. The present and future values in Tables 1.10 through 1.13 are *pretax* calculations. Unless we have put our money into an investment where it is permitted to compound tax-free, we must factor the debilitating effect of taxes into our calculations. When we do so, we then refer to:
• After-Tax: Now you have your $100 (pretax) return and have braced yourself to settle up with Uncle Sam, who wants his share of the profit, gain, or return on your investment. In the 28% bracket, the tax on the $100 gain is $28. What's left for you—$72—is your *after-tax return*. This is the sum you actually get to keep. Your true after-tax return on the $100 is $72, or 7.2%—not 10%. In the final analysis, the after-tax return is the important measure of the net value of an investment. To help you estimate future after-tax values, the appropriate factors are shown in Table 1.14.

OK. We've spent several pages explaining the wonders of compounding. But in certain types of investments, money grows by another process, one that generally gives us an even greater overall gain. This process is:

LEVERAGING

A most remarkable feature of real estate investments, leveraging allows us to control a large asset with a small amount of invested cash. We define leveraging as the use of "other people's money" (OPM). The more OPM you use, the larger your asset control or ownership can be. The unique advantage of leveraging lies in the growth of the value of the *entire* asset, not just of the originally invested cash portion. The concept is depicted in (I) of Figure A-3.

In Figure A-3, (II) shows the results of a full $2,000 cash investment in a non-leveraged product. The profit of $300 represents a 15% return. But look what happens when we put the same $2,000 in a *leveraged* investment, as shown in the right side of the same figure.

There are a number of advantages in the leveraged investment. First, we have acquired a $10,000 asset through a cash outlay of only ⅕ of its cost, or $2,000. Second, we receive a 15% yield ($1,500) on the *whole* asset ($10,000)—$300 on the initial cash outlay and $1,200 on the leveraged portion. We must pay interest on the financed portion of the investment, and, after deducting the interest, or the cost of borrowing, from the total $1,500

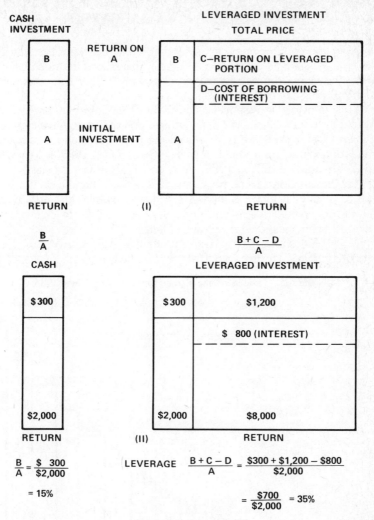

Figure A-3: Leverage

profit, we have the true gain—$700. The payoff: the return on the leveraged investment is 35% ($700), versus 15% in a standard non-leveraged investment.

That's not all. Uncle Sam may make leveraging even sweeter. The cost of using other people's money (OPM) may be tax-deductible. In a 28% tax bracket, the deduction on $800 interest is $224 (28% × $800). That leaves only $576 net cash out of your pocket, not $800. Uncle Sam may pick up the rest of the tab.

This discussion dramatizes the value of leveraged buying. It further compels us to investigate how we are taxed and consider the consequences of taxation for each of us.

HOW ARE WE FINALLY TAXED?

You know that your income is taxed, and you may be aware that it has been done on a *progressive* tax system for years. This means that the higher your income, the higher the percentage of tax you pay. The IRA implements this system by using *tax brackets*.

This principle is essentially sound in theory, but in practice it has confused the average taxpayer. Only professionals seem to have a grasp of it. But even fiscal experts are reeling from the recent regulations reducing the number of tax brackets from fourteen in 1986 to five in 1987 and then to two (and a "shadow" third) by 1988. This third bracket will be clarified in the 1988 tax explanation several pages ahead. Getting a handle on the specifics of this big change is tricky. But if you step back, examine the principles, and come to understand them, you can adapt to any future changes in the number, percentages, or size of the brackets.

Figure A-4 shows the 14 tax brackets that were used to calculate tax obligations in 1985. The first $3,540 of your taxable income, if you were married

Figure A-4: Taxable Income-Married Couples Filing Jointly 1985

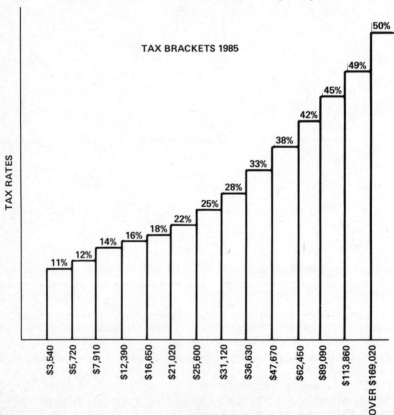

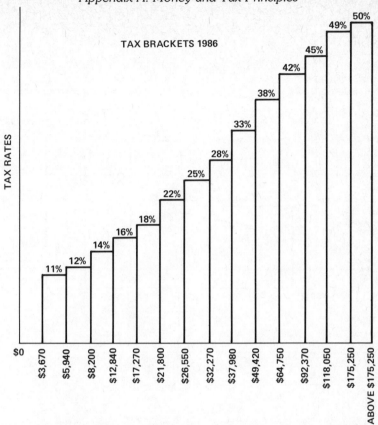

Figure A-5: Taxable Income-Married Couples Filing Jointly 1986

and filed jointly, was tax-free. The next $2,180 ($5,750-$3,540) was taxed at the rate of 11%. This stepladder approach was repeated for each bracket until your total tax bill was arrived at. If your taxable income in 1985 was $36,630, the last segment—$5,510 ($36,630-$31,120)—was taxed at the rate of 28%. If you were able to reduce your taxable income from $36,630 to $34,630, your tax savings would have been $2,000 × .28, or $560.

Figure A-5 provides the tax brackets for the same married couple in 1986. The number of brackets and the tax rates are the same, but you'll notice the dollar levels have risen in each bracket. This was done to avoid "bracket creep": If your salary rose at a rate that matched inflation, you "crept" into the next higher tax bracket and found that the IRS had increased your tax bill. The net effect was negative. To eliminate this inequity, the dollar range of each tax bracket was increased. In 1985, the 28% rate started at $31,120 and ended at $36,630. In 1986, this bracket encompassed incomes from $32,270 to $37,980. An increase of 4% in your taxable income would not cause you to creep into a higher tax percentage.

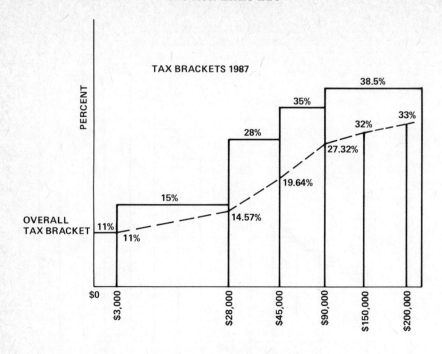

Figure A-6: Taxable Income-Married Couples Filing Jointly 1987

Despite this fair adjustment by the IRS, the multiple tax brackets confused tax preparers and taxpayers alike. Badly needed simplification was part of the tax reform legislation of 1986. By 1988, the number of tax brackets is reduced to two (but more accurately, to three, as we'll see shortly). To make this dramatic change palatable, 1987 is a transitional year in which five tax brackets are used before the final two go into effect in 1988.

The tax brackets for 1987 are shown below in Table 1.15 and plotted for married taxpayers filing jointly in Figure A-6.

Table 1.15: 1987 Taxable Income Brackets (Dollars)

Tax rate	Married, (filing jointly)	Heads of Household	Singles
11%	0-3,000	0-2,500	0-1,800
15%	3,000-28,000	2,500-23,000	1,800-16,800
28%	28,000-45,000	23,000-38,800	16,800-27,000
35%	45,000-90,000	38,000-80,000	27,000-54,000
38.5% ..	Above 90,000	Above 80,000	Above 54,000

The zero tax bracket was eliminated but compensated by increased personal deductions. These new tax schedules are certainly simpler and should

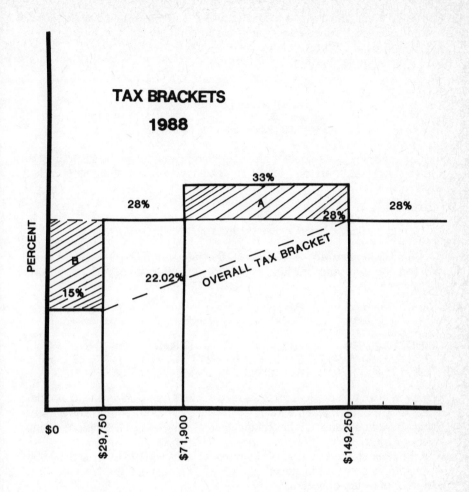

TAXABLE INCOME

Figure A-7:   Taxable Income-Married Couples Filing Jointly 1987

eliminate many of the creative financial tactics that some people used to evade income taxes.

In 1988, your calculations will be much easier when the two (or three) tax-bracket schedule becomes effective (Figure A-7).

For married individuals filing jointly with taxable income of less than $71,900, the tax calculations will become easier. As shown in Figure A-7, all taxable income up to $29,750 will be taxed at 15%. From that point on, the tax rate is 28% up to $71,900. At that figure, the 28% rate is increased in order to recapture the difference between 28% and the 15% tax in the original tax bracket. Notice in A-7 how at $149,250, the 15% bracket is eliminated for all practical purposes and the total income is taxed at 28%. This is accomplished by increasing the tax obligation by 5% on income from $71,900 to $149,250.

For example, the total *additional* tax at $149,250 is 5% of the total range, or:

> 5% of ($149,250 − $71,900)
> 5% of $77,350
> $3,867.50 (Shaded area A in Figure A-7)

The $3,867.50 is equal to the tax difference between the 28% bracket and 15% bracket (therefore, 13%). To verify this, the loss of the first bracket advantage is:

> 13% of $29,750
> $3,867.40 (Shaded area B in Figure A-7)

On all income above $149,250, the rate returns to 28%. The basic two and the adjusting bracket—33%—for the other taxpayers are shown below.

	Married, filing jointly	Head of Household	Single	Married, filing separately
15%	$0-29,750	$0-23,900	$0-17,800	$0-14,875
28%	29,750-71,900	23,900-61,650	17,800-43,150	14,875-35,950
33%	71,900-149,250	61,650-123,790	43,150-89,560	35,950-113,300

However, even two or three brackets may confuse many citizens who wonder what percent of their income they pay in taxes. Everyone should know his or her tax burden because it is important when making financial decisions of any kind.

The bar chart in Figure A-7 demonstrates that in 1987, the first $3,000 of taxable income will be taxed at 11% ($330). If your taxable income is $28,000, your tax obligation is:

> 11% of $ 3,000 = $ 330
> 15% of $25,000 = $3,750
> Total: $4,080

The overall *percentage* of your tax in relation to your $28,000 income is:

$$\frac{\$4,080}{\$28,000} = 14.57\%$$

At $45,000, the tax *additional* to the above is:

> 28% of $17,000 = $4,760

for a total tax bill of $8,840 ($4,760 + $4,080)

At this $45,000 taxable income level, the percentage of tax you pay is:

$$\frac{\$8,840}{\$45,000} = 19.65\%$$

These percentages are plotted as a dotted line in Figure A-7, showing that you can count on keeping 80% of your $45,000 taxable income for yourself in 1987.

This overview of basic financial and tax terms and calculations is, of course, only an introduction to a highly complex subject. The investment world is complicated and ever-changing, so to keep up with it, you will have to be alert to the changes that will take place frequently. But you should absorb the principles we have discussed here. Their essence will change very little, and they can serve you well as a basic guide to understanding the stream of tax and investment information you will always be wading through.

Appendix B: How The IRA Works

In this appendix, we will review the government rules, regulations, and restrictions that affect your IRA. Our purpose will be to explain these conditions thoroughly so that you can make your IRA perform as a valuable ally in your search for financial security in retirement. First, though, let's take a step back in history to understand precisely how and why the IRA evolved.

THE EVOLUTION OF RETIREMENT INCOME

The concerted search for financial security developed and intensified after World War II, when worker demand for private pension plans accelerated. A decade earlier, during the Great Depression of the 1930s, the Social Security system had been launched. But since Social Security was intended and designed as only a rudimentary support base, employees of private corporations pressed their bosses for extra help. Seeking reward for their services, they petitioned for corporate or private pension plans to supplement their Social Security benefits, and many such plans were put into effect.

With two retirement programs now in position—one public, one private—millions of workers in postwar America enjoyed a new confidence. They felt a new assurance about their retirement and anticipated the day when they would leave the work force in comfort.

This rosy optimism began to fade in the early 1970s. With far more people receiving Social Security payments than the program's original planners had ever expected, an overload of benefits jeopardized the program, and its administrators had to overhaul and reinforce the entire system. Today, some pessimists suggest Social Security is still threatened. But the system seems likely to survive well into the next century before really facing any threat to its existence; this is good news because, without Social Security, millions of senior citizens would find themselves dependent on friends and relatives or on spot welfare programs.

Thousands of the pension plans created since World War II did not fare as well as Social Security. Large numbers of workers with many years of service who enrolled in such programs received little or none of the benefits promised them. Abuses, deception, and fraud hounded these plans.

Many pension plans were designed to pay only those employees with long service to the organization. But someone who had worked for an organization for thirty years could be denied a pension if he or she had taken a short leave of absence. The "fine print" stipulating that the thirty years be "continuous service" deprived many unsuspecting employees of the retirement income they had dreamed of for so long.

Another common abuse was the deceptive presentation of eligibility requirements. After long years, many people found that they were not eligible to receive benefits under their plans. In addition, many individuals were dismissed just before they were to qualify for their pension payments. Management often found it cheaper to fire a long-term employee and train a new one than to permit a veteran worker to receive his or her pension; this would have committed the company to pay retirement benefits for an indefinite period.

Furthermore, some corporations underfunded their pension plans. Investigations often revealed that monies available in these plans were insufficient for meeting their obligations to retirees. If the corporation became insolvent, the chances that the retired workers would receive any benefits were slim. In the early 1970s, some large corporations owed as much as 60% to 120% of their total asset value to their pension plans. Indeed, an underlying reason for major loans to the giant Lockheed Corporation a few years ago may have had a good deal to do with unfunded obligations to its pension plans. Many other firms simply went bankrupt in an effort to abandon previously unfunded obligations.

Such rampant abuses led the federal government to take corrective action. In 1974, Congress passed ERISA (The Employee Retirement Income Security Act). This legislation addressed the serious issues of pension structure, pension management, funding requirements, and employees' rights vis-a-vis pensions.

The government does not compel corporations to offer a pension plan. However, it can withhold approval of a plan that fails to meet the criteria of structure and operation set by ERISA. ERISA approval allows a company to take immediate tax deductions on all plan contributions. If denied plan approval, on the other hand, the company is stripped of this tax advantage, and no firm can economically manage a plan without such favorable treatment of its plan monies. Furthermore, since a pension plan is also a major employee benefit, denied plan approval could put the company at a disadvantage in attracting and keeping competent employees.

ERISA has set up specific guidelines for eligibility, vesting, and funding, and it has devised many other regulations necessary to assure pension stability. For people covered by pension plans, these changes have been big steps in the right direction.

But what of the millions of people who were self-employed, or whose employers had no pension plan, or whose pension benefits were totally inadequate? Alas, ERISA's reforms and improvements of existing pension plans did not help them. To compensate somewhat for this problem, ERISA also inaugurated a program that was meant to become a powerful component of the 1974 legislation—the Individual Retirement Account (IRA).

Originally, the IRA was available only to those people *not* covered by an ERISA-approved pension plan, regardless of the plan's quality. (The government cannot control or comment on the quality of plans; it can only stipulate that they conform to ERISA rules and regulations. For example, plans cannot discriminate. This means that the benefits may be meager, and that's all right, so long as all employees are treated equally.) Thus an employee who was due to receive as little as $50 to $100 per month in retirement benefits was disqualified for an IRA. Clearly, further changes were in order. And such changes soon arrived, under the Economic Recovery Tax Act (ERTA) of 1981. This legislation permitted virtually every working American, regardless of his or her existing pension coverage, to participate in the IRA program.

Since 1982, the IRA has been of special benefit to employees who: Are not covered by formal pension plans, have pension plans that provide insufficient benefits, or want to enhance their existing benefit plan. The tax reforms of 1986 altered the IRA for many participants; we shall discuss these changes shortly.

An IRA is neither a pension plan nor technically a deferred compensation program—such as the 403(b) and 401(k)—although it closely resembles the latter. Deferred compensation programs are available only when the employer originates them; adopting an IRA, on the other hand, is a purely personal decision. The individual also controls his IRA contribution levels—within legal limits, which we shall cover below. The basic procedure is simple: The individual chooses an IRA investment plan, makes the contribution to his or her account, and if able to under the 1986 law, takes the appropriate tax deduction. Any untaxed contribution and the yield on it are tax-deferred until distribution.

Regulations require that participants adopt only plans that the IRS has approved. When the program was introduced in 1974, banks, insurance companies, and brokerage houses rushed to gain IRS approval in order to sell their own IRAs. Approval was granted if their prototype plan met the guidelines set forth by ERISA. Consequently, all approved plans are basically similar.

The basic advantages, restraints and potential pitfalls of the IRA may be clarified if we picture it as a fortress (see Figure B-1) that the IRS cannot penetrate. Since this fortress is invulnerable to an IRS onslaught, conventional tax treatments do not apply to money that has been contributed to it. To many taxpayers' disappointment, expenses related to the IRA investment—such as IRA brokerage commissions, real estate taxes, or manage-

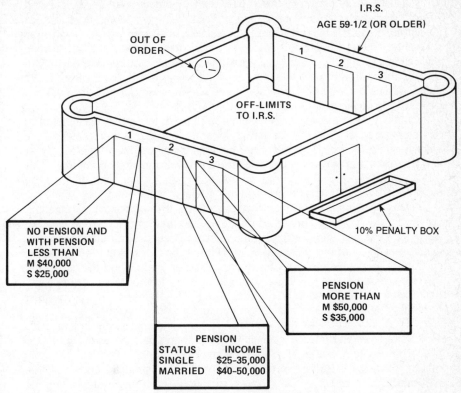

OUT OF ORDER

I.R.S.
AGE 59-1/2 (OR OLDER)

OFF-LIMITS TO I.R.S.

10% PENALTY BOX

NO PENSION AND
WITH PENSION
LESS THAN
M $40,000
S $25,000

PENSION
MORE THAN
M $50,000
S $35,000

PENSION
STATUS	INCOME
SINGLE	$25-35,000
MARRIED	$40-50,000

Figure B-1: The IRA Fortress

ment fees—cannot be tax-deductible because the IRS has no presence within the fortress.

Another unusual condition inside the fortress is the absence of IRS "tax time." Because the tax clock does not tick here, there can be no deductions for depreciation, which is dependent on the passage of investment time. Because IRA funds have witnessed no passage of time in the eyes of the IRS, IRA benefits will be taxed as ordinary income when they emerge from the fortress at distribution.

This leads us to an important point: Although the IRS can't get into the fortress, it's always waiting right outside the walls and will pounce on the unsuspecting person who thinks the coast is clear. So, in order to stay out of the IRS's clutches, we must understand the rules and standards that it dictates in order to nurture and better protect our own IRA. We can conveniently divide these regulations into four specific areas:

1. Rules that concern eligibility, ownership (vesting), contribution levels, adoption procedures and trustee regulations.
2. Rules governing types of assets and asset accumulations.
3. Regulations governing penalties for premature and/or improper distribution.
4. Regulations that cover the tax status of IRA benefits.

188   *The Real Estate IRA*

All you need to qualify for an IRA is earned income. Hourly, salaried, and self-employment income are all considered earned income. Yields from investments, rents, dividends, and interest are *unearned* income, and they cannot be factored into the IRA formula. All working Americans are eligible. Only after reaching 70½ are you prohibited from contributing to an IRA.

Rent

Contributions to an IRA may be made only in the form of cash. No "cash equivalent" is allowed; assets such as bonds, stocks or CDs must first be converted to cash before being put into an IRA.

Initially, the maximum allowable contribution to an IRA was limited to the lesser of $1,500 or 15% of earned income. In 1982, this sum rose to the smaller of $2,000 or 100% of earned income. If you earn less than $2,000—say $1,500—then you can deposit that entire amount into your IRA. This action may not be wise from a practical perspective, but it may be advantageous for a married person who works part-time but files jointly.

1986

This uncomplicated regulation concerning IRA qualifications and tax-deferral of contributions prevailed until 1986. At that time, Congress enacted the most sweeping and simplifying tax reform in decades, reducing tax rates, decreasing the number of brackets, and closing dozens of tax loopholes and shelters. The changes were long overdue; but in simplifying the tax code, Congress made a few modifications to the IRA. And the thrust of simplification did not prevail when Congress turned its attention to this popular program. Let's examine what "improvements" were enacted.

The new law states that all wage earners can still qualify for an IRA. That's simple enough. But, while all IRA participants can still contribute up to $2,000 every year, some people will be contributing non-taxed dollars while others will now use after-tax dollars. Prior to this "simplification," all IRA participants entered the IRA fortress through the same gate; everyone contributed tax-deferred dollars. In 1987, there are now *three* gates to the fortress, each with different admission requirements. Let's look at each of these gates:

Gate 1: Full Tax Deduction: Any wage earner *not* covered by a pension plan, regardless of income, can contribute to an IRA and deduct the full contribution from his or her taxable income. If you are covered by a pension plan and file a joint return with your spouse, you can also take the full deduction, if your adjusted gross income is less than $40,000. If you're single and your adjusted gross income, (AGI) is $25,000 or less, you can enter through this gate as well. If you can use gate #1, no changes have occurred; you can proceed as you did before 1987.

Gate 2: Partial Tax Deduction: This is reserved for couples covered by a pension plan and whose adjusted gross income is between $40,000 and $50,000, and for single persons with a pension plan and an AGI between $25,000 and $35,000. People who enter the fortress through this gate can contribute the maximum allowed to their IRA, but they will only be granted a partial tax deduction. The deduction will be reduced $200 for each $1,000 earned over $40,000 for couples filing jointly or $25,000 for single people. For example, a single woman who earns $30,000 can deduct $1,000 of her IRA contribution.

Gate 3: No Tax Deduction: This gate is for wage earners who are covered by a pension plan and whose AGI exceeds $35,000 if single or $50,000 if married and filing jointly. Their IRA contributions must be made entirely with after-tax dollars.

While these people receive no tax deduction, they can still enjoy tax-free asset growth within the IRA and not pay any taxes on the earnings until withdrawal.

Whichever gate you use, your IRA is held in trust and all IRA assets belong to you. That is, they are vested in you. An official of the trust company with whom you place your IRA is designated as the trustee. The trust must maintain a separate account for you. In the case of a bank or brokerage house, an official is appointed in the institution's trust division to carry out this responsibility on your behalf.

For a given year, IRA funds can be contributed anytime until the filing date for that year's income taxes—April 15 of the following year. Thus, for example, you can pay money into your IRA for 1987 at any point until April 15, 1988.

Most IRA participants mistakenly believe that IRAs are the sole province of banks, probably because of the massive advertising campaigns that these institutions launch during the tax season. This misapprehension about permissible IRA investments may prove costly to participants. And it's not only the general public who's in the dark. Even some professionals have misconstrued ERISA's position on investments because of their experience in 1962–1974, when a published list of savings and investment vehicles was approved for Keogh dollars.

When Congress undertook to reform abuses under IRA, it avoided this rigid, restrictive approach. It did not post or approve any list. Some limitations on IRA investments are still dictated by legislation, though. At the outset, for instance, ERISA banned the purchase of life insurance with IRA funds (as explained why in Chapter Six). In 1982, TEFRA (The Tax Equity Fiscal Responsibility Act) extended this prohibition to investing in collectibles such as gold, silver, coins, art, antiques, stamps, diamonds, and gems. (To confuse matters, the 1986 modifications now permit the purchase of U.S. silver and gold coins. This is the only exception to the exclusion of collectibles).

A major reason for the exclusion of collectibles was that there are no regulatory agencies to control the actions of salespersons or agents for these products. (Conventional investments such as stocks, bonds, insurance, and real estate are monitored by authorities who police their particular fields of expertise and are empowered to revoke licenses and take punitive actions against unethical practices or acts of misrepresentation). Therefore, any investment of IRA dollars in collectibles will be deemed a distribution of funds and will be subject to payment of both the 10% penalty before age 59½ and the standard income tax.

Aside from these products, the range of IRS-sanctioned IRA investments is all-inclusive. Investments can be made in stocks, commodities, certificates of deposit (CDs), bonds, mutual funds, mortgages, and real estate.

However, a very real restriction does arise in that institutions that offer IRS-approved IRAs tend to limit the choices of investments you can select. For example, banks permit IRA investments only in passbook accounts, CDs, and various bank instruments. Insurance companies offer only annuities, that are basically savings accounts. Brokerage houses approve investment only in stocks, bonds, or mutual funds.

Of course, as an organization's product line increases, so do your investment options in its IRA. Some financial institutions have recently responded to a trend toward offering total financial services. They have combined as many products as their business plan dictates. Banks now service stock and bond orders; some even sell insurance. Similarly, brokerage houses have essentially entered the banking profession. Formerly clear-cut boundaries have blurred. The gradual movement to full-service activity will provide "one-stop" financial shopping for all types of clients. And the broader the variety and flexibility of the financial institution, the easier it will be for the IRA holder to respond to changes in the economy and in fiscal policy.

In a typical bank IRA, you open an account and make deposits into it. Your investment options may be as restrictive as the choice between a 12- or 36-month CD. In the heyday of the 18% return, the rewards of such an account were comforting. But if you have to accept a 6% or 7% return, your enthusiasm may well wane. You might want to switch to another investment, but you have no flexibility since no other approved product with a higher return is possible in a bank IRA.

Self-Directed IRAs

But there's another less-publicized type of IRA that gives you even more flexibility: You can control your own portfolio adopting a *self-directed IRA* through a trust company. Such a trust sells no insurance, stocks, bonds, annuities, or any other product. It *does* provide administrative services for self-directed IRAs and Keoghs. It will neither offer investment advice nor invest your finds until it receives instructions from you. *You're* the boss.

If you participate in a self-directed plan, you have a wide range of options from which to select. You may move a CD into a "hot" mutual fund or opt for an annuity. Direct purchase of stocks through a discount house may strike your fancy. Or you may, of course, buy real estate. If so, you could sell your stocks, bonds, or other investments to acquire it. In short, with a self-directed IRA, you have the freedom and flexibility to decide where and when you invest.

To change investments within the self-directed IRA, a mere request to the trustee suffices. The trust is not a product marketer and therefore has no particular interest in any specific investment option. It simply will not benefit from use of your money, as a bank does. Consequently, the trust levies fees for its services, since it is in business for *some* profit! (Chapter Six showed typical fee schedules.) The cost is reasonable when you consider what you gain in personal control, investment options, and flexibility.

A common misconception is that your IRA contributions are irretrievable until you reach age 59½, the minimum age for distribution. Many people have shied away from an IRA, fearing that their monies will be locked away until some distant date.

This is not technically true. IRAs can be terminated any time. However, the IRA may impose a 10% penalty on any funds taken out prior to age 59½. It will also collect the deferred income taxes due on premature withdrawals.

Premature IRA Distribution

Earned Income = $2,000
Contribution = $2,000 (one-time)
Annual Yield = 8%

\$.08 X .85 = 1.068 In̄come (AFTer TAX Rate)

		IRA			CONVENTIONAL	
					Tax Brackets	
			Tax Brackets		15%	28%
		Penalty			(1,700)	(1,440)
Year	Cumm.	@ 10%	15%	28%		
1	2,160	216	1,620	1,339	1,816	1,523
2	2,333	233	1,750	1,446	1,920	1,611
3	2,519	252	1,890	1,562	2,031	1,703
4	2,721	272	2,041	1,687	2,148	1,802
5	2,939	294	2,204	1,822	2,271	1,905
6	3,174	317	2,380	1,968	2,402	2,015
7	3,428	343	2,571	2,125	2,541	2,131 *Break even YR*
8	3,702	370	2,776	2,295	2,687	2,254
9	3,998	400	2,999	2,479	2,842	2,384
10	4,318	432	3,238	2,677	3,005	2,521
11	4,663	466	3,497	2,891	3,179	2,666
12	5,036	504	3,777	3,123	3,362	2,820
13	5,439	544	4,079	3,372	3,555	2,982
14	5,874	587	4,406	3,642	3,760	3,154
15	6,344	634	4,758	3,933	3,977	3,336

Figure B-2: Premature IRA Distribution

Taxes should have no bearing on your decision to avoid opening an IRA. You will have to pay them sooner or later anyway.

The sole drawback to consider is the penalty that must be paid on early withdrawal. Be aware that after a certain point, this ceases to be a disadvantage. Figure B-2 plots the effects of the penalty and indicates the breakeven year when a premature cash-in will be no more costly or punitive than a conventional after-tax investment.

We have assumed an 8% investment return on both the IRA and the conventional investment, and we have placed our IRA holder in the 28% tax bracket. The columns on the left show the contribution, its yield, the assumed penalty of 10%, the taxes of 28%, and the *net* amount for the withdrawal. The two columns to the right reflect the dollars invested in a conventional vehicle ($1,440 that are left after the 28% tax treatment of a $2,000 investment) and the net return. Note that in the seventh year, the early IRA distribution begins to fare as well as or better than the conventional investment. Withdrawal before the seventh year means a *net* loss of the IRA's return in relation to that of the conventional investment. At a 10% tax bracket the breakeven point occurs in the 10th year.

Another penalty confronts those who fail to take distributions after age

70½. Before December 31 of the year in which they reach that age, participants must begin to take receipt of the accumulated funds under the following guidelines:

1. If you have designated no beneficiary, the yearly distributions must be calculated so that no funds are left by the end of your life expectancy.
2. If you have named a beneficiary, the distributions may be based on leaving 50% of the funds for that person, if you wish.

You *must* adhere to the schedule of payments you elect. Any distribution that results in an excess balance in the account will trigger a penalty of 50% on the surplus.

IRA distributions that have not been previously taxed are treated as ordinary income. As discussed earlier, you must remember that no tax clock ticks in the IRA fortress, so time-dependent treatment does not apply.

ROLLOVERS AND CASH TRANSFERS

To facilitate asset transfer from one retirement program to another without penalty and taxation, the IRS has designed the protected transfer and rollover procedure. The regulations that govern this process are specific and inflexible; any deviation will result in immediate taxation and if you're younger than 59½, possible penalty. Be advised here: An inadvertent mistake can be costly. You must plan, execute, and monitor an anticipated transfer carefully and properly.

Two types of transfers are available. In one, you move assets from a pension plan to an IRA. In the other, your assets are switched directly from one IRA to another. These processes are shown in Figure B-3.

Let's say you want to move funds from your pension plan or Keogh into your IRA. You contact your bank or corporate benefits officer and arrange for funds to be distributed. The moment the asset or check is issued to you, *constructive receipt* is said to have occurred and tax consequences can ensue.

Figure B-3: Transfer and Rollover

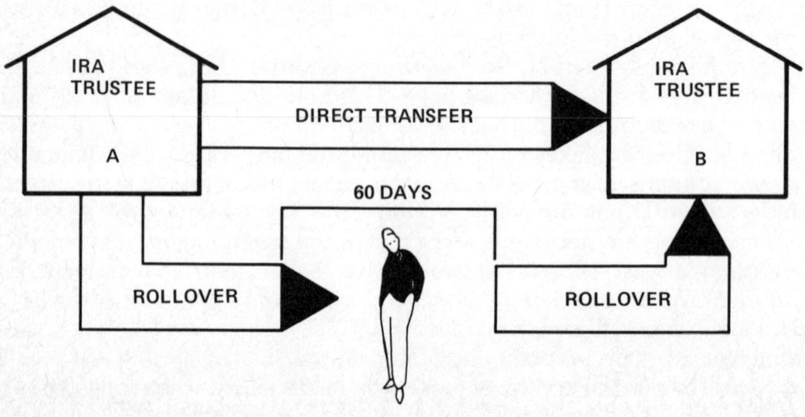

No excuse will be accepted even if a check has not been cashed or used. To avoid taxation, you must deposit it into your IRA within *60 days*. The clock starts ticking the day the original trustee writes the check, *not* the day you receive it. Since this rule is inflexible, be diligent when you request a distribution. Make certain that you receive it promptly: If you don't, take action. If you hold the assets for *61* days, for whatever reason, the IRS *must* impose penalties and taxes.

In addition to referring to a general procedure, the term "rollover" also designates a specific type of IRA, the "rollover IRA." If money has been distributed from a qualified pension plan and deposited into an IRA within 60 days, then these assets are allowed to be rolled over at a later date into another employer's approved pension plan. Note, though, that this is not permissible if any other IRA money has been mixed in with the funds in question.

To qualify for rollover protection, any assets (cash, stock, and so on) switched from your pension plan must be either the asset itself or its cash value. For example, my pension from Company A is 100 shares of its stock. I can roll over the stock, or sell it and roll over the receipts as cash to Company B.

You need not transfer all of your original assets to qualify for this tax-protected procedure, but any portion you do not deposit in your new IRA will be considered a distribution and will be taxed. During the 60-day grace period, you can use the funds at your discretion. But remember that the original funds must be deposited into your new IRA by the end of this period, or else they will be taxed. Furthermore, any profit or interest earned on the funds during this period may not be rolled over, but is taxable income and must be reported in the same year; the maximum that you can redeposit is the amount you withdrew. You can roll over a distribution from a pension plan or Keogh only once a year.

Moving assets directly from one IRA trustee to another is the more popular method of transfer. The once-a-year rollover limitation does not apply in this case because a trustee-to-trustee transfer does not involve the individual. Since no constructive receipt of the assets by the individual takes place, regulations permit unlimited numbers of these transfers.

THE SPOUSAL IRA

An exception to the rule that an IRA must be paid for with qualified earned income is the spousal IRA, which really is two separate IRAs. To qualify for a spousal IRA, your spouse need not have earned any income, as long as you have. The two of you are simply required to be married at the end of the year and must file a joint tax return. You can set aside $2,250 a year, or $250 more than in a standard single IRA.

The total contribution to a spousal IRA is allocated between the two partners in proportions that the couple themselves determine. The only limitation is that one account can accept no more than $2,000, with the $250 balance credited to the other. Directing the $2,000 maximum into the non-working spouse's account is not only legal, but may make more sense. Remember, contributions into an IRA are prohibited for wage earners after age 70½. But if the nonworking spouse is younger than the wage earner, he or she should be allocated the larger amount. This will make it possible to maintain the tax shelter for a *longer* period of time if desired. The younger spouse can either take immediate distribution or delay it until he or she reaches 70½.

SEPs

There is a unique type of pension plan—the Simplified Employee Pension (SEP)—that behaves very much like an IRA. It was introduced under the 1978 Revenue Act, in response to criticism that Keogh plans were too expensive to manage. Unlike a Keogh plan—in which funds are pooled under a trustee who has complete control over and responsibility for monies—the SEP is set up so that the employer contributes funds into each employee's account but gives each employee control of his or her pension funds under the employer's SEP plan. A SEP, like a Keogh, can be implemented only if the employer elects to subscribe to and adopt a plan pre-approved by the IRS.

In the SEP, unlike the IRA, the *employer* pays the *employee's* contribution based on a percentage of his or her salary. As with other pension plans and Keoghs, the rate of contribution must not discriminate in favor of employees who are officers or owners of the organization; the employer must provide the allocated percentage for all employees regardless of their salary. This contribution is credited and vested immediately into the account of the employee, who has the right to withdraw the employer's contribution without penalty.

Using the SEP, employers divest themselves of the responsibilities of fund management and also avoid the onerous reporting required of conventional Keogh pension accounts. On the downside for the employer, the employee enjoys immediate 100% vesting and the right to move his or her funds, including those that the employer has contributed.

The SEP permits integration of pension benefits with the Social Security benefits that the employer pays. If such integration is chosen, everyone in the firm, including the owner/employer, must have it.

Interesting though the SEP is, we will leave a more detailed analysis of it to the pension plan books. We will be better off if we focus our attention on the IRA itself so as to evaluate its advantages and disadvantages with respect to our total financial objectives. To help us to achieve this understanding, we must determine what our financial needs in retirement will be. We'll calculate these in Appendix C.

Appendix C:
Retirement Need Analysis

We must resolve many problems before we can retire from work comfortably. Besides preparing psychologically and emotionally for retirement, our most important practical concern will be its financial impact. If we do not have a sufficient income, we can forget our dream of a quiet, contented retirement. This basic point dictates that we establish, as soon as possible, a personal financial plan designed to deliver economic security in retirement. And then we must act on our plan.

What do we mean by a plan? The dictionary defines the word "plan" as "any detailed program worked out beforehand for the accomplishment of an objective." Some 95 of 100 American workers today will not be able to afford to retire in reasonable comfort when they reach age 65. This overwhelming majority has obviously failed to plan or act for retirement.

This shocking statistic points out that we must pay far more attention to undertaking financial planning at the very outset of our working years. Only through effective planning and action can a retiree enjoy a satisfactory retirement lifestyle, instead of "dodging bullets," as so many senior citizens do now.

Personal goals for retirement vary widely, but most people tend to envision a life equal or superior to their present one. If this is your view, your first step toward making it a reality is to establish the *financial objective* for your retirement. You must define and quantify this seemingly distant goal before you can devise and implement any plan.

The basis for determining our retirement objective is our current earned income. We must examine this income which is a barometer of our present lifestyle, in order to predict our spending patterns in retirement.

In addition, as we progress toward retirement, our lifestyle changes will be reflected in our changing patterns of demand for the goods and services we buy. And as time marches on, it will be accompanied by a constant nemesis—inflation—which will boost the cost of these goods and services. Accordingly, both the changes in our spending patterns and the rising costs of what we purchase must be factored into the calculation of our retirement needs.

THE CONSUMER PRICE INDEX (CPI)

As individuals, we have no systematic means of predicting the impact of our future spending patterns or of inflation. But the government does. Its primary method of tracking and recording spending patterns and costs is the body of data known as the Consumer Price Index (CPI), devised by the U.S. Labor Department. The CPI tracks two conditions: The pattern of use of the seven major categories of goods and services on which American consumers spend their income, and the price changes in all these goods and services.

Spending Patterns

The seven major categories of consumer goods and services are itemized in Figure C-1. This chart breaks down by percent how much Americans spend in each category. The national CPI is compiled from in-depth figures from numerous regions throughout the country; it represents the national norm, as it were. Brief analysis shows that almost four of every five dollars (79.6%) are spent in three categories—housing, transportation, and food.

These averages may in no way resemble your own experience. Nor are they meant to indicate that you should conform to them. They simply reflect the overall national experience and can be helpful as a guide for you. However, you probably are curious—and ought to be—about how closely the national CPI mirrors your own lifestyle, and you may well wish to evaluate your own personal CPI. This is not difficult to calculate.

To assist you, we have designed an expenditure analysis checklist (Figure C-2). You can estimate your expenses and enter them in the appropriate space in the column. Completing these entries will require you to refer to your checkbook, cash receipts, and any other records of your expenditures. You more than likely have to do some enlightened "guesstimating" in order to list all your expenses, especially cash purchases. Do the best you can to post each expense in the category in column one that best approximates that item's general description. If you are uncertain about an item, place it in the category marked "Other." Add the components and fill in the total. Complete column two by dividing the amount of each category in column one by the total of column one. This tells you the percent of your total expenditures that you have allocated to each of the seven categories.

Now you can compare your personal spending pattern to the national average. Figure C-3 will help you to ascertain your personal CPI. In column two of Figure C-3, list your expenditures as a percentage of all you spent

Personal CPI

CPI Components	Total	% of Total
Food & Beverages	20.069	
• Food at home		12.866
• Away from home		6.097
• Alcoholic beverages		1.106
Housing	37.721	
• Shelter		21.339
(Including rent & owners' equivalent rent)		
• Fuel & utilities		8.377
• Household furn. & operation		8.005
Apparel and Upkeep	5.205	
Transportation	21.791	
• Private (gas, maintenance, insurance, fees)		20.250
• Public transportation		1.541
Medical Care	5.995	
• Commodities (pres. drugs, etc)		.976
• Services (Doctors, dentists, etc.)		5.019
Entertainment	4.206	
• Commodities (newspapers, magazine hobbies, sporting goods)		2.485
• Services (admission fees, sporting events)		1.721
Other Goods & Services	5.014	
• Tobacco		1.387
• Personal Care		1.857
• Educational, Misc.		1.770
	100.%	100.%

Figure C-1: Personal CPI

(data from Figure C-2). Compare your percentage with the national standard, listed in column one. Post the difference in column three, "Deviation from National." For each category, the total deviation (plus or minus) from the 100% base is your personal CPI. For example, if you grow some of your own food then your food component may be only 15%. Your deviation from the national average of 20% for that category is 5% less. Perform this evaluation for each of your personal CPI components, and you can total the results to find your *net* deviation.

If the total of all your variations is, let's say, 20% less than the national norm, your personal CPI will then be only 80% (100 − 20%) of the basic standard. Interpreted more meaningfully, if the CPI components increase 6%

Expenditure Analysis

Income = _____	Current Year Expenditures	% of Net Income
Housing		
Mortgage		
Taxes		
Insurance		
Maintenance		
Heating		
Utilities		
Furnishings		
Appliances		
Subtotal		
Food & Liquor		
At home		
Out-of-home		
Subtotal		
Apparel		
Clothing		
Transportation		
Purchase of auto		
Gasoline		
Maintenance		
Auto insurance		
Misc. costs		
Subtotal		
Public transportation		
Medical		
Care service		
Insurance		
Dental		
Medicine, glasses		
Subtotal:		
Entertainment		
Movies, theatre,		
Sports		
Books, magazines		
Subtotal:		
Other		
Personal care		
Gifts, charities, misc.		
TOTAL:		

Figure C-2: Expenditure Analysis

Personal CPI

CPI Components	National Percent	Personal Expenditure Percent	Deviation From National
Food & Beverages	20.069	15%	−5
• Food at home	12.866		
• Away from home	6.097		
• Alcoholic beverages	1.106		
Housing	37.721	27%	−11
• Shelter	21.339		
(Including rent & owners' equivalent rent)			
• Fuel & utilities	8.377		
• Household furn. & operation	8.005		
Apparel and Upkeep	5.205	5%	—
Transportation	21.791	22%	—
• Private (gas, insurance, fees, maintenance)	20.250		
• Public transportation	1.541		
Medical Care	5.994	4%	−2
• Commodities (pres. drugs, etc.)	.976		
• Services (Doctors, dentists)	5.018		
Entertainment	4.206	3%	−1
a • Commodities (newspapers, magazine hobbies, sporting goods)	2.485		
b • Services (Admission fees, sporting events)	1.721		
Other Goods & Services	5.014	4%	−1
• Tobacco	1.387		
• Personal Care	1.857		
• Educational, misc.	1.770		
	100.000	80%	−20%

Figure C-3: Personal CPI

during the year, *your* increased rate will have been only 4.8% (.80 × 6.0). More important, the inflation rate *is* the increase in these prices. When the national rate is 6%, yours will be only 4.8% if you spend 80% of the norm.

Now you know your own CPI. But this figure reflects only today's data. CPI patterns, both nationally and individually, are always changing. The course of your own life will reflect those shifts. Over time, your outlay of dollars for each of the CPI components will ebb and flow. Major life events may cause your spending in one component to diverge markedly from the national average. Buying a home, raising your children, paying their college tuition—these are all important expenditures that can lead to significant personal variations from the norm.

Inflation

As we noted earlier, price changes in the cost of goods and services will also alter the CPI. Carefully researching and documenting these changes are the major purposes of the CPI, and they tell us the effect of the purchasing power of our dollars.

The CPI reports fluctuations in the cost of all goods and services, and these figures are published monthly. These statistics comprise the yardstick that determines the national inflation rate, which we must monitor closely and factor into any formula to ascertain future costs correctly. If you are to win in the relentless economic struggle, your salary and investment yields must move ahead at a pace that surpasses the inflation rate—that is, the rise in the CPI. If your earnings merely match inflation, they will grow—but only at a level that keeps you just afloat, not swimming, in the shark-infested ocean of economic change.

CALCULATING YOUR PRE-RETIREMENT INCOME

To calculate your future inflation-adjusted income, we again use your present salary as a base. Then, through a corrected-for-inflation process, we estimate the salary that you will have to earn to equal the spending power of your income today. Should your salary climb to an even higher level, you will have outrun inflation. For planning purposes, we will *not* be that optimistic. We will base our predictions only on keeping pace with inflation.

Crystal-ball forecasting of inflation is unscientific and at best uncertain. But we must start somewhere, from some base. Helpful to our estimates is the future value chart we encountered in Table 1-11. To calculate your inflation-adjusted pre-retirement salary, multiply your current salary by the factor at the intersection of the row that coincides with the number of years until you retire *and* the column that lists the probable inflation rate over that period. Picking this rate is a judgment call at best, but no plausible alternative exists.

For example, consider Mr. Jones. He presently earns $30,000 a year and intends to retire in 20 years. To maintain dollar-value equivalency, his future salary has to increase to keep pace with anticipated inflation. Assuming an oversimplified constant rate of 7%, we can use the factors in Table 1-11 to make the adjustment. The future value inflation factor at 7% for 20 years is 3.87. Thus Mr. Jones's target salary in the year before he retires must be:

$$\$30,000 \times 3.87 = \$116,000$$

If Mr. Jones could retire in 15 years rather than 20, his pre-retirement salary at the same inflation rate would be:

$$\$30,000 \times 2.76 = \$82,800$$

At an inflation rate of 8%, his pre-retirement salary would be:

In 15 years: $30,000 × 3.17 = $ 95,100
In 20 years: $30,000 × 4.66 = $139,800

Tracking Your Salary Against Inflation

These projections presume that Mr. Jones's spending patterns will remain relatively constant. As we saw earlier, this is rarely the case. To simplify our calculations, proceed as if all changes will occur at retirement.

However, to track the theoretical against the all-too-real, it is advisable to compare your target salary projections with *actual* performance figures. Figure C-4 will facilitate this task. You can use it to post both your salary increases and the projected salary you will need to keep up with inflation.

In the column labeled "Starting Salary," insert your actual work earnings at the start of this year. This is a reference point for comparisons. Subsequent entries in this column will be not actual salaries but theoretical ones derived from column three.

In column two, place the inflation-rate factor found under the appropriate year's inflation rate in Figure C-4. Six percent would be 1.06, for example. The actual year-end rate is easily obtainable; it is widely reported in the mass media.

Next, multiply your starting salary by the inflationary factor to fill in column three. The product of these two numbers is the income you need to keep pace with inflation in that year. In column four, insert the actual salary you earned; simply record the salary you reported to the IRS that year.

Column five is the most important. It shows the deviation between the inflation-corrected salary and your actual year-end salary. Calculate this difference, positive or negative, and enter it in column five.

To demonstrate this procedure, we have projected ourselves into the 1990s in Figure C-5, using Mr. Jones's 1985 salary of $30,000. We estimated theoretical inflation rates of 5% in 1986, 8% in 1987, 7% in 1988, 6% in 1989, and 5% in 1990. In column two, we insert the factors listed in line 1 of Table 1-11. Multiplying Mr. Jones's actual $30,000 salary by 1.06 produces a theoretical inflation-corrected salary of $31,800—the sum needed to match

Figure C-4: Earned Income Record

Earned Income Record

Year	(1) *Starting Salary*	(2) *Inflation Factor*	(3) *Inflation Corrected Salary*	(4) *Actual Year End Salary*	(5) *Deviation (+) (−)*
1985					
1986					
1987					
1988					
1989					
1990					

Earned Income Record

	(1)	(2)	(3)	(4)	(5)
			Inflation	*Actual Year*	
	Starting	*Inflation*	*Corrected*	*End Salary*	*Deviation*
Year	*Salary*	*Factor*	*Salary*		*(+) (−)*
1985	30,000	1.06	31,800	32,000	+200
1986	31,800	1.05	33,390	33,000	−90
1987	33,390	1.08	36,061	36,000	−01
1988	36,061	1.07	38,586	39,000	+414
1989	38,586	1.06	40,901	42,000	+1099
1990	40,099	1.05	42,946	45,000	+2054

Figure C-5: Earned Income Record

the year's inflation in 1986. Observe that in column four, we record that Mr.
Jones' salary has increased to $32,000 in 1986. Fortunately, this exceeds the
theoretical amount he needs to keep up with inflation. Mr. Jones is $200
ahead (see column five).

Let us continue to trace Mr. Jones's career in Figure C-5. We insert his
inflation-corrected 1985 salary (column three) in column one for 1986. As the
years pass, we place the actual factor for inflation in column two and repeat
the procedure we followed for 1985 through each year: Calculate the
inflation-corrected salary, and enter it in Column three. This will tell you what
Mr. Jones must earn at the reported CPI inflation rate just to break even and
not fall behind in purchasing power.

Column four contains the actual salary Mr. Jones earned in each year.
We then compare these data to those in column three to see how he has fared
in the inflation war. If his *actual* year-end salary is less than the inflation-
corrected sum he needs, he has lost ground. Column five renders the verdict
in positive or negative dollar amounts and records the deviation for each year.
Note that Mr. Jones lost fractionally in two years and won in the others,
especially 1990. That year's $2,054 gain represents the additional discretion-
ary income he can divert to investment and/or savings.

Following this tracking and analysis procedure will help you make many
financial decisions along the way. It will also assure you that your actual
salary's performance is fulfilling your projections. Of course, you should
adjust your initial calculations each year to correct the actual, rather than
projected, inflation. But the estimated figures presented here are planning
targets and are valuable as such.

CALCULATING YOUR RETIREMENT NEEDS

Having determined our inflation-adjusted income at retirement, we can now
estimate our financial retirement need, that is our key objective in this
appendix. Because of changes in your lifestyle after you retire, the number of
goods and services you need will alter over the course of many years. As you
move toward and achieve various life goals, your spending will tend to shift

to a more *personal* emphasis. It will also decrease, so much so that, by retirement, your expenditures will drop commensurately with your income.

As you near retirement, saving becomes easier, since your personal CPI diminishes, making more dollars available. In the decade or so before they retire, many people find themselves able to save or invest more than at any previous time in their lives.

There are many reasons why you need less income in your golden years. A host of needs and expenditures dwindle or disappear completely. Your expenditures for transportation, clothing, housing, education, and food will decline considerably. You no longer have a long and costly commute to

Figure C-6: Retirement Renters CPI
Retirement/Renters CPI

CPI Components	National Percent	Retirement Percent	Renter in Retirement
Food & Beverages	20.069	15%	15%
• Food at home	12.866		
• Away from home	6.097		
• Alcoholic beverages	1.106		
Housing	37.721	16%	36%
• Shelter	21.339		
(Including rent & owners' equivalent rent)			
• Fuel & utilities	8.377		
• Household furn. & operation	8.005		
Apparel and Upkeep	5.205	2%	2%
Transportation	21.791	13%	13%
• Private (gas, insurance, fees, maintenance)	20.250		
• Public transportation	1.541		
Medical Care	5.994	8%	8%
• Commodities (prescriptions, etc)	.976		
• Services (Doctors, dentists)	5.018		
Entertainment	4.206	8%	8%
• Commodities (newspapers, magazine hobbies, sporting goods)	2.485		
• Services (Admission fees, sporting events)	1.721		
Other Goods & Services	5.014	3%	3%
• Tobacco	1.387		
• Personal Care	1.857		
• Educational, misc.	1.770		
TOTAL	100.000	65%	85%

and from work. Mileage on your car decreases, your maintenance costs diminish, and you consequently don't have to replace your car so often. The size of your wardrobe also shrinks—you no longer need all those business suits. Best of all, if you're a homeowner, your mortgage will likely be paid off and your children's college costs will be distant memories. The cost of food goes down, too, as you prepare and eat more of your meals at home.

If we compile all of these factors, we find that the typical retiree needs far less to live on than he or she did as a member of the work force; this is quantified and demonstrated in Figure C-6.

In fact, we can conclude encouragingly from Figure C-6 that you will need only 65%, less than *two-thirds*, of your last working year's income as a retiree. For example, if your pre-retirement salary is $93,000, you will find the following retirement income sufficient to maintain your lifestyle:

$$.65 \times \$93,000 = \$60,450$$

To calculate your own probable personal retirement income, use the following procedure:

- Present Salary (A)   _____
- Future-value
  inflation factor
  from Table 1-10
  (B)   _____
- Future
  Pre-retirement
  Salary (A × B):   _____
                                        × .65
- Retirement Income: _____

The projections and calculations we have just explored will enable you to define your retirement planning objectives more accurately. Your personal CPI and your projected retirement CPI are powerful tools with which you can plan and build sensibly and logically toward economic independence in your retirement years.

Questions and Answers

Eligibility

1. **Who is Eligible for an IRA?**

   Every working American is still eligible.

2. **Didn't Congress Recently Change the Eligibility of Wage Earners to Adopt an IRA?**

   No. Every worker is still permitted to contribute to the IRA under the tax reform legislation of 1986. However, the tax deductibility of the contributions has been changed. People are covered by a pension plan at work, as well as singles with adjusted gross incomes below $25,000 and marrieds under $40,000, still enjoy the full tax deduction of the maximum $2,000 contribution to a single IRA, or $2,250 for a spousal IRA. For pension-covered workers, no deduction for an IRA is allowed for adjusted gross income over $35,000 for singles and $50,000 for marrieds. Partial deduction is permitted between $25,000 to $35,000 for singles and $40,000 to $50,000 for marrieds. At both maximum levels, deductions are phased out completely.

3. **What Kinds of IRAs are There and What are Their Contribution Levels?**

There are two types: The single IRA and the spousal IRA. The single IRA allows a working individual to contribute up to a maximum of $2,000 of earned income each year to his account. The spousal IRA permits a working spouse to contribute the same $2,000 each year plus an additional $250 for a non-working spouse, for a total of $2,250. If a married couple works, they can establish their own individual IRAs and have $4,000 in contributions working for them.

4. Do I Have to Work a Minimum-Hour Requirement to Have an IRA?

No. Any qualified wage earner, regardless of hours worked or length of employment, can contribute to the IRA.

5. Is There a Minimum or Maximum Age to Establish an IRA?

There is no minimum age, but individuals cannot start an IRA after age 70½.

6. Does a Two-Income Couple Who File Jointly Establish One or Two IRAs?

Each working spouse can have his or her own IRA, for a combined contribution of $4,000. Whether they file separately or jointly has no bearing. For the record: There is no such entity as a *joint* IRA.

7. Does My Spouse Own any Part of My IRA?

No. An individual's IRA assets are owned only by the participant.

Contributions

8. What is the Deadline for Contributing to My IRA?

An Ira must be established and funded before the tax filing deadline of April 15 of the year <u>following</u> the year for which the contribution is made.

9. Do I Have to Make a Lump-Sum Contribution to My IRA or Can I Make Periodic Payments?

You may make either. But a lump-sum contribution early in the year is to your distinct advantage as shown in Chapter Five (p. 54). If it is not possible for you to make a lump-sum payment, you can make periodic payments on a monthly, quarterly or semi-annual basis, whichever is most convenient for you.

10. Can I Have Automatic Payments Made to My IRA by My Employer?

Yes. This is a matter between your employer and your IRA trustee, and must be taken up where you work.

11. Must I Contribute Each Year to an IRA?

No. You can skip your contribution any year. However, if you purchase real estate requiring a long-term debt obligation, then contributions must be continued for that term. If that is not possible, the payments can be discontinued and the real estate sold, with the proceeds placed in your IRA account.

12. Can I Borrow Money to Fund My IRA?

Yes.

13. May I Have More than One IRA?

Yes. You can have as many as you like. The only condition is that your combined contributions to them do not exceed the annual maximum allowed.

14. If I Only Put $1,200 into My IRA This Year, Can I Make up for the Undercontribution Next Year by Depositing My Regular $2,000 *plus* the $800 Underpayment for a Total of $2,800?

No. You cannot make up for undercontributions the next year. If you do, you will incur a 6% penalty on the overcontribution amount in any year.

15. If I Accidentally Overcontribute to My IRA, Is There Any Way I Can Escape a Penalty?

Yes. You can withdraw the excess amount prior to the tax-filing date for the given year to avoid the penalty.

16. What Events or Conditions Can Incur a Penalty in My IRA?

Three come to mind:

1. Overcontribution: If you contribute more than $2,000 (single) or $2,250 (spousal), you will be assessed 6% annually on any overage until it is removed from your account.
2. Premature distribution: If you make withdrawals from your IRA before age 59½, you will be taxed at ordinary income rates and also assessed at a 10% penalty.
3. Non-withdrawal past age 70½: If you fail to begin distribution by age 70½, you

will be subject to a 50% penalty on any portion of funds that should have been withdrawn each year, and are not, under IRS life expectancy tables.

17. What Are Typical Fees or Costs of Self-Directed IRA Plans?

There are generally three types of fees for a self-directed IRA: An establishment or set-up fee, which usually is between $25 and $50; a maintenance or administrative fee that can range up to $75 yearly; a one-time termination charge that could be $100. These totals are modest in view of the overall benefits of a self-directed IRA.

Taxes

18. We See the Terms "Tax-Free" and "Tax-Deferred" Used Interchangeably About the IRA. Which is More Accurate?

"Tax-deferred." Since you will eventually pay taxes on your original untaxed contributions and the accumulations, it is not "tax-free."

19. If My IRA Investment Choices Show a Value Decline, Can I Claim the Losses as a Tax Deduction?

Sorry. You can't deduct such losses in your IRA investments because there is no tax treatment in the IRA.

20. Can I Lose any Tax Protection by Moving Funds from One IRA to Another?

No. You are free to switch IRA assets or funds anytime, but the transfer or rollover must be accomplished within 60 days to avoid penalty and taxation.

21. In a Spousal IRA, Does the Working Partner Who Makes the Contribution Also Take the Tax Deduction?

That's a moot point, if you are filing jointly. If you are filing separately, the spouse whose account received the contribution must claim the deduction. This reinforces the distinction that the non-working spouse's account is indeed separate from that of the working spouse.

Rollovers

22. What's the Difference Between Transfers and Rollovers of IRA Funds?

A transfer is the movement of funds from one IRA custodian to another plan by your request to the current trustee. Your trust handles the transaction, directly switching the assets from one custodian to another.

You may authorize transfers as often as you wish in any year. However, in a rollover, you request that the assets be sent directly to you. You take personal receipt of what may be funds from your IRA, Keogh, pension or profit-sharing programs. Under rollover regulations, you must place the funds in your possession in another IRA within 60 days to avoid penalties and taxes. You can make only one rollover per calendar year.

23. Can I Switch IRAs from One Trustee to Another?

Yes. You may transfer your IRA to another trustee or custodian any time you wish. You may ask your existing IRA trustee to transfer your assets to another IRA, or you can roll over the assets to another IRA.

24. Can I Roll Over Part of the Funds Distributed from a Pension Plan Into an IRA and Keep the Rest?

Yes. By so doing, you defer taxes on the rollover portion into the IRA, allowing those tax dollars to grow untaxed until distribution. The segment of pension funds you receive and keep for yourself is subject to ordinary income rates.

25. Can I Roll Over Funds Received from a Qualified Plan into an IRA and then to Another Qualified Plan?

Yes. But they must be rolled into a separate IRA until you become eligible to take part in another pension plan.

Distributions

26. How are IRA Funds Taxed when Withdrawn?

They are taxed at ordinary income tax rates—either 15% or 28%, or at whatever rates Congress legislates at that time.

27. When Can I Legally Receive IRA Distributions?

Anytime. However, you may be penalized 10% of your distribution if you withdraw before age 59½.

28. Can I Withdraw IRA Funds *Before* Age 59½ Under any Condition that Does Not Impose a Penalty?

Yes, under certain medical circumstances. If you can prove a mental or physical disability that prevents gainful employment of any kind, you can receive distribution during that period without penalty.

29. May I Use My IRA as Collateral for a Loan?

No. This is a forbidden practice in the IRA. The IRS is harsh in treating such use of funds meant for retirement. The tax agency will consider any amount designated for loan collateral as a premature withdrawal and tax and penalize it as such.

30. What Happens to My IRA if I Die Before Age 59½?

If your spouse is your beneficiary, he or she may continue the account in your name or roll it over into his or her name. If the account is left in your name, no penalty will be exacted on withdrawals made after you would have become age 59½. To avoid penalties, distribution must start no later than when you would have reached age 70½.

31. Does an IRA Beneficiary have to Report Anything to the IRS?

Yes. If funds are still in the account, their status must be reported. A beneficiary must file each year with the IRS until the account is zero balance.

32. If I Inherit an IRA, Can I Roll it Over into My IRA?

No, unless you are the surviving spouse.

33. What Happens if I Fail to Name a Beneficiary for My IRA?

Your IRA funds will be dispersed by the trustee to your estate.

Investments
34. What Investments Can I make in the IRA?

You can invest in just about anything. There are just two prohibitions—life insurance and collectibles, with the exception of U.S. gold and silver coins.

35. Can I Switch a CD I Already Own into My IRA?

No, you cannot. You can only contribute cash into an IRA except if the CD or any other investment is being transferred from another IRA.

36. Are There any Guarantees that My IRA Assets and Their Accumulation in Bank Instruments are Safe or Insured until Retirement?

Generally, yes. In the main, most banks and S&L's insure funds under FDIC and FSLIC membership up to $100,000.

Can The monthly Payments on The Rental Properties Qualify as IRA Contributions?

37. Can I Purchase Real Estate with only Part of My IRA Funds?

Yes. You can use all or any portion you wish and invest any remainder in another vehicle of your choice.

38. Why Should I Buy Real Estate with My IRA Instead of a CD, Stock, Annuity or Mutual Fund?

Because real estate has historically proven to be the best hedge against inflation of all investments. The comparison chart in Chapter Four (p. 43) is convincing evidence of real estate's superiority.

39. What Kind of Real Estate Can I Buy?

You can technically buy any type you wish. No restrictions are set on the kind of real estate.

40. How Much Real Estate Can I Afford?

That depends on two things: The amount of your accumulated IRA assets, and the maximum sum that your IRA contribution limit can finance. (Examples are shown in Chapter Ten.)

41. Can I Purchase a Home with My IRA?

Yes, as long as you have accumulated sufficient IRA assets.

42. From Whom Can I Buy Real Estate in an IRA?

From any seller willing to sell to you under the rules and regulations of a self-directed IRA.

43. Can I Deduct the Interest on the Property Financing?

No. While this is allowable in a conventional purchase, interest is not deductible in an IRA purchase because of the IRA's non-taxing environment.

44. Can I Pay for any Real Estate Maintenance or Property-Operating Costs out of My IRA Funds?

Yes. In fact, these costs *must* be satisfied from IRA funds since these expenses are ruled as part of the real estate asset held in the IRA.

45. Are Property Taxes and Maintenance on an IRA Lot Tax-Deductible?

No. They are considered part of the asset's cost in an IRA, and no IRA asset can be tax-treated. (See discussion in Appendix B.)

46. Can I Transfer Funds from other IRA Assets to Make a Larger Down Payment for a More Expensive Property?

Absolutely. But be sure any transfers do not incur a sponsor's penalty for premature withdrawal. You should maximize your return from any time-sensitive investments before using such funds for real estate.

47. Must I Use Property at Distribution or Can I Sell it and Invest the Funds in Other Financial Products, if I Should Change My Mind in Using the Real Estate IRA as a Retirement Home?

You are not obligated to use the property. You can sell the property and have the funds sent to your IRA trustee, who will follow your instructions in subsequent investment choices with the funds. Or you may withdraw any portion of them if you wish.

48. If I Change My Mind on a Retirement Locale, Can I Sell the Lot and with the IRA Funds Buy Another Lot Elsewhere Later?

Yes, anywhere and any time.

49. What's the Procedure to Sell Real Estate within the IRA?

Upon instruction from you, your IRA trustee will place your property for sale just like any other real estate, preferably using a local broker. The receipts from the sale must be returned to your IRA account if you are to escape taxation and possible penalties.

50. When the Real Estate in My IRA is Sold, Who Keeps the Profits?

In all IRA transactions, assets and any profits must remain in the IRA until you begin distribution after age 59½.

51. How do I Figure the Income Tax I'll Owe on My Property when I Take it out of My IRA to Build on?

The market value of your property must be determined at the time the asset is distributed out of the IRA. That sum is added to your income and the ordinary tax rate for that combined total is applicable.

52. Who Gets the Deed to My Real Estate Purchase?

Your *trustee* will receive the deed since, under IRA regulations, all assets must be held by the IRA trust during build-up. The deed is herein considered an IRA asset and will remain in the custody of your trustee until you take distribution.

53. In the Event Circumstances Prevent Continuing the Payoff of the IRA Property, Can I Sell it?

Yes, you can sell anytime during the payoff period. You may be in competition with other lot sales, so be prepared to meet a possible challenge.

Index

SPECIAL PRE-PUBLICATION OFFER

THE REAL ESTATE IRA HAS FOCUSED ON ONLY ONE BUILDING BLOCK OF A REAL ESTATE-FINANCIAL PLAN, IDENTIFIED AS HOUSEPOWER. HOUSEPOWER USES YOUR HOUSE (AND OTHER REAL ESTATE) TO MEET YOUR MAJOR FINANCIAL OBLIGATIONS AND GOALS. THE PLAN IS SIMPLE, REQUIRES NO EXPERTISE AND CAN BE SELF-MANAGED.

This is a
BONUS OFFER
to readers
of this book

- -

YES! PLEASE SEND ME ____ BOOK(S) AT $14.95
PLUS SHIPPING AND HANDLING AT $2.00 EACH.
☐ CHECK OR MONEY ORDER (PAYABLE TO HOUSEPOWER)
☐ BILL MY CREDIT CARD:
   [VISA/MC/AMEX] _____
(SIGNATURE) _____
NAME _____
(City) _____ (State) _____ (Zip) _____

SEND TO **HOUSEPOWER**
P.O. BOX 1679
WEST CALDWELL, NJ 07007